Sophie M Hollinshead

Sept. 30th 2009

Georgian geographies

Published in our
centenary year
2004
MANCHESTER
UNIVERSITY
PRESS

GEORGIAN GEOGRAPHIES

Essays on space, place and landscape in the eighteenth century

edited by
Miles Ogborn &
Charles W. J. Withers

Manchester University Press
Manchester and New York

distributed exclusively in the USA by Palgrave

Published by Manchester University Press
Oxford Road, Manchester M13 9NR, UK
and Room 400, 175 Fifth Avenue, New York, NY 10010, USA
www.manchesteruniversitypress.co.uk

Distributed exclusively in the USA by
Palgrave, 175 Fifth Avenue, New York, NY 10010, USA

Distributed exclusively in Canada by
UBC Press, University of British Columbia, 2029 West Mall,
Vancouver, BC, Canada V6T 1Z2

British Library Cataloguing-in-Publication Data
A catalogue record for this book is available from the British Library

Library of Congress Cataloging-in-Publication Data applied for

ISBN 0 7190 6510 0 *hardback*

First published 2004

11 10 09 08 07 06 05 04   10 9 8 7 6 5 4 3 2 1

Typeset in Minion fonts
by Graphicraft Limited, Hong Kong
Printed in Great Britain
by Biddles Limited, King's Lynn

Contents

ℰ

List of figures

𝒞

Notes on contributors

ℰ

Daniel Clayton is Lecturer in Human Geography at the University of St Andrews, Scotland. His research and teaching focus on the geographies of colonialism and empire, and Native–Western contact in the north Pacific. He is the author of *Islands of Truth: The Imperial Fashioning of Vancouver Island* (2000), and he is currently working on a book entitled *Colonialism's Geographies*.

Rosie Dias is a Teaching fellow in the Department of the History of Art at the University of York. She has recently completed her PhD thesis, entitled 'John Boydell's Shakespeare Gallery and the Promotion of a National Aesthetic', which examines the Gallery in terms of its reformulation of artistic ideologies, exhibition culture and visual style.

John Gascoigne was educated at the universities of Sydney, Princeton and Cambridge and has taught at the University of New South Wales since 1980. His published works have dealt with two main themes: the role of the early modern university in the promotion and diffusion of knowledge, and the nature of the English-speaking Enlightenment. Recent books include *Science in the Service of Empire* (1998) and *The Enlightenment and the Origins of European Australia* (2002).

Karen Harvey is Lecturer in Cultural History at the University of Sheffield. She has published articles on the body, masculinity and erotica and her book *Bodies and Gender in Eighteenth-Century English Erotic Culture* for Cambridge University Press will be published in 2004. She is also editor of *The Kiss in History* (Manchester University Press, to be published in 2004). Her current project explores eighteenth-century men and the home.

Vladimir Jankovic is a Wellcome Research Lecturer at the Wellcome Unit and the Centre for the History of Science, Technology and Medicine at the University of Manchester. He is the author of *Reading the Skies: A Cultural History of English Weather* (2000). His current research is on the history of modern environmental medicine.

David Lambert is Lecturer in Human Geography at Royal Holloway, University of London. He is the author of several articles on White Caribbean identities and the cultural politics of anti-humanitarianism. He is currently engaged in research on the geographies of post-imperial 'loyalism' in Britain's overseas territories.

Luciana Martins is Lecturer in Luso-Brazilian Studies at Birkbeck, University of London, and author of *O Rio de Janeiro dos Viajantes: O Olhar Britânico, 1800–1850* (2001). She has published widely on the visual culture of tropicality, world cities and modernity and is co-editor, with Felix Driver, of *Tropical Views and Visions* (forthcoming).

Miles Ogborn is Reader in Geography at Queen Mary, University of London. He is the author of *Spaces of Modernity: London's Geographies, 1680–1780* (1998). He is currently researching the ways in which the production, distribution and consumption of different forms of script and print were involved in the workings of the English East India Company in the seventeenth and eighteenth centuries.

Robert Mayhew is Lecturer in Human Geography at the University of Wales, Aberystwyth. He is the author of *Enlightenment Geography* (2000), and of numerous articles on the history of geographical thought. He is currently writing a book on geography's role in the humanities from antiquity to the present and undertaking research on geography in Victorian Britain.

Cynthia Wall is Associate Professor of English Literature at the University of Virginia. She is the author of *The Literary and Cultural Spaces of Restoration London* (1998), and has published editions of Pope's 'Rape of the Lock' and Defoe's *A Journal of the Plague Year*. She is currently working on an anthology of eighteenth-century literatures in English (with J. Paul Hunter), and on a history of space, objects and narrative description in eighteenth- and nineteenth-century literature.

Charles Withers is Professor of Historical Geography at the University of Edinburgh. Recent publications include *Geography and Enlightenment* (1999) (co-edited with David Livingstone), *Geography, Science and National Identity: Scotland since 1520* (2001), and, co-edited with Paul Wood, *Science and Medicine in the Scottish Enlightenment* (2002).

Preface and
acknowledgements

℮

This book has its origins in a conference entitled 'Georgian Geographies' held in September 2000 at the Paul Mellon Centre for Studies in British Art in London, in association with the departments of geography of Queen Mary, University of London and the University of Edinburgh. The conference brought together scholars from a variety of disciplines whose research interests cohered around understanding culture and society in the eighteenth century. Our motivation for bringing people together lay in the recognition that, in various ways, terms such as 'space', 'place', 'mapping' and 'national identity', are a subject of enquiry for historians, scholars in cultural and literary fields and for historians of art and of science as well as for geographers. There are, for example, common concerns across these disciplines not just with the nature of the eighteenth-century public sphere but with the particular location and constitution of the social activities and their audiences subsumed within that term. The idea and constitution of empire in the eighteenth century was also a matter of geography, one of the political control of distant lands and peoples. Further, historians of science have paid attention to the 'geographical turn' in their studies of the making of geographical knowledge, and have examined the audiences and the sites of reception for such knowledge. As in the case of science, what was understood as art took place in specific settings such as public galleries and private drawing rooms. Ideas and audiences, processes not just patterns of change, the particularities of the imperial world, the circumstances of cultural consumption not simply the facts of economic production: each, we would argue, had its geographies in the eighteenth century.

These new interdisciplinary concerns with public and private spaces, with landscape and its meanings, with cultural consumption, knowledge production and imperial power and politics have both shifted the terrain of debate for those interested in the eighteenth century and brought into focus a new range of geographical questions. This is not to claim a disciplinary centrality for geography as a way of understanding the eighteenth century. This collection is certainly not an investigation of geography in the Georgian period. The book is intended, rather, as a contribution to the interdisciplinary reorientation of eighteenth-century studies by considering both how different forms of geographical knowledge about spaces, places and landscapes were constituted in the eighteenth century and how ideas and practices – of empire, of art, of natural history and of the public sphere to name but a few – had their own geographies.

The editors and contributors would like to thank the anonymous readers for their comments, and members of the conference audience for their critical engagement with the substance of the chapters. We would like to thank Brian Allen and the staff at the Mellon Centre for making the conference possible, and Michael Bravo, Chloe Chard, Stephen Daniels, Paul Glennie, Mark Overton and David Solkin for their contributions to it. We particularly acknowledge the help of Christopher Fleet, Andrew Grout, Penny Fielding, Susan Manning, Paul Wood, Carol Gibson-Wood and Edward Oliver (for drawing Figure 5.1). For permission to reproduce illustrations, we acknowledge the Royal Botanic Gardens, Kew; Reading Museum and Art Gallery; the Trustees of the British Museum; the Trustees of the Victoria and Albert Museum; the British Library; the Trustees of the Sir John Soane Museum; the UK Hydrographic Office; the Guildhall Museum in Boston, Lincolnshire; the University of British Columbia Press; the Department of Special Collections, University of British Columbia Library; and the John Rylands Library, the University of Manchester. The conference could not have happened without the generous financial support of the British Academy, the Mellon Centre for Studies in British Art, the Voltaire Foundation and the Historical Geography Research Group of the Royal Geographical Society (with the Institute of British Geographers). Miles Ogborn gratefully acknowledges the award of a Philip Leverhulme Prize from the Leverhulme Trust, and Charles Withers gratefully acknowledges the award of a British Academy Research Readership that made possible much of the work on this volume. Our thanks also go to staff at Manchester University Press for their support and guidance. Our final thanks are to the contributors for their scholarship and for their forbearance.

Miles Ogborn, London
Charles W. J. Withers, Edinburgh

1

Introduction:
Georgian geographies?

ℰ

Miles Ogborn &
Charles W. J. Withers

THIS BOOK is about the geographies of the eighteenth century, or, put
another way, the eighteenth century understood geographically. It draws
upon and, we hope, advances interdisciplinary interests in a period understood as fundamental to the making of the modern world through transformations in science, the state and the idea and meaning of empire, commerce,
culture and national identity. The book does not pretend to completeness.
Rather, and simply, we hope to point to themes that have brought geographical matters and questions to do with geographical knowledge to the
fore in studies of eighteenth-century Britain and its place in the world, and
to elaborate upon them.

These themes and our interest in them converge around the ideas of 'space',
'place' and 'landscape', terms we see to be central to the attention of several
disciplines in understanding the eighteenth century. In the first part of this
introduction, we draw attention to something of that recent work which,
from a variety of perspectives, has examined the geographical nature of the
eighteenth century. Following this brief historiographical survey, the second
and larger part of the introduction highlights the three themes we have used
to order the collection. These are: the geographies of the British Empire in
the eighteenth century, the geographical nature of the public sphere and the
Enlightenment understood geographically including the role of geographical
knowledge in the Enlightenment. The introduction signals to the individual
arguments made by contributors and illustrates, with reference to specific
spaces, places and landscapes, how particular narratives and general themes
are connected.

GEOGRAPHIES OF THE EIGHTEENTH CENTURY

The most significant recent transformations in eighteenth-century studies have, we argue, been animated by an attention to questions of space, place and landscape. This turn to questions of geography has been prompted less by historians becoming interested in the work of historical geographers (although that has certainly happened), than a more general engagement across a range of disciplines with bodies of theory that have brought geographical issues to the fore. For example, both in eighteenth-century studies and more broadly within the humanities, it is possible to trace the increasing influence of, for instance, Michel Foucault's notions of the connections between space, knowledge and power; Jürgen Habermas's theory of communicative action and the public sphere; Raymond Williams's cultural politics of landscape; Edward Said's understanding of the discursive power of imaginative geographies, and Bruno Latour's elaboration of the production of knowledge within networks and their centres of calculation.[1]

As these new geographical perspectives have cross-pollinated with existing versions of historical geography and of the geography behind history, scholars from several disciplines have, in turn, furthered insights into what may be thought of collectively as the geographies of the eighteenth century. This is apparent in numerous ways. Renewed attention to the making of Britain's empire in this period has, as the editor of one collection on this topic notes, involved a recognition that later eighteenth-century Britain in particular was 'a global power'. The increasing awareness of this new geography was a matter of enormous importance within and beyond the British Isles.[2] The making of empire and its representation has been reviewed as a matter of geographical exploration.[3] In one particular imperial context, the local and global dimensions of the encounter between the British, the Spanish and the indigenous inhabitants of Vancouver Island in the late eighteenth century have been set out to challenge orthodox colonial chronologies.[4] The importance of Joseph Banks's management of geographical knowledge to the connections between science and empire has been demonstrated.[5]

Other recent developments in the history of ideas and the history of science have also reconsidered the eighteenth century through an attention to geography and geographical knowledge. The connections between geography and the Enlightenment have been examined, and arguments have been advanced for Enlightenment Britain's leading role in the creation of the modern world.[6] Historians of science are paying particular attention to the sites in which science was produced in the eighteenth century and the ways in which scientific knowledge moved successfully from the spaces of its making to the public and private sites of its reception.[7] Among historians of geography, there have been studies of the geographical nature of the Scottish

Enlightenment and of the political languages of Enlightenment geography.[8] For historians of eighteenth-century natural history, Banks's management of Kew as a royal centre of imperial calculation for Britain has its parallels in recent work on the place of natural history in revolutionary France.[9] Two broader collections have considered the place of science and of medicine more generally in Enlightenment Europe.[10]

Studies of Georgian art and literature have also found new questions by exploring space, place and landscape. Historians of art have illustrated how important certain new spaces were for the display of visual culture and the constitution of a 'viewing public'.[11] Historical geographers have likewise examined the aesthetic nature of landscape in the eighteenth century, and discussed major figures in the production of the landscape garden.[12] Literary scholars have paid attention to the connections between exploration and cultural exchange, and to travel accounts as a particular genre of geographical representation.[13] Travel writing as well as natural history collecting provided new geographies of the exotic and challenged the authority of the 'Old World'. New forms of visual representation brought new ways of seeing and imagining geography to the fore.[14]

There are similar developments in many other areas of eighteenth-century studies. Economic historians have examined the geographies of the agricultural revolution in England and the intricate local and regional geographies that made up the industrial revolution.[15] Political historians have studied the territoriality of the eighteenth-century British state, and urban historians and historical geographers have detailed the production and use of new city spaces.[16]

It is clear, even from this partial review, that much of this work is informed by a sensitivity to the geographies *of* the eighteenth century. This, we would argue, is apparent in the use of geography's language – a language of 'nation', 'territory', 'place' and 'space' – even when such usage is, perhaps, metaphorical. It is more substantially apparent, however, in the recognition that questions of geography make a difference in understanding the material constitution in the eighteenth century of things such as 'empire', 'Enlightenment', 'national identity' and 'the public sphere'. These questions have in part been recognised by some historians of the eighteenth century: in Linda Colley's account of the making of 'Britishness' after 1707, and her exposition of the importance of scale in the shaping of the British empire before 1850; in Kathleen Wilson's attention to the local differences subsumed within the rise of the articulate middling rank; or in J. H. Plumb's and John Brewer's examinations of the social spaces of polite sociability.[17] In a review of some of this work, Roy Porter has written of a 'new eighteenth-century social history' characterised by attention to social difference and to multiple processes of cultural production in different public spheres.[18] This new social history also offers alternative subjects for study from those who have considered the eighteenth century in terms of religion and politics.[19]

We share something of these concerns in advancing here ideas for a 'new historical geography' of the eighteenth century. This is, however, to build upon rather than depart from the concerns of 'traditional' historical geography in its attention either to cross-sectional analyses of landscapes at particular dates or to thematic change over time. The insights afforded by geographical assessment of historical change in such ways remain considerable.[20] Our intention is to add to this by showing how ideas, social processes and cultural practices – of empire, the public sphere, or Enlightenment – had material expression in the geographies that they shaped and themselves varied between places and in different social spaces. It is also to strengthen connections between geography and those other subjects that have taken seriously the importance of thinking geographically in explanation of historical context. We argue that it is precisely the importance of geography and of differences in geography that make the study of such matters in the eighteenth century so stimulating. There are, we suggest, different geographies of empire and of the public sphere, and so on, and that any study of imperialism or of cultural production must take them into account. Peter Burke has argued for a social history of knowledge with its emphases in professing, establishing, locating, classifying, controlling, selling, acquiring and trusting knowledge.[21] It is also possible to think of a historical geography of knowledge in the eighteenth century in which differences over space and between places matter in interpreting landscape, in debating the workings of empire, or in assessing information and social relations in the public sphere. By the same token, it is possible to think of geographical knowledge as itself having a discernible geography, in which, for example, what was held to be geography was the result of encounters with particular parts of the imperial realm. Books of geography – and, of course, works in other subjects – were published in certain places and not in others, moved across space as cultural artefacts and were consumed by audiences in other locations. In such ways, and we illustrate this further below, the eighteenth-century public sphere was a matter of connected geographies: of production, of movement and of spaces of consumption.

Such concerns with the importance of space and place are part of what has been more widely thought of as a 'spatial turn' in the humanities. Attention to geographical difference and to the situatedness of discourse in, for example, moral philosophy and social anthropology parallel that 'geographical turn' evident in the historical study of science.[22] Two examples may serve to highlight what we mean by this sensitivity to geography in interdisciplinary study of the eighteenth century.

John Brewer's *The Pleasures of the Imagination* (1997) offers a wideranging account of the state of English culture in the eighteenth century. The book is organised geographically and chronologically. He argues that the production of culture in Georgian England was less the preserve of kings and courtiers and was more the property of a larger public. He discusses, for example, the shifting sites of cultural production in England from the later seventeenth century when 'high culture moved out of the narrow confines of the court and into diverse spaces in London'.[23] London was the key location in the nation for new forms of cultural production, but it was also a city of difference in which high culture was being made, and attended by diverse publics in new places and sites.

The patronage of the monarchy, the aristocracy and the church were less important to the worlds of letters, art and theatre in eighteenth-century London than new commercial spaces for culture's production and consumption: coffee houses, reading societies, debating clubs, assembly rooms, art galleries and pleasure gardens. In such spaces, new identities could be forged – identities which both challenged existing values and were determined by the dictates of that polite behaviour appropriate and necessary to the spaces of commercialised pleasure. Thus, the creation of the Royal Academy under the direction of Joshua Reynolds helped transform the relationship between British artists and their publics so that their art might be seen in what Brewer calls 'a space of cultural edification and not of private commerce'.[24] The Academy was a place in which new standards of taste, new forms of public opinion, even new ideas of what it meant to be British, could be formed. Such matters of cultural production were also evident elsewhere in England, in the emergence of distinct cultural forms in the provinces and in the ways in which London's influence was more widely felt across the country. In sum, Brewer's interpretation of the changes in culture and in cultural production 'depends upon understanding those changes through a series of urban, regional and national geographies which shaped the new forms of public engagement with the arts'.[25]

For historians of science, the edited collection by William Clark, Jan Golinski and Simon Schaffer, *The Sciences in Enlightened Europe* (1999), reflects a wider recognition that the Enlightenment witnessed the definition of both a European and a global sphere for the conduct of scientific activities while noting how science took a different shape in different places. As the editors note, such concerns 'have informed work on the sites where particular knowledges were made, and the linkages that allowed them to be distributed, shared, and challenged. Operations of knowledge making have then been mapped across the dimensions of physical space and in relation to human understandings of locality and distance'.[26]

Part Four of that collection is made up of four chapters whose collective focus is on the making of science in the 'provinces and peripheries' of enlightened Europe: Italy, the Netherlands, the Baltic region and

Brandenburg-Prussia. To take one of these chapters as an example, Lissa Roberts's study of Dutch science in the Enlightenment is, in effect, a study of science's production in, and dissemination from, four specific sites: the anatomy theatre, the physics theatre, the private lecture and the private scientific society. These sites, she argues, provided key places in which various social classes could participate in enlightened science and socialise in doing so, and she illustrates how, over time, the Dutch scientific Enlightenment was differently evident in each of these four sites.[27] Other scholars have also shown how the audiences for medical learning were carefully controlled in eighteenth-century Dutch anatomy theatres: dissection was, for some, a moral question about the proper constitution of the human being and of the state.[28] Larry Stewart's attention to the geographies of scientific debate in London's coffee-houses in the early eighteenth century reminds us that differences in location often reflected differences of social rank between those persons judged to be credible practitioners of natural philosophy and others who were not.[29] No less than art, commercial exchange and musical performance, eighteenth-century science had its sites of production and consumption, sites which provided new spaces for debate and for the emergence of new forms of social and intellectual identity.

Attention to the ways in which eighteenth-century culture and society was made in place, to the consideration of particular geographies – of empire, of knowledge, of public art and so on – and to the forms of geographical knowledge itself is, we suggest, of considerable interest and significance. Thinking geographically about the eighteenth century in such ways provides both a new agenda for the historical geography of the period and new opportunities for interdisciplinary study. This claim is elucidated in the individual contributions here and in the ways in which their work is situated with reference to the study of empire, the public sphere and the Enlightenment.

IMPERIAL GEOGRAPHIES

Georgian Britain was an imperial power. Its geographies were ones that increasingly tied the fortunes of those in the North Atlantic archipelago to other places across the globe. When George I came to the throne in 1714 Britain had just gained, through the Treaty of Utrecht that ended the War of Spanish Succession (1702–13): Gibraltar and Minorca in the Mediterranean, St Kitts in the Caribbean, and Hudson Bay, Nova Scotia and Newfoundland in North America to add to the islands and coastal colonies established since the early seventeenth century. This war-driven process of imperial rivalry and expansion, primarily at the expense of France and Spain, continued throughout the century. In the Seven Years War (1756–63), Britain gained control over Florida, Canada and Cape Breton in North America; the

Caribbean islands of Tobago, Grenada, St Vincent and Dominica; and significant portions of West Africa and, as tax-gatherers, India. By 1815, the empire
had been extended to the Pacific, with settlements in New South Wales and
Van Diemen's Land (Tasmania) as well as claims over many Pacific islands.

This Georgian empire was a varied one. It incorporated very different ways
of life and labour – enslaved Africans on plantations in the sugar islands,
peasant farmers and weavers of cloth in India, and European yeomen and
fur-trading Indians in North America – and a variety of forms of imperial authority and administration, from the fractious politics of governors,
councils and assemblies in the Caribbean to government by the mercantile
East India Company in Bengal. All of this was loosely held together under the
notion that this was an 'Empire of Trade' secured through naval control of
maritime trade routes, and that Britain's empire was somehow different from
the universal monarchy dreamed of by Spain and then France. It also offered
a changing scene. The fortunes of war were never certain and were always
a matter of political debate. Support within Britain for the slave trade and
for plantation slavery was challenged in the later eighteenth century, as it
had been for much longer by those subjected to it, leading to the abolition of
the trade in 1807 and the emancipation of the slaves in 1834. North America
moved from migration to revolution, changing the shape of the empire and
what it meant to be British. This switched the focus to India, where imperial
interests were shifting from trade to territory and raising new questions about
appropriate forms of governance. Scientific exploration in the Pacific also
provoked debate about who the British were and where they fitted into the
world.[30] Empire in the eighteenth century is, therefore, about power, identity
and the forms of representation which bring them together. These are concerns that may be pursued by considering the historical geographies of imperial practices, identities and representations.

First, it is important to distinguish different imperial practices. These are
the varied ways in which the work of empire was done, guided by ideological
and instrumental objectives and shaped by the responses and resistances that
they met.[31] In part this is simply a matter of seeing that things were done
differently in different places. For example, the nature of trade in the Atlantic
world – based on a large number of merchants, ship captains and agents, all
in open competition with each other – was quite different from the large
monopoly companies that controlled Britain's trade elsewhere, particularly
with India and China. Each required different skills of management, different forms of knowledge and different relationships of trust and credit.[32] On a
smaller scale, differences in geography, topography, population density and
the relative numbers of white settlers and African slaves meant that the colonial authorities in Jamaica fought wars against organised bands of runaway
slaves (known as maroons) throughout the eighteenth century, whereas those

on Barbados faced no organised slave rebellion between 1692 and 1816.[33] Yet this is also a matter of the geographies of those imperial practices themselves.

As Daniel Clayton shows in Chapter 2, Vancouver Island was the site of different relationships between 'King George men' and the native peoples of the coast. Scientific exploration, fur trading and imperial geopolitics each brought different techniques for the production of imperial spaces, and created varied geographies of engagement and effacement with the indigenous population. All were the spatial practices of empire building, but the particularities of each deserve interrogation. James Cook's expedition sought to encounter and understand people and places both through Enlightenment science's humanitarianism and its reconnoitring of potential imperial territory and trade. The fur traders also met natives face to face in their attempts to establish and coordinate webs of capital and exchange up and down the Pacific northwest coast. In so doing, they found that their engagements with native polities had to be attentive to the demands of local power relations and ritual practice. Native leaders such as Wickaninish at Clayoquot Sound were able to shape the trading encounter. Finally, the mapping of the coast, and its place within late eighteenth-century geopolitics, reveals a set of imperial practices which relied upon abstraction and effacement, producing a set of geographies over which native people had very little influence.

Secondly, imperial identities were based on particular conceptions of geography that involved various imaginings of Britain and its relationship to the world. Britishness was forged not only in the 1707 Act of Union between England and Scotland, but also in opposition to a Catholic continental other, absolutist and then revolutionary France.[34] This always had an imperial dimension, both in a struggle for global hegemony between European powers that shaped political identities 'at home', and in the notions of difference that sustained imperial ambitions and ideologies there and elsewhere.[35] As a result, Georgian imperial identities were kaleidoscopic. For example, identities in the Atlantic colonies were time and space specific, differing between Ireland, New England, Georgia and the Caribbean islands, and changing over time as the interaction between settlers on the land, indigenous peoples, imported labour (enslaved or free), and the metropole unfolded. For political elites in the Americas, claims to a Britishness which rested on a shared transatlantic political language of law, liberty and the pursuit of freedom might lead them into rebellion against Britain's authority.[36] At the other end of the social spectrum, the circuits of empire brought together the disenfranchised and dissatisfied of all corners of the worlds, and among this picaresque proletariat might be found the glimmerings of a multicultural and anti-imperial internationalism.[37] Elsewhere identities were deeply ambivalent.[38] As David Lambert shows in Chapter 3, the attempt by white Barbadians to negotiate a position for themselves within late-Georgian imperial identity was full of tensions. Through an interpretation of the construction of creole identities via the violent and polemical attacks on Methodism in Barbados in the early 1820s, and in the context of increasing anti-slavery campaigning and the redefinition of Britishness in terms of humanitarianism, he shows that white Barbadian identities oscillated between ultra-loyalty to Britain and resistance to imperial authority.

Thirdly, these questions of imperial practice and identity were bound up with representations of empire in words and images. Within this array of representations, depictions of space, place and landscape were central as part of both self-understanding and the imperial governance of others.[39] However, the lands and landscapes of the Americas, Asia, Africa and the Pacific posed substantial problems of representation to which conventional modes of textual and visual depiction – mapping, drawing, painting and travel writing – had to respond. Cartographic techniques had to be devised, adapted and combined with indigenous knowledge to produce detailed maps of India and of the Pacific islands and coasts.[40] The aesthetic conventions of the georgic and the picturesque needed to be reworked in contradictory attempts to manage the meanings of productive landscapes on plantations in the Caribbean, European travellers' responses to Indian scenes, and the curious nature of the Pacific islands.[41] In each case, understanding these forms of 'imperial' representation requires attention to the specific material geographies of their production and of their consumption or display.

As Luciana Martins demonstrates in Chapter 4, the depiction of tropical landscapes is a more complex process than can be captured by recourse to the 'imperial eye'. Her reconstruction of the connections between techniques of visualisation, the making of scientific knowledge and the experience of travel focuses on the work of the artist William Havell. She demonstrates the material grounding of his artistic production in forms of sketching 'on the spot' which can be conceived of as on-going experiments in the representation of the tropics – experiments which required innovations in materials, composition and colour. The often critical response to Havell's work in London signalled both the risks in the representation of empire, and the ways in which such representations of Georgian imperial geographies were part of that world of public exhibition – as theatre, art or curiosity – which was constructing new relationships between cultural production and public space.[42]

GEOGRAPHIES OF THE PUBLIC SPHERE

The towns and cities of eighteenth-century Britain were reshaped through changes in the ways people understood, acted out and negotiated the idea of the 'public'. New spaces such as the coffee house, the assembly rooms and the pleasure garden were created by and for these 'publics', and these places were animated by new activities, encounters and experiences shaped by a rapidly-expanding marketplace for culture in print, paint and music, and by the ideas and practices of polite sociability.[43] At the same time, there were transformations in domestic life – as detected in furnishings, floor plans and foodstuffs, as well as in parenting, portraiture and periodical essays – towards a more comfortable domesticity based, again, on new consumer goods.[44] Yet within these broad parameters, the precise nature of these historical geographies of public and private need to be understood through close attention to the specific spaces which came into being.

By examining public spaces one begins to uncover multiple public spheres, which may have intersected but which each had its own rules of entry and engagement. There were, for example, many coffee houses and many faces of the coffee house. Jonathan's sold to stockbrokers, Old Slaughter's was patronised by artists, Tories sipped at the Smyrna, and Whigs supped at Arthur's. There were paintings to be seen at the Barbadoes coffee house in Exchange Alley, while the nearby Marine hosted lectures on Newtonian natural philosophy.[45] Theatres, opera houses, concert halls, parks, assembly rooms, pleasure gardens, debating societies, circulating libraries and exhibition halls, not to mention the newly planned streets, squares and circuses of Bath, London, Edinburgh and Dublin which held, connected and framed these new sites of leisure, may have shared a broad culture of politeness, but this culture was one with an intricate topography. As Rosie Dias demonstrates in Chapter 5, the geography of the exhibition of art in the capital in the 1780s and 1790s was a complex one.[46] By recovering the array of exhibition spaces on and around Pall Mall (and the coffee houses, clubs and print-shops which surrounded them), and by studying the relationship between the viewing public and British history painting and its tense and politicised relationship with the Royal Academy at Somerset House, she both illustrates the ways in which different public spheres were created in and through different public spaces, and discusses the implications that this has for understanding gender, politics and cultural production.

Compared to the attention that has been paid to the public sphere and public spaces in the eighteenth century, there has been relatively little scrutiny of the domestic sphere and of how its more intimate geographies were figured. This requires an understanding of the household as a social and material space as well as a demographic or economic unit. Questions of identity and social status, of authority and autonomy, can be understood through the geographies of the home. Where and how were domestic commodities such as tea tables, coffee-pots, cutlery, cupboards, clocks, pictures, books and musical instruments bought, placed, used and replaced? How did their design and display change with architectural style? How did they give domestic spaces particular meanings, such as making dining rooms and kitchens fit for polite conversation with visitors, or dealings with tradespeople? What were the implications for the relationships of power and intimacy between men and women of different understandings of domestic space and their negotiation and contestation through things in and out of place – boots on the sofa, or romantic novels in the library?[47]

For Cynthia Wall in Chapter 6, these understandings of domestic space underwent a dramatic transformation within the narratives of historians and of novelists over the course of the eighteenth century. By considering the history of description, particularly the description of interiors, she shows how writers moved away from the classical view that description unnecessarily disrupted narrative for an audience understood to have a common frame of reference. What replaced it were novels and histories where descriptions of space were, for audiences which increasingly understood themselves and others in terms of the differentiation of spaces and things, a vital part of the depiction of character, motivation and subjectivity.

It is clear, however, that none of this should be used to reinforce a strongly gendered distinction between 'public' and 'private'. Eighteenth-century versions of the public/private dichotomy, as 'spheres' or as 'spaces', cannot be shoehorned into either a neat division of the worlds of men and women, or a simple linear history of their separation and of the increasingly strict sequestration of the body, sex and death.[48] The particular configurations of public and private, and the ways in which the boundaries between them were drawn or blurred both discursively and in practice, were different in different situations. The very nature of 'public' and 'private' were worked out in contrasting ways in the parlour, on the pavement, or at the polls, and questions of rank and status were as crucial as issues of gender.[49]

As Karen Harvey argues in Chapter 7, the study of eighteenth-century erotica offers both a challenge to our expectations about 'public' and 'private' in terms of reading practices and provides evidence of deep-seated and iniquitous power relations between men and women. She shows how the model of the solitary female reader consuming erotica in private, which was constructed by authors of such texts, was part of the immobilisation and sexualising of female bodies. These privately-situated bodies were then consumed by elite men reading aloud and inspecting women's bodies within homosocial and public (if exclusive) gatherings. As Harvey also shows, the male audience for erotica was one that constructed its masculinity through an engagement with geographical knowledge. She demonstrates the satirical uses of cartography and travellers' tales in the construction of erotic texts, of women's bodies as landscapes and territories to be surveyed and explored, and of masculine identities as witty and enlightened.[50] Indeed, such texts were part of a more general making of Enlightenment geographies.

ENLIGHTENMENT'S GEOGRAPHIES

Where it has been so recognised at all, the Enlightenment understood geographically has mainly been studied in national context. Roy Porter and Mikulas Teich's collection, *The Enlightenment in National Context* (1981), is illustrative here. The book was prompted by a recognition that earlier accounts had been insufficiently attentive to what the editors termed the Enlightenment's 'geographical, social, and political *location* as a cultural movement'.[51] Their book sought in thirteen chapters to consider the different national expressions of Enlightenment in England, Scotland, France, the Netherlands, Switzerland, Italy, Germany (the subject of two chapters), Austria, Bohemia, Sweden, Russia and America.

More recently, scholarship on what, collectively, may be termed the geographies of the Enlightenment has moved in several ways beyond the nation as a scale of analysis (something which Porter and Teich anyway saw as problematic). The European Enlightenment was moulded by geographical contact with other parts of the world, notably with the Americas and with the peoples of the Pacific. Those Enlightenment ideas and ideals embodied in the stadial theory of historical difference and development were, in truth, matters of geography since what lay 'before Europe' (and, indeed, what lay differently *within* individual European countries) also lay 'beyond Europe'. Peter Hulme and Ludmilla Jordanova noted that such concerns about the global and local nature of the Enlightenment meant that 'The Enlightenment's self consciousness was to some extent a geographical consciousness based on the distinctiveness of the part of the world that came to be called Europe'.[52] Further work has examined the place of geography as a discipline in the Enlightenment and, in so doing, has revised the understanding of the discipline's history in the period.[53]

Of greater significance to the concerns of this volume is that work on understanding the Enlightenment geographically which can, for convenience, be considered under two general headings. First, there is work which has discussed geographical knowledge *and* the Enlightenment – that is, the various intellectual practices such as mapping and naming through which European navigators encountered and represented the rest of the world. Second, we may distinguish renewed attention to the geographical nature *of* the Enlightenment, in which context both the local settings of the Enlightenment's making and reception and its international nature have been stressed at the relative expense of the national scale of enquiry.[54] Both historiographical trends are apparent to one degree or another in several of the following chapters.

It is now more widely recognised that geographical knowledge was central to the form and the content of the Enlightenment. For this reason, it is important to distinguish more clearly the processes by which geographical knowledge was accumulated during the Enlightenment, the ways in which such knowledge was employed and for whom and, finally, the routes and means of its dissemination. Too firm a typological demarcation between gathering, using and disseminating new forms of geographical knowledge should be avoided, of course, since such terms may suggest a strict separation of the production and consumption of knowledge that the authors here would wish to challenge. As others have shown of mapping, for example, eighteenth-century map making, in Britain and France at least, was underpinned by distinct social and practical hierarchies, yet the resultant maps had different audiences and uses. Those who looked upon maps as purportedly accurate documents of the real world did so in different ways from audiences in other places where the map was an accompaniment to public lectures or private instruction in geography. Elsewhere, the contribution of indigenous populations within and beyond Europe to new maps of the world were effaced by the very documents they helped produce.[55]

Several of these issues underpin John Gascoigne's attention in Chapter 8 to Joseph Banks's understanding of maps and of mapping. For Banks and for those with whom he worked, the map was an instrumental device by which the form of distant lands such as Vancouver Island and New Holland (Australia) could be given a more exact shape. The map was also a means to classification, a form of taxonomic control of the global natural knowledge that Banks sought to place in order. At the same time, Banks was locating himself at the centre of the map of learning concerning Enlightenment geography and natural history. If, then, as Gascoigne notes here, 'Maps and empires were made to appear natural allies', we should not forget that such appearances of alliance depended upon (as they also obscured) social networks of reliance and of credibility. Map makers in the field had to trust themselves, their instruments and their informants. Map users elsewhere had to trust that maps faithfully reproduced a geography that they had not themselves encountered.

Banks was concerned, as Gascoigne and others have shown, that the new knowledge gathered in the eighteenth century should be useful in one way or another.[56] 'Utility' and its surrogate, 'improvement', are, however, terms which permit subdivision and some attention as to who found what useful. On the one hand, notions of utility embraced material 'improvements' – in such things as agricultural yield (or in the texts which promoted it), in the accuracy of the map, the performance of scientific instruments or the mathematisation of natural philosophical discourse. On the other hand, utility encompassed issues of public (and private) edification in which, for example, facts learned from a public lecture, or new discoveries learned through conversation in a coffee house might have no more immediate benefit than an increase in public sociability and individual education.[57]

As Vladimir Jankovic shows in Chapter 9, rural Britain may have been the place in which ideas of material improvement in Georgian agriculture took root. It was not, however, a space in which respectable and edifying ideas of natural philosophy were expected to emerge – not, anyway, from those who actually worked the ground or tended livestock. In its many landscape gardens and in its associations with Virgilian indolence and pleasure, rural Britain in the Georgian period was, for the upper ranks at least, a space of aesthetic pleasure and Arcadian virtue. Yet as Jankovic shows, for some eighteenth-century commentators, the doing of scientific enquiry and even what was held to be legitimate philosophical discourse about things like the weather depended upon where the work was undertaken and by whom. In that sense, rustic science was a subject that demanded attention to questions of lore and tradition, and to the moral economy and truths resulting from the virtuous labour of people not usually deemed credible producers of reliable natural knowledge.

Making sense of the utility inherent in the new facts of geography, epistemology and economy during the eighteenth century depended in part upon the circulation of relevant books, be they works of agrarian instruction from men like Adam Dickson, manuals of survey produced by James Rennell to guide Banks and others like him, or books of geography designed to instruct and to entertain. Work by historians of the book in the eighteenth century, looking principally at scientific and medical works, has drawn attention to a number of themes including the idea of the 'communications circuit', the location of book production and of authorship and the networks of book exchange.[58] For a later period, different 'geographies of reading' have been mapped for one scientific text.[59]

In these terms, it is clearly as relevant to think of a 'book geography' as a book history in the eighteenth century. It is also important that we do not lose sight of the distinctions contemporaries recognised between different genres of books of geography. As Robert Mayhew documents in Chapter 10, books of geography – gazetteers and grammars alike – were regarded as works of useful knowledge, in both the practical and philosophical senses. Geography books such as William Guthrie's *New Geographical, Historical and Commercial Grammar* incorporated and disseminated the political theories of the Enlightenment. For the Enlightenment philosopher and historian William Robertson in his *History of America* (1788), geographical knowledge was essential to an understanding of America's history, both in terms of its discovery by Europeans and from the internal geographical matters that had to be overcome in forging American nationhood. The work had prefatory maps by Thomas Kitchin, Hydrographer Royal, in order that readers could locate the formative events of Robertson's historical narrative. Mayhew's attention to Rennell's *Hindoostan* memoir also reminds us that, as Lambert shows of Barbados and Gascoigne of Banks, interests in geography and imperial expansion were interrelated, and the map as a form of Enlightenment geographical knowledge depended upon a close association with the textual memoir.

Yet what was held by readers as a geography book during the Enlightenment was not straightforwardly a work encompassing the body of useful geographical knowledge. As Karen Harvey shows, Stretser's *A New Description of Merryland* (1741) had a different body in mind in its geographical references and illustrative map. As Harvey shows, the work was partly a satire of 'proper' geography books, notably of Patrick Gordon's *Geography Anatomiz'd: or, A Compleat Geographical Grammar,* first published in London in 1693. Gordon's work, corrected and enlarged, was one of the most popular works of geography in Georgian Britain and ran to twenty editions by 1760. Taken together, these two books illustrate the different languages of geography and the connections between the geographies of the Enlightenment and of the public and private worlds during the Georgian period. Between the particular anatomical geographies of Stretser's satire and the enduring success of Gordon's *Geography Anatomiz'd,* and in the specific places, both public and private, that they were read, geographical knowledge connected the worlds of eroticism and of practical utility.

CONCLUSION: THE GEORGIAN GLOBE

The themes of imperialism, Enlightenment and the public sphere that we have used to organise this book and the ways in which the contributors have elaborated upon them in their different approaches to space, place and landscape can be brought together by considering the geographies of the Georgian globe. As both the shape of the world and as a representation of it, the globe was made, transformed, consumed and studied in new ways in the eighteenth century.

In the imperial realm, the scale of Britain's colonial expansion in the eighteenth century – especially from the beginning of the Seven Years War in 1756 to the end of the Napoleonic Wars in 1815 – was global, a fact often overlooked in the attention paid to the British Empire as a phenomenon of the later nineteenth century. The making of this Georgian empire brought almost one quarter of the world's population under British authority, at the same time as Britain's material and intellectual culture was more and more embedded in circuits that connected Western Europe, Africa, Asia and the Americas.[60] Global economic, political and cultural geographies were reconfigured. Yet despite the globe being an arena for imperial politics – indeed, precisely because of that – questions of empire were not a matter of single geographical entities, either everywhere held together in similar ways or containing within their bounds 'essential' colonial subjects. Britain's global political reach depended upon accommodating and creating different geographies across the globe.

If the eighteenth century was a period of unparalleled imperial expansion, so it was also a period of unprecedented empirical exploration of the age, shape and content of the terraqueous globe.[61] By the end of the century, the globe was immeasurably older than it had been in 1700. Systems of classification, in botany, in geology and in stratigraphy, aimed to put nature's diversity to order. Voyages of exploration sought to chart the geography of the world as never before. In being at least partly concerned with the astronomical issue of the transit of Venus, for example, Cook's first voyage was also concerned with understanding the terraqueous globe in its celestial context. The fact that he sailed with secret orders to extend Britain's commercial interests where he could, serves only to emphasise the connections in the Georgian period between global knowledge, mercantilism, imperial science and geographical discovery.

Cook's geographical endeavours across the globe were made easier by advances in scientific instrumentation. He was supplied with some instruments for his first voyage by George Adams Senior, who with others had run an instrument-making business in London from the 1750s. Adams's precision instruments travelled the globe the better to know it. For those people who stayed put, Adams and others supplied the developing market for globes in later eighteenth-century London with the symbolic means to know the world as an object of geography. As maps depended for their credibility upon an associated memoir, so globes also needed accompanying texts. Adams's *Treatise Describing and Explaining the Construction and Use of New Celestial and Terrestrial Globes* (1766), promoted his work as an instrument maker and offered instruction in viewing the world or the heavens in model form. Understanding the Georgian globe depended upon an association between the instrument, the text and the geographical knowledge they both contained and represented.

That there were different markets for different scientific instruments and different local geographies of scientific engagement means we must be sensitive to the different audiences, or publics, for scientific knowledge.[62] Globes were limited in their capacity for large-scale public spectacle and display. Panoramas, produced first in 1789 and established in London's Leicester Square in the 1790s, were a more significant vehicle for the grand visual dramatisation of geographical knowledge.[63] Yet, in other settings in Georgian Britain, different types of globes afforded people different opportunities for geographical knowledge. Instrument makers like Nathaniel Hill, who had a shop at 'The Globe and Sun' in London's Chancery Lane in 1754, prominently displayed globes of several sorts and dimensions on his trade card.[64] These might be divided into two kinds: sophisticated globes, which were used to demonstrate scientific phenomena, and decorative but less accurate globes which were deployed within less specialist modes of education and display. Of the latter sort, one particularly English late eighteenth-century globe was highly popular among certain social ranks – the pocket globe. This was a sphere, usually of wood or pasteboard, inside two hinged hemispheres, with the terraqueous globe being printed on the sphere and the celestial globe being printed on the interior surface of the case. These may have been for the education of children in geography and astronomy, expensive status symbols or, simply, amusing playthings.[65] Whatever is the case, for a price the Georgian world could be kept in one's pocket, toyed with, or admired on display in the drawing-room or nursery.

That other globes were objects of domestic admiration and their use a matter of polite accomplishment is clear from the advertisement for those made by John Senex, appended to Thomas Wright's 1740 work, *The Use of the Globes*, which aimed to sell them as pairs in order 'to adorn the Libraries of the Curious'. As Alice Walters has shown, geography and astronomy taught to men and women and boys and girls through use of terrestrial and celestial globes as conversation pieces helped to advance notions of politeness. The globe was used in the home in private lessons, often in association with maps and books of geography. In one sense, civil society and geographical enquiry were held together through the facts of conversation and mannered tutelage about the globe. But, as Walters has also shown, domestic spaces were not just reserved for conversations and activities of a geographical nature. Men's interest in globes as instruments of delight and pleasure could extend to an erotic interest in the female form – globes had many meanings, and the transit of Venus was not just an astronomical phenomenon.[66] As Denis Cosgrove argues more generally for the western geographical imagination, the enlightened globe was an object of domestic display and delight, Newtonian philosophy and precision, cartographic power and the imaginative reach of European empires.[67]

The Georgian globe, at once material and symbolic, fashioned by imperialism and mediating between public and private worlds of geographical knowledge, is a fitting figure for bringing together concerns with the geographies of Georgian Britain, its place in the world, and the nature of eighteenth-century geographical understanding. As the following essays reveal, other significant ideas and practices in the Georgian world need to be understood through their geographies, geographies which we hope are illuminated here in ways which will stimulate further enquiry.

NOTES

1 M. Foucault, *Discipline and Punish: The Birth of the Prison* (London: Allen Lane, 1977); J. Habermas, *The Structural Transformation of the Public Sphere: An Inquiry into a Category of Bourgeois Society* (Cambridge: Polity Press, 1989); R. Williams, *The*

Country and the City (London: Chatto & Windus, 1973); E. W. Said, *Orientalism* (Harmondsworth: Penguin, 1978); B. Latour, *Science in Action: How to Follow Scientists and Engineers Through Society* (Milton Keynes: Open University Press, 1987).

2 P. J. Marshall, 'Preface', in P. J. Marshall (ed.), *The Oxford History of the British Empire. Volume 2: The Eighteenth Century* (Oxford: Oxford University Press, 1998), x. On empire, see also K. Wilson, *The Sense of the People: Politics, Culture and Imperialism in England, 1715–85* (Cambridge: Cambridge University Press, 1995).

3 See, for example, D. P. Miller and P. H. Reill (eds), *Visions of Empire: Voyages, Botany, and Representations of Nature* (Cambridge: Cambridge University Press, 1996).

4 D. W. Clayton, *Islands of Truth: The Imperial Fashioning of Vancouver Island* (Vancouver: University of British Columbia Press, 2000).

5 J. Gascoigne, *Science in the Service of Empire: Joseph Banks, the British State and the Uses of Science in the Age of Revolution* (Cambridge: Cambridge University Press, 1998).

6 D. N. Livingstone and C. W. J. Withers (eds), *Geography and Enlightenment* (Chicago: University of Chicago Press, 1999); R. Porter, *Enlightenment: Britain and the Creation of the Modern World* (London: Allen Lane for the Penguin Press, 2000).

7 See, for example, J. Golinski, *Science as Public Culture: Chemistry and Enlightenment in Britain* (Cambridge: Cambridge University Press, 1992), and his *Making Natural Knowledge: Constructivism and the History of Science* (Cambridge: Cambridge University Press, 1998); L. Stewart, *The Rise of Public Science: Rhetoric, Technology, and Natural Philosophy in Newtonian Britain, 1660–1750* (Cambridge: Cambridge University Press, 1992). On audiences for eighteenth-century science, see, for example A. G. Morton (ed.), 'Science lecturing in the eighteenth century', *British Journal for the History of Science*, 28 (1995), 1–100.

8 C. W. J. Withers, *Geography, Science and National Identity: Scotland since 1520* (Cambridge: Cambridge University Press, 2001); R. J. Mayhew, *Enlightenment Geography: The Political Languages of British Geography, 1650–1850* (London and New York: Macmillan and St Martin's Press, 2000).

9 E. C. Spary, *Utopia's Garden: French Natural History from Old Regime to Revolution* (Chicago: University of Chicago Press, 2000).

10 W. Clark, J. Golinski and S. Schaffer (eds), *The Sciences in Enlightened Europe* (Chicago: University of Chicago Press, 1999); C. W. J. Withers and P. Wood (eds), *Science and Medicine in the Scottish Enlightenment* (East Linton: Tuckwell Press, 2002).

11 D. H. Solkin, *Painting for Money: The Visual Arts and the Public Sphere in Eighteenth-Century England* (New Haven: Yale University Press, 1993). For France, see T. Crow, *Painters and Public Life in Eighteenth-Century Paris* (New Haven and London: Yale University Press, 1985), and his *Emulation: Making Artists for Revolutionary France* (New Haven and London: Yale University Press, 1995).

12 S. J. Daniels and D. Cosgrove, 'Introduction: iconography and landscape', in D. E. Cosgrove and S. J. Daniels (eds), *The Iconography of Landscape* (Cambridge: Cambridge University Press, 1988), 1–10; S. J. Daniels, 'Revisioning Britain: mapping and landscape painting 1750–1830', in K. Baetjer (ed.), *Glorious Nature: British Landscape Painting, 1750–1850* (New York: Hudson Hills, 1994), 61–72; S. J. Daniels, *Joseph Wright: Art and Enlightenment* (London: Tate Gallery, 2000); S. J. Daniels, *Humphry Repton: Landscape Gardening and the Geography of Georgian England* (New Haven: Yale University Press, 2001); R. Mayhew, 'Landscape, religion, and knowledge in eighteenth-century England', *Ecumene*, 3 (1996), 454–71.

13 See, for example, C. Chard and H. Langdon (eds), *Transports: Travel, Pleasure, and Imaginative Geography, 1600–1830* (New Haven and London: Yale University Press, 1996); J. Lamb, *Preserving the Self in the South Seas, 1680–1840* (Chicago: University

of Chicago Press, 2001); J. Lamb, V. Smith and N. Thomas (eds), *Exploration and Exchange: South Seas Anthology, 1680–1900* (Chicago: University of Chicago Press, 2000); J. Renwick (ed.), *L'Invitation au Voyage: Studies in Honour of Peter France* (Oxford: Voltaire Foundation, 2000); N. Leask, *Curiosity and the Aesthetics of Travel Writing, 1770–1840* (Oxford: Oxford University Press, 2002).

14 Spary, *Utopia's Garden*. On travel and exoticism, see T. Fulford and P. J. Kitson (eds), *Romanticism and Colonialism: Writing and Empire, 1780–1830* (Cambridge: Cambridge University Press, 1998); T. Fulford and P. J. Kitson (eds), *Travels, Explorations and Empires: Writings from the Era of Imperial Expansion, 1770–1835* (London: Pickering and Chatto, 2001); A. Gilroy (ed.), *Romantic Geographies: Discourses of Travel, 1775–1844* (Manchester: Manchester University Press, 2000). On artistic encounters and visual representation, see B. Smith, *European Vision and the South Pacific, 1768–1850: A Study in the History of Art and Ideas* (Oxford: Clarendon Press, 1960), and his *Imagining the Pacific: In the Wake of the Cook Voyages* (New Haven: Yale University Press, 1992); B. M. Stafford, *Voyage into Substance: Art, Science and the Illustrated Travel Account, 1760–1840* (London: MIT Press, 1984); A. R. W. Meyers and M. B. Pritchard (eds), *Empire's Nature: Mark Catesby's New World Vision* (Chapel Hill and London: University of North Carolina Press, 1998); N. Thomas and D. Losche (eds), *Double Vision: Art Histories and Colonial Histories in the Pacific* (Cambridge: Cambridge University Press, 1999).

15 M. Overton, *Agricultural Revolution in England: The Transformation of the Agrarian Economy, 1500–1850* (Cambridge: Cambridge University Press, 1996); P. Hudson (ed.), *Regions and Industries: A Perspective on the Industrial Revolution* (Cambridge: Cambridge University Press, 1989); M. Berg and P. Hudson, 'Rehabilitating the industrial revolution', *Economic History Review*, 45 (1992), 24–50.

16 J. Brewer, *Sinews of Power: War, Money and the English State, 1688–1783* (London: Unwin Hyman, 1987); J. R. Kent, 'The centre and the localities: state formation and parish government in England, *circa* 1640–1740', *Historical Journal*, 38 (1995), 363–404; P. Borsay, *The English Urban Renaissance: Culture and Society in the Provincial Town, 1660–1770* (Oxford: Clarendon Press, 1989); M. Ogborn, *Spaces of Modernity: London's Geographies, 1680–1780* (New York: Guilford Press, 1998).

17 L. Colley, *Britons: Forging the Nation, 1707–1837* (New Haven and London: Yale University Press, 1992); L. Colley, *Captives: Britain, Empire and the World, 1600–1850* (London: Jonathan Cape, 2002); Wilson, *The Sense of the People*; J. H. Plumb, *Georgian Delights* (London: Weidenfeld & Nicolson, 1980); J. Brewer, *The Pleasures of the Imagination: English Culture in the Eighteenth Century* (London: Fontana Press, 1997). See also J. Black, *An Illustrated History of Eighteenth-Century Britain, 1688–1793* (Manchester: Manchester University Press, 1996); G. Sutton, *Science for a Polite Society: Gender, Culture, and the Demonstration of Enlightenment* (Boulder, CO: University of Colorado Press, 1996).

18 R. Porter, 'The new eighteenth-century social history', in J. Black (ed.), *Culture and Society in Britain, 1660–1800* (Manchester: Manchester University Press, 1997), 29–50.

19 In particular, J. C. D. Clark, *English Society, 1688–1832* (Cambridge: Cambridge University Press, 1995). On politics and religion, see also J. Black, *The Politics of Britain, 1688–1800* (Manchester: Manchester University Press, 1993); K. Haakonsen (ed.), *Enlightenment and Religion: Rational Dissent in Eighteenth-Century Britain* (Cambridge: Cambridge University Press, 1996); B. W. Young, *Religion and Enlightenment in Eighteenth-Century England: Theological Debates from Locke to Burke* (Oxford: Clarendon Press, 1998); J. G. A. Pocock, *Barbarism and Religion. Volume 2: Narratives of Civil Government* (Cambridge: Cambridge University Press, 1999).

20 These methods and their enduring significance are discussed in H. C. Darby, *The Relations of History and Geography: Studies in England, France and the United States* (Exeter: Exeter University Press, 2001).

21 P. Burke, *A Social History of Knowledge from Gutenberg to Diderot* (Cambridge and Oxford: Polity Press, 2000).

22 On the spatial turn in these and other subjects, see D. N. Livingstone, 'The spaces of knowledge: contributions towards a historical geography of science', *Environment and Planning D: Society and Space*, 13 (1995), 5–34; D. N. Livingstone, 'Making space for science', *Erdkunde*, 34 (2000), 285–96. On the 'geographical turn' in the history of science, see C. Smith and J. Agar, 'Introduction: making space for science', in C. Smith and J. Agar (eds), *Making Space for Science: Territorial Themes in the Shaping of Knowledge* (London and New York: Macmillan, 1998), 1–23.

23 Brewer, *Pleasures of the Imagination*, 3.

24 *Ibid.*, 245.

25 M. Ogborn, 'Georgian geographies?', *Journal of Historical Geography*, 24 (1998), 218–23, quote on p. 220.

26 Clark, Golinski and Schaffer (eds), *Sciences in Enlightened Europe*, x.

27 L. Roberts, 'Going Dutch: situating science in the Dutch Enlightenment', in Clark, Golinski and Schaffer (eds), *Sciences in Enlightened Europe*, 350–88.

28 J. Rupp, 'The new science and the public sphere in the premodern era', *Science in Context*, 8 (1995), 487–507.

29 L. Stewart, 'Other centres of calculation, or, where the Royal Society didn't count: commerce, coffee-houses and natural philosophy in early modern London', *British Journal for the History of Science*, 32 (1999), 133–53.

30 For overviews, see Marshall, *The Oxford History of the British Empire. Volume 2*; D. Armitage, *The Ideological Origins of the British Empire* (Cambridge: Cambridge University Press, 2000); L. Stone (ed.), *An Imperial State at War: Britain from 1689 to 1815* (London: Routledge, 1994); P. J. Marshall and G. Williams, *The Great Map of Mankind: British Perceptions of the World in the Age of Enlightenment* (London: Dent, 1992); R. Blackburn, *The Making of New World Slavery: From the Baroque to the Modern, 1492–1800* (London: Verso, 1997) and his *The Overthrow of Colonial Slavery, 1776–1848* (London: Verso, 1998); P. J. Marshall, *The New Cambridge History of India, Volume 2 Part 2, Bengal: The British Bridgehead, Eastern India, 1740–1828* (Cambridge: Cambridge University Press, 1987); M. Lincoln (ed.), *Science and Exploration in the Pacific: European Voyages to the Southern Oceans in the Eighteenth Century* (Woodbridge: Boydell & Brewer, 1999); Wilson, *The Sense of the People*, and her *The Island Race: Englishness, Empire and Gender in the Eighteenth Century* (London: Routledge, 2002).

31 One important set of objectives was understood as 'improvement': see R. Drayton, *Nature's Government: Science, Imperial Britain, and the 'Improvement' of the World* (New Haven: Yale University Press, 2000); R. Grove, *Green Imperialism: Colonial Expansion, Tropical Island Edens and the Origins of Environmentalism, 1600–1860* (Cambridge: Cambridge University Press, 1995).

32 D. Hancock, *Citizens of the World: London Merchants and the Integration of the British Atlantic Community, 1735–1785* (Cambridge: Cambridge University Press, 1995); K. N. Chaudhuri, *The Trading World of Asia and the English East India Company, 1660–1760* (Cambridge: Cambridge University Press, 1978); H. V. Bowen, M. Lincoln and N. Rigby (eds), *The Worlds of the East India Company* (Woodbridge: Boydell Press, 2002).

33 H. McD. Beckles, *A History of Barbados: From Amerindian Settlement to Nation-State* (Cambridge: Cambridge University Press, 1990); M. Craton, *Testing the Chains: Slave Resistance in the British West Indies* (Ithaca: Cornell University Press, 1983).

34 Colley, *Britons*; C. Kidd, *Subverting Scotland's Past: Scottish Whig Historians and the Creation of an Anglo-British Identity, 1689–c. 1830* (Cambridge: Cambridge University Press, 1993); P. Langford, *Englishness Identified: Manners and Character, 1650–1850* (Oxford: Oxford University Press, 2000).

35 Wilson, *Sense of the People*; R. Wheeler, *The Complexion of Race: Categories of Difference in Eighteenth-Century British Culture* (Philadelphia: University of Pennsylvania Press, 2000).

36 N. Canny and A. Pagden, *Colonial Identity in the Atlantic World, 1500–1800* (Princeton: Princeton University Press, 1989); J. P. Greene, 'Empire and identity from the Glorious Revolution to the American Revolution', in Marshall (ed.), *Oxford History of the British Empire. Volume 2*, 208–30; J. C. D. Clark, *The Language of Liberty, 1660–1832: Political Discourse and Social Dynamics in the Anglo-American World* (Cambridge: Cambridge University Press, 1994).

37 P. Linebaugh and M. Rediker, *The Many-Headed Hydra: Sailors, Slaves, Commoners, and the Hidden History of the Revolutionary Atlantic* (Boston: Beacon Press, 2000); M. Rediker, *Between the Devil and the Deep Blue Sea: Merchant Seamen, Pirates and the Anglo-American Maritime World, 1700–1750* (Cambridge: Cambridge University Press, 1987); W. J. Bolster, *Black Jacks: African American Seamen in the Age of Sail* (Cambridge MA: Harvard University Press, 1997); J. Roach, *Cities of the Dead: Circum-Atlantic Performance* (New York: Columbia University Press, 1996).

38 For the Pacific, see Lamb, *Preserving the Self*. For the Caribbean, see K. Sandiford, *The Cultural Politics of Sugar: Caribbean Slavery and Narratives of Colonialism* (Cambridge: Cambridge University Press, 2000).

39 See, for example, B. F. Tobin, *Picturing Imperial Power: Colonial Subjects in Eighteenth-Century British Painting* (Durham: Duke University Press, 1999); K. D. Kriz, 'Curiosities, commodities and transplanted bodies', in Hans Sloane, *Natural History of Jamaica', William and Mary Quarterly*, 57 (2000), 35–78; Lamb, *Preserving the Self*.

40 M. H. Edney, *Mapping an Empire: The Geographical Construction of British India, 1765–1843* (Chicago: University of Chicago Press, 1997); K. Raj, 'Colonial encounters and the forging of new knowledge and national identities: Great Britain and India, 1760–1850', *Osiris*, 15 (2000), 119–34; R. Sorrenson, 'The ship as a scientific instrument in the eighteenth century', *Osiris*, 11 (1996), 221–36; Clayton, *Islands of Truth*.

41 S. Seymour, S. J. Daniels and C. Watkins, 'Estate and empire: Sir George Cornewall's management of Moccas, Herefordshire and La Taste, Grenada, 1771–1819', *Journal of Historical Geography*, 24 (1998), 313–51; Leask, *Curiosity and the Aesthetics of Travel Writing*; Smith, *European Vision and the South Pacific*.

42 G. Dening, *Mr Bligh's Bad Language: Passion, Power and Theatre on the Bounty* (Cambridge: Cambridge University Press, 1992); Roach, *Cities of the Dead*; N. Thomas, *Entangled Objects: Exchange, Material Culture and Colonialism in the Pacific* (Cambridge MA: Harvard University Press, 1991).

43 Borsay, *English Urban Renaissance*; Brewer, *Pleasures of the Imagination*; M. Hallett, *The Spectacle of Difference: Graphic Satire in the Age of Hogarth* (New Haven: Yale University Press, 1999); L. E. Klein, *Shaftesbury and the Culture of Politeness: Moral Discourse and Cultural Politics in Early Eighteenth-Century England* (Cambridge: Cambridge University Press, 1994); Solkin, *Painting for Money*; A. Vickery, *The Gentleman's Daughter: Women's Lives in Georgian England* (New Haven: Yale University Press, 1998).

44 C. Shammas, 'The domestic environment in early modern England and America', *Journal of Social History*, 14 (1980), 3–24; L. Weatherill, *Consumer Behaviour and Material Culture in Britain, 1660–1760* (London, Routledge, 1998).

45 B. Cowan, 'What was masculine about the public sphere? Gender and the coffeehouse milieu in post-Restoration England', *History Workshop Journal*, 51 (2001), 127–57; H. Berry, 'Rethinking politeness in eighteenth-century England: Moll King's coffeehouse and the significance of "flash talk"', *Transactions of the Royal Historical Society*, fifth series, 6 (2001), 65–81; Stewart, 'Other centres of calculation'.

46 See also D. H. Solkin (ed.), *Art on the Line: The Royal Academy Exhibitions at Somerset House, 1780–1836* (New Haven and London: Yale University Press, 2001).

47 For clocks, see N. J. Thrift and P. Glennie, 'The spaces of times', in P. Joyce (ed.), *History and the Social Sciences* (Manchester: Manchester University Press, forthcoming). Both Vickery, *The Gentleman's Daughter* and Hancock, *Citizens of the World* consider the significance of bespoke mahogany furniture for the northern provincial elite and London Atlantic merchants respectively. On architecture, see E. McKellar, *The Birth of Modern London: The Development and Design of the City, 1660–1720* (Manchester: Manchester University Press, 1999).

48 A. Vickery, 'Golden age to separate spheres: a review of the categories and chronology of English women's history', *Historical Journal*, 36 (1993), 383–414; H. Barker and E. Chalus (eds), *Gender in Eighteenth-Century England: Roles, Representations and Responsibilities* (London and New York: Longman, 1997); P. Carter, *Men and the Emergence of Polite Society, Britain 1660–1800* (London and New York: Longman, 2001); N. Elias, *The Loneliness of the Dying* (Oxford: Basil Blackwell, 1985); T. Hitchcock, *English Sexualities, 1700–1800* (Basingstoke: Macmillan Press, 1997).

49 Vickery, *The Gentleman's Daughter*, Chapter 6; Ogborn, *Spaces of Modernity*, Chapter 3; P. Langford, *Public Life and the Propertied Englishman, 1689–1798* (Oxford: Clarendon Press, 1991).

50 For similar attention to the allegorical role of cartography in promoting new ideals of femininity in eighteenth-century France and England, see F. Reitinger, 'Mapping relationships: allegory, gender and the cartographical image in eighteenth-century France and England', *Imago Mundi*, 51 (1999), 106–30.

51 R. Porter and M. Teich (eds), *The Enlightenment in National Context* (Cambridge: Cambridge University Press, 1981), vi (original emphasis).

52 P. Hulme and L. Jordanova (eds), *The Enlightenment and its Shadows* (London: Routledge, 1990), 7.

53 See, for example, Mayhew, *Enlightenment Geography*; R. J. Mayhew, 'Geography in eighteenth-century British education', *Paedagogica Historica*, 34 (1998), 731–69; C. W. J. Withers and R. J. Mayhew, 'Rethinking "disciplinary" history: geography in British universities', *Transactions of the Institute of British Geographers*, 27 (2002), 11–29.

54 For a review of such work, see C. W. J. Withers and D. N. Livingstone, 'Introduction: on geography and Enlightenment', in Livingstone and Withers (eds), *Geography and Enlightenment*, 1–28.

55 On these issues, see, for example, M. H. Edney, 'Mathematical cosmography and the social ideology of British cartography', *Imago Mundi*, 46 (1994), 101–16, and his 'Reconsidering Enlightenment geography and map making: reconnaissance, mapping, archive', in Livingstone and Withers (eds), *Geography and Enlightenment*, 165–98; A. M. C. Godlewska, *Geography Unbound: French Geographic Science from Cassini to Humboldt* (Chicago: University of Chicago Press, 1999). On Enlightenment mapping 'writing out' indigenous knowledge, see K. Brealey, 'Mapping them "out": Euro-Canadian cartography and the appropriation of the Nuxalk and Ts'ilhqot' in First Nations' Territories, 1791–1916', *The Canadian Geographer*, 39 (1995), 140–56; M. Bravo, 'Ethnographic navigation and the geographical gift', in Livingstone and Withers (eds), *Geography and Enlightenment*, 199–235; P. Carter, *The Road to Botany Bay: An Essay in*

Spatial History (London: Fontana, 1987); A. M. C. Godlewska, 'Map, text and image: the mentality of enlightened conquerors – a new look at the *Description de l'Egypte*', *Transactions of the Institute of British Geographers*, 20 (1995), 5–28.

56 On Banks, see also Gascoigne, *Science in the Service of Empire*; Drayton, *Nature's Government*; D. P. Miller, 'Joseph Banks, empire, and "centers of calculation" in late Hanoverian London', in Miller and Reill (eds), *Visions of Empire*, 21–37; Grove, *Green Imperialism*.

57 This distinction is taken from L. Daston, 'Afterword: the ethos of Enlightenment', in Clark, Golinski and Schaffer (eds), *The Sciences in Enlightened Europe*, 495–504.

58 On the 'communications circuit', see R. Darnton, 'What is the history of books?', *Daedalus*, 111 (1982), 65–83; more generally, see M. Frasca-Spada and N. Jardine (eds), *Books and the Sciences in History* (Cambridge: Cambridge University Press, 2000).

59 See J. A. Secord, *Victorian Sensation: The Extraordinary Publication, Reception and Secret Authorship of* Vestiges of the Natural History of Creation (Chicago and London: University of Chicago Press, 2000), 153.

60 S. Thorne, 'The conversion of Englishmen and the conversion of the world insepar-able: missionary imperialism and the language of class in early industrial Britain', in F. Cooper and A. L. Stoler (eds), *Tensions of Empire: Colonial Cultures in a Bourgeois World* (Berkeley: University of California Press, 1997), 238–62; H. V. Bowen, 'British conceptions of global empire, 1756–1783', *Journal of Imperial and Commonwealth History*, 26 (1998), 1–27.

61 R. Porter, 'The terraqueous globe', in G. S. Rousseau and R. Porter (eds), *The Ferment of Knowledge* (Cambridge: Cambridge University Press, 1980), 285–324.

62 See, for example, Porter, 'The new social history'; P. Elliott, 'The birth of public science in the English provinces: natural philosophy in Derby, c. 1690–1760', *Annals of Science*, 57 (2000), 61–100; A. Morrison-Low, ' "Feasting my eyes with the view of fine instru-ments": scientific instruments in Enlightenment Scotland', in Withers and Wood (eds), *Science and Medicine in the Scottish Enlightenment*, 17–53. On instruments in eighteenth-century science, see G. L'E. Turner, 'Eighteenth-century instruments and their makers', in R. Porter (ed.), *The Cambridge History of Science. Volume 4: The Eighteenth Century* (Cambridge: Cambridge University Press, 2002), 583–609. Globes were used, for example, as diplomatic gifts as well as scientific instruments: see D. L. Cranmer-Byng and T. H. Levere, 'A case study in cultural collision: scientific apparatus in the Macartney embassy to China, 1793', *Annals of Science*, 38 (1981), 503–25.

63 See A. Bermingham, 'Landscape-o-rama: the exhibition landscape at Somerset House and the rise of popular landscape entertainments,' in Solkin (ed.), *Art on the Line*, 127–44. We thank Luciana Martins for this point.

64 E. Decker and P. van der Krogt, *Globes from the Western World* (London: Zwemmer, 1993), 105–6. More widely, see M. A. Crawforth, 'Evidence from trade cards for the scientific instrument industry', *Annals of Science*, 42 (1985), 453–554.

65 E. U. Dahl and J.-F. Gauvin, *Sphaerae Mundi* (Montreal: Septentrion and McGill-Queen's University Press, 2000), 87–90, 93.

66 A. N. Walters, 'Conversation pieces: science and politeness in eighteenth-century England', *History of Science*, 35 (1997), 121–54, see esp. 139–40. Denis Cosgrove makes this point, for example, in discussing the portrayal of globes in Pietro Longhi's paint-ing 'The Geography Lesson' (1750–52) in terms of sexual intrigue, social difference and the iconography of domesticated polite learning. D. E. Cosgrove, *Apollo's Eye: A Cartographic Genealogy of the Earth in the Western Imagination* (Baltimore and London: Johns Hopkins University Press, 2001), 176–7.

67 Cosgrove, *Apollo's Eye*, Chapter 7: The enlightened globe, 176–204.

2

Georgian geographies
'from and for the margins':
'King George men' on the northwest
coast of North America

℮

Daniel Clayton

I F IT IS POSSIBLE to talk of 'Georgian (or Napoleonic or Enlightenment)
geographies' – of geographies that shape and characterise particular ages –
then the geographies of empire should be accorded a prominent place in our
understanding of the Georgian age and Britain's 'long eighteenth-century'
(1689–1815).[1] Since the late 1980s, our perception of eighteenth-century Britain
has been significantly revised, or decentred, by a range of work that explores
the constitutive role that empire played in the making of the nation.[2] It has
become commonplace to argue that the history of empire should not be
separated from the history of the British nation. Linked to the wider postcolonial project of renewing European history 'from and for the margins',
recent scholarship on the Georgian period challenges nation-centred and
Eurocentric narratives that treat metropolitan societies and states as self-
generated and hermetically-sealed entities, and explores the reciprocal (albeit
asymmetrical and hierarchical) constitution of metropole and colony.[3] There
has been a plethora of work on how Britain and Europe were constructed
'from the outside in', through diverse relationships between different peoples
and parts of the world.[4]

There are a range of perspectives on the ties between nation and empire.
Some have focused on Britain and examined how empire permeated Georgian
politics and culture. Kathleen Wilson, for example, has tried to show that
Britain's eighteenth-century imperial endeavours were 'believed by contemporaries to maximise trade, liberty, prosperity and national power, and

thus appealed to a heterogenous range of interests, grievances, and aspirations at any given moment'.[5] Others, cautious about such generalisations, have called for more nuanced assessments of the links between imperial and national history.[6] It has been pointed out that empire's national impress was more strongly felt in some decades and areas of Georgian life than in others, and that the global power of the British is often exaggerated and oversimplified. Only in the age of George III (1760–1810), and especially in the wake of the Seven Years War (1756–63) and the War of American Independence (1775–83), did the British start to see themselves as a truly global power, and to see empire as integral to national identity.[7] Even then, the myriad territorial gains and losses that Britain made against her European rivals heightened concern about the unity, efficacy, profitability and legitimacy of empire.[8] Edmund Burke and other contemporaries observed that the British had created an exploitative territorial empire as well as an empire of trade that exemplified William Blackstone's adage that the British were 'a quiet and commercial people'.[9] Recognition of the geographical, racial and constitutional heterogeneity of empire frustrated attempts to discern an integrated imperial system, a collective imperial subject (yoked in the image of the freeborn Englishman), or a uniform native Other against whom ideas of Englishness and Britishness could be clearly projected. Thus, it has been suggested, empire was an important but by no means straightforward or stable arena in which eighteenth-century Britons made sense of themselves and their place in Europe and the world.

Others have argued that this focus on empire raises difficult questions about how the marginalised periphery is to be incorporated into mainstream-metropolitan history. The view that the impulses of empire emanated solely from the imperial metropolis has been challenged on numerous counts. David Cannadine, for example, suggests that empire 'was not exclusively (or even primarily) about what the British decided and did', but that it was about 'the assorted and multifarious experiences of many peoples in many parts of the world', and complex relations of sameness (or affinity) and difference (or otherness).[10] Yet it is a vexed truth that much scholarship that decentres Georgian Britain by attending to the margins of empire and unpacking the imperial discourses that shaped and accompanied British expansion remains stuck in a nation-centric and Eurocentric mould. The agendas, experiences and texts of British and European adventurers and agents of empire remain of intrinsic interest (and often of exclusive concern), and the inter-subjective dimensions of contact and colonialism get comparatively short shrift. Scholars unwittingly reinforce the authority of the Western discourses that they seek to question by focusing solely on the British (imperial, white and usually male) record, overstating the capacity of European systems of representation to foster dominance and hegemony, and sidelining native influences on what was decided and done. We are learning a great deal about how empire was conceived in metropolitan terms, but less about what Britain and Europe meant to people living at the near and far reaches of empire. In this sense at least, Edward Said's elementary – and now well-rehearsed – postcolonial point that the interpretation of European history and metropolitan culture has been 'insufficiently weighted toward the expansion of Europe' has only been partially realised.[11] Philip Morgan has noted that work on the relationship between the British and indigenous peoples struggles fully to come to terms with the idea that the British Empire was a 'vast interactive system'.[12] As Dipesh Chakrabarty has argued in a more general vein, 'Europe' has not been fully 'provincialised'.[13]

Let me highlight two matters that relate directly to what follows. First, one of the defining features of geography as it was practised and conceived by eighteenth-century Britons and Europeans was its embrace of Enlightenment precepts of science, reason and progress, and their duplicitous deployment in the exploration of the Pacific.[14] Bounded imaginatively by the search for *Terra Australis* and the Northwest Passage, and economically and politically by Britain's changing imperial relationship with North America and East Asia, the Pacific became both a testing ground for the ambitions of European empirical science and a focus of European imperial aggrandisement.[15] Vincent Harlow and Bernard Smith (working, respectively, on political and artistic dynamics) were among the first scholars to demonstrate that scientific, commercial and political motives for the exploration of this vast region were deeply intertwined. Many others have since probed the interplay between knowledge and power in the eighteenth-century opening of the Pacific.[16]

European explorers – most famously Cook and Vancouver for the British, Bougainville and La Pérouse for the French, and Malaspina for the Spanish – did not simply exemplify the Enlightenment's thirst for objective knowledge and humanist commitment to peaceful contact and the spread of European civilisation. They also fostered new visions of empire. The practices of navigation, mapping, surveying, collecting, classification and ethnographic description and depiction that were brought to, and honed in, the Pacific worked as tools of material and intellectual appropriation. They encoded cultural difference in European terms, supported capitalist expansion, and were bound up with the creation of new forms of governmentality.

Secondly, scholars from a range of disciplines have stressed the need to think about the places and spaces in which imperial and colonial identities and relations of power were forged. The culturally situated, spatially constructed, hybrid and contested aspects of imperial and colonial power, knowledge and subjectivity are now routinely emphasised. Geographical concepts and metaphors have an important place in postcolonial efforts to expose and subvert binary and essentialist models of centre and periphery, coloniser and colonised, civilisation and savagery, and so on. Postcolonial thinkers such as Chakrabarty have argued that attempts to rework imperial conceptions of world history necessarily involve the recognition that both the margins and the centres are plural and diverse. He notes that 'postcolonial scholars, speaking from their different geographies of colonialism, have spoken of different Europes', and that empire 'appears different when seen from within the experiences of colonization or inferiorization in specific parts of the world'.[17] Recent work on native–Western relations in the Pacific pursues many of these ideas. Scholars from a range of disciplines have challenged Western historicist schemes that treat indigenous people as the dupes of an expanding imperial system, and fatal impact scenarios that romanticise natives and demonise Europeans. Nicholas Thomas and Marshall Sahlins have powerfully argued that we need to work through the context-specific ways in which Europeans and Pacific Islanders encountered one another, exchanged elements of their cultures, and created mutual webs of coercion and complicity.[18]

This chapter traces these issues and concerns to the northwest coast of North America in the late eighteenth century. It explores the beginnings of native–Western contact and empire there and how cross-cultural and imperial dynamics revolved around a series of geographical struggles over the use, control, ownership and representation of native territory. I will trace the specific ways in which the native people and territory of the northwest coast – and, more particularly, the Nuu-chah-nulth people of Vancouver Island – came into contact with Western explorers, traders and a more distant set of metropolitan-based discourses and imperial conflicts. This chapter considers the geographical fashioning of knowledge and power at a variety of scales, and plays particular attention to questions of native agency and the role that the geography of the coast played in the making of Western knowledges about, and plans for, the region.

I start by outlining the events and processes that culminated in the colonisation of the northwest coast by the British and Americans in the mid-nineteenth century. I then take a more detailed look at the formation of two spaces of power that worked at different scales and had radically different implications for native people: spaces of cultural engagement and of cultural effacement. Finally, I will point to some of the implications of the story I outline for work on the northwest coast and Georgian geographies.

THE NORTHWEST COAST FROM CONTACT TO COLONIALISM[19]

The northwest coast was one of the most densely populated regions of native North America, and one of the last regions of the world to be reached by Westerners.[20] In the 1770s and 1780s, the diverse native groups of this coastal region (who spoke different languages and had differing socio-political systems) started to come into contact with three sets of forces that were of general importance in Britain's and Europe's eighteenth-century imperial outreach. These were scientific projects of exploration, capitalist processes of commercial expansion, and the geopolitics of nation-state rivalry.

Britain's illustrious explorer James Cook visited Nootka Sound on Vancouver Island in 1778. George Vancouver mapped the coast and island that bears his name for the British between 1792 and 1795. Spanish and French explorers reconnoitred the region between 1775 and the 1790s. Exploration was infused with the scientific and humanitarian spirit of the Enlightenment. Cook, for example, was instructed to 'observe the Genius, Temper, Disposition, and Number' of the peoples he met, to 'cultivate a friendship with them' through trade and to show them 'every Civility and Regard'.[21] His one-month sojourn at Nootka Sound was, for the most part and on most accounts, a peaceful affair. Historians have seen in it the beginnings of a contact process that, until the onset of formal colonialism, was mutually beneficial for natives and newcomers.[22] But Cook's third voyage was not sealed off from wider commercial and imperial currents that in time brought the coast and mainland under the imperial aegis of the European powers. Cook came to the northwest coast in search of the Northwest Passage – the fabled water route across North America that Europeans thought would transform the structure of European trade with Asia.[23] He cast doubt on its existence, but his and his officers' observations about the resources of the coast and the trading propensities of its native people encouraged a lucrative trade in sea otter furs that provided a new venture for British and American capital in the immediate aftermath of the War of American Independence.[24] British and American trade vessels (and some Spanish, French and Russian outfits) flocked to Nootka Sound and other native villages, where they exchanged sea otter furs for iron bars, copper kettles, jewellery, firearms and other commodities. American traders, who dominated the business by the end of the century, sold their furs to Chinese merchants in Canton and Macao and returned to Boston and other New England ports with silk, porcelain and tea. Their British counterparts, some of whom had been trained by Cook, traded at Canton through East India Company supercargoes and returned to London with bills of exchange that were recoverable on the Company's account.

With the dawn of the sea otter trade in the mid-1780s, the terms of contact changed. Explorers and traders were hooked into different modes of contact and circuits of power. Interaction was now driven by profit rather than framed by science, and violence and trickery were endemic features of commercial contact.[25] Traders were instructed to avoid conflicts with native people, but they were not expected to be humanitarians and few of them were specifically instructed to study native life.[26] Native people were incorporated into a hands-on order of capitalist exchange. Native fortunes became conditioned by a capitalist logic of uneven development, and there were native attacks on (especially American) trade vessels. Traders had to visit native villages to get furs and go through native leaders to get them. Yet when furs and profits dried up in one location, traders went elsewhere. In the 1780s and 1790s, Vancouver Island was one of the main areas of trade, but by 1805, it had largely been abandoned by the British and the Americans. As the commercial potential of this barely-charted corner of the Pacific began to be harnessed, geopolitical disputes over rights of sovereignty arose between Britain and other imperial powers. The sea otter trade sparked a diplomatic dispute between Britain and Spain over rights of trade and sovereignty in the Pacific that brought the two countries to the brink of war.

The 'Nootka crisis' (January–October 1790) stemmed from an altercation between British traders and a Spanish official who had been posted to Nootka Sound to safeguard Spain's imperial claim to the Pacific littoral of North America.[27] This imperial fracas on distant shores emphasised that the world economy was an international imperial space of assumed rights and competitive drives as well as a global commercial network. British and Spanish politicians derived imperial claims from explorers' and traders' activities, and started to create a different, imperial, space. Commercial contact became entangled with imperial strategies of representation and knowledge production that reterritorialised native territory from afar.

War between Britain and Spain was averted by the Nootka Convention of October 1790, which granted the two countries joint commercial access to the coast and left questions of sovereignty in abeyance. Political and diplomatic tension over the spoils of trade and empire inaugurated a process of imperial appropriation that extended into the nineteenth century and turned to the continental penetration of the Cordillera by British and American fur-trading companies.[28] Between 1818 and 1846, Britain and the United States of America became embroiled in another vitriolic territorial dispute – this time over the vast region west of the Rockies between Alaska and California known as the Oregon Territory – which culminated in the Oregon Treaty of 1846.[29] By 1846 American pioneers had started to occupy the area south of the 49th parallel, the international border established by the treaty, and, in 1849, Britain established a colony on Vancouver Island under the proprietorship of the Hudson's Bay Company.[30]

This, in outline, is how the northwest coast was contacted by Westerners and gradually incorporated into empire. We can now take a closer, if inevitably limited, look at the geographical make-up of the sea otter trade and the imperial processes of reterritorialisation that encompassed it, and see how native and Western interests became intertwined through commerce and then diverged as this region was fashioned as imperial space. The connections that Western explorers, traders and empire-builders made with this region worked through circuits of knowledge and power that had different spatial and temporal ranges. Some of these circuits were global in scope, and others were utterly local. The following discussion underscores the importance of thinking about the links between contact projects and relationships in particular native places and the grander spaces that constituted the economic and geopolitical reach of empire's global networks.

SPACES OF CULTURAL ENGAGEMENT

Commercial contact was shaped by two geographies of cultural engagement. The first of these geographies was about place. The contact process revolved around native villages and trade vessels, and was mediated by a complex set of cross-cultural perceptions: about whether the native could trust the trader, and vice versa. Traders also had to attune themselves to native geographies if they wanted to make a profit. There is insufficient space here to discuss these geographies fully, but it is important to say something about native agendas.

In Nuu-chah-nulth societies, the 'local group', consisting of a family of chiefs owning territorial rights, houses and other privileges (songs, family legends, and so on), was the centrepiece of native social organisation.[31] Such groups were built on ties of kinship and hereditary rank and, more specifically, on one or more family lines. Each of these had dwellings and place names that were owned and occupied by chiefs who were ranked according to their generational proximity to a common ancestor (who was remembered in spiritual origin stories).[32] There were aggregations of native people larger than the local group – tribes (two or more local groups sharing a winter village) and confederations (shaped by trade, marriage and tributary ties) – and native people entered into inter-group arrangements for a number of reasons. Mutual protection was important; so was the desire to elevate one's social standing within a local group. The size, security, longevity and prestige of local groups hinged on the success of chiefly strategies of resource procurement, trade, marriage and warfare. Chiefs sought to attract followers in order to exploit their economic privileges fully, and the social reproduction of chiefly power and social cohesion of the larger kin group revolved around the redistribution of food, resources and privileges in the feast (or potlatch) system. Crucially from our perspective, chiefs and local groups wanted to trade with each other and foreigners, because wealth was a form of chiefly prestige. The social and martial pursuit of wealth and territorial privileges was a basic way of averting and combating scarcity, and an important means by which lesser chiefs and native commoners could enhance their position in family lines.[33] It thus follows that the sudden influx of alien wealth (in the form of traders' commodities) encouraged competition within and between native groups, as well as between natives and traders. In short, traders encountered intricately stratified native groups, and people who had strong ideas about the ownership and control of territory and resources. According to the ethnographer Philip Drucker, the Nuu-chah-nulth 'carried the concept of ownership to an incredible extreme'.[34]

The sea otter trade injected new wealth into native communities, and, according to some, nurtured an efflorescence of native culture.[35] Yet this wealth was unevenly distributed, both socially and geographically, and native chiefs did not all pursue the same strategies of trade with foreigners. As Figure 2.1 suggests, commercial contact at Nootka Sound and Clayoquot Sound was quite different, in part because these two native places were shaped by different local group and tribal relationships. Right along the coast of Vancouver Island, however, the sea otter trade heightened inter-native competition and warfare, and ignited native violence towards Westerners.[36] Traders (and the first historians of this mode of contact) saw these native attacks as the products of an innate native savagery.[37] It is now more common to see them as native responses to traders' violent impulses, and as attempts to plug those gaps in native prestation, prestige and subsistence systems that were created by traders' comings and goings.[38]

Traders picked up the edges of these native agendas and relationships, but few journalists discerned them very fully, and written and visual images of conflict and tension abound in the archive (see Figure 2.2). Endlessly opportunistic, and without quite the time, energy or talent to observe native people carefully, traders frequently resorted to platitudes about 'the market' for furs, 'the native mind', and the 'inconstancy of native demands'. In traders' journals, this focus on place often disintegrates into stereotypes about native people as savage, fickle and whimsical precisely because of traders' commercial objectives. It was also the case that native people had to study traders if they wanted to benefit from the trade, and contact involved the formation of inter-personal relationships between captains and chiefs. Like the traders, native people saw their commercial interlocutors in more aggregate terms, and called British explorers and traders 'King George men'. The Americans were dubbed 'Boston men'. Nuu-chah-nulth people had long regarded 'the English as a large tribe, whose principal village is distant', G. M. Sproat reported in the 1860s.[39] John Walbran reported that King George III was 'so frequently mentioned by British subjects and others that in the native mind his name became synonymous with power and authority'.[40] Such appellations belonged to what Greg Dening has described as 'a time of intense theatre of the civilised to the native . . . [and] the civilised to one another' in the Pacific.[41]

Traders hoped that native people would be irresistibly attracted to Western goods, but as a British merchant, John Etches, reported in 1790, it was 'an incontrovertible fact that in newly discovered countries the natives are remarkably capricious; articles in demand one day will be rejected the

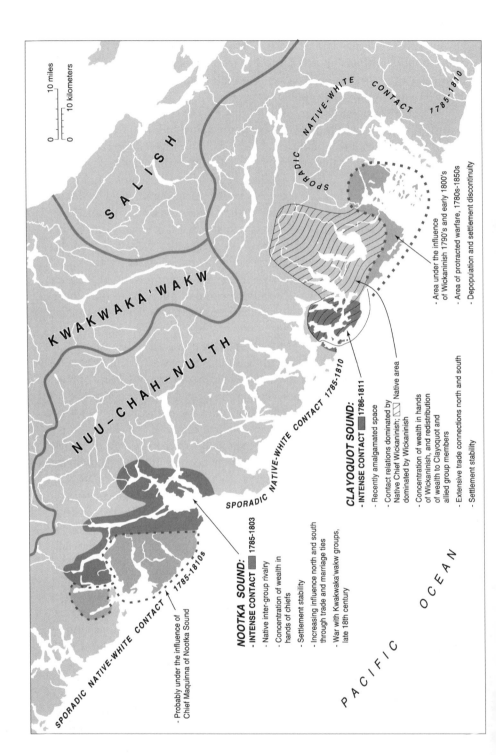

NOOTKA SOUND:
- INTENSE CONTACT ▓ 1785-1803
- Native inter-group rivalry
- Concentration of wealth in hands of chiefs
- Settlement stability
- Increasing influence north and south through trade and marriage ties
- War with Kwakwaka'wakw groups, late 18th century

- Probably under the influence of Chief Maquinna of Nootka Sound

SPORADIC NATIVE-WHITE CONTACT 1785-1810s

CLAYOQUOT SOUND:
- INTENSE CONTACT ▓ 1786-1811
- Recently amalgamated space
- Contact relations dominated by Native Chief Wickaninish; ▨ Native area dominated by Wickaninish
- Concentration of wealth in hands of Wickaninish, and redistribution of wealth to Clayoquot and allied group members
- Extensive trade connections north and south
- Settlement stability

- Area under the influence of Wickaninish 1790's and early 1800's
- Area of protracted warfare, 1780s-1850s
- Depopulation and settlement discontinuity

SPORADIC NATIVE-WHITE CONTACT 1785-1810

S A L I S H

K W A K W A K A ' W A K W

N U U - C H A H - N U L T H

SPORADIC NATIVE-WHITE CONTACT 1785-1810

P A C I F I C   O C E A N

10 miles
10 kilometers

facing] **2.1** Nuu-chah-nulth geographies and agendas during the early contact period. (Courtesy of Eric Leinberger and Graeme Sandeman)

2.2 'The *Columbia* attacked by Indians'. From a drawing by George Davidson, in F. W. Howay (ed.), *Voyages of the 'Columbia' to the Northwest Coast, 1787–1790 and 1790–1793* (1941), 404

following'.[42] Likewise, a prominent Boston trader, William Sturgis, recognised that the traffic in furs could only partly be accounted for using Western notions of supply and demand, price and profit.[43] What Nicholas Thomas terms 'just-so' stories about the allure of Western goods – stories that essentialise interaction from Western perspectives, with trade as the constitutive transaction of cultural and civilisational exchange – did not work well on the northwest coast.[44] The root of the problem was the exchange process itself, and the difficulties of cultural perception were compounded by the physical dangers and psychological problems incurred by traders working in cramped and leaky vessels, on a wet and treacherous coast, and amidst alien people that they struggled to understand.

Traders' and natives' perceptions of each other were bound up with the way goods were owned, given, used, exchanged, circulated and valued, and many traders recognised that distinctions between need and fancy, gift and commodity, were unstable.[45] The inter-subjective space that was commercial contact was not easily bridged, and matters were exacerbated by the fact that British and American traders purposely misled one another, verbally and in print, about their transactions and the 'savagery' of particular native groups.[46]

The facts of competition, and traders' needs to size up a broader set of business opportunities and tendencies leads us to our second geography. This is a more anomalous sense of commercial space, a different envisioning of capital. Traders rarely expended all of their time or trade goods at one location. They had to be attentive to new commercial possibilities and locales, and wherever they went they entertained risk and anticipated danger. Today's chief, known to a trader by name and fêted as a dignitary, could become tomorrow's savage. Equally for native people, a trader could turn his guns on their villages and become an instant enemy.

And so it was that traders' representations of native people were not simply drawn from metropolitan imaginative geographies, projected on to the coast, and embellished intact. They were actively built on the coast, out of the contact process and the tension between place and space that I have been describing. Traders' representations were hybrid and contradictory. They made statements about native people that simultaneously recognised and disavowed cultural difference, and grudgingly acknowledged native agency in the business. Imported binary models of civilisation and savagery that putatively placed Westerners and their commodities in a position of command vis-à-vis the native became fractured and irresolute. One trader wrote that, 'The Savage, who is nevertheless dishonest, pretends to be Scrupulous, and exact in his dealings.'[47] Another informed his Boston boss that, 'These cunning savages . . . are great Merchant traders.'[48] Yet another informed his British readers that 'we found at our cost that these people . . . possessed all the cunning necessary to the gains of mercantile life'.[49]

In these statements we can detect what Homi Bhabha sees as the constitutive ambivalence of colonial discourse: an incessant 'mixing and splitting' of signification. Bhabha reasons that the stereotype, a common trope of colonial discourse, is an 'arrested, fixated form of representation' characterised both by the recognition and disavowal of difference, and the fraught interplay of mastery/pleasure and anxiety/defence. To borrow and reorient his image of this conflictual economy of representation, many traders viewed natives as 'mystical, primitive, single-minded yet the most worldly and accomplished of liars'.[50]

I conclude this section with a detailed example of the volatility of commercial contact. In the 1780s and 1790s the area between Meares Island and Barkley Sound became increasingly dominated by the Clayoquot chief Wickaninish and his family. A range of archaeological and ethnographic evidence suggests that in late pre-contact times, Wickaninish gained tremendous influence over neighbouring local groups through a series of wars, and trade and marriage alliances (see Figure 2.1). In the early years of contact this influence was extended beyond Clayoquot Sound, and the arrival of traders arguably had a good deal to do with this. Traders discovered that there was a large supply of furs at Clayoquot Sound and quickly learned that Wickaninish and his chosen attendants controlled the exchange process and expected traders to follow native protocol.

When Captain Robert Gray of the American vessel *Columbia* reached the Sound in August 1788, he was cordially received by Wickaninish and trade prospects looked good. But as one of Gray's officers noted, 'greatly to our mortification there was nothing in our vessel except muskits [which he] would perchace . . . [and] that was an article we were not supplied with'.[51] Gray left the Sound empty-handed. Traders did little business unless they took stock of Wickaninish's desires. His influence on the terms of trade was almost unparalleled on the coast, and confounded the idea, related by Sturgis, that the natives of the coast wished to 'imitate their somewhat more polished visitors'.[52]

The exchange process was the basic source of tension at Clayoquot Sound. The British trader John Meares sensed that present-giving was an integral part of native protocol. When he first reached the Sound in June 1788, he was invited to a feast with Wickaninish at his winter village of Opitsat, and he presented the chief with blankets and copper kettles. Meares reported that fifty natives then stepped into the middle of Wickaninish's enormous house, each displaying a six-foot long sea-otter skin, and stood to attention while Wickaninish informed the British trader that the skins were 'the return he proposed to make for our present'.[53] 'Our royal host appeared entirely satisfied with our homage,' Meares surmised, 'and we . . . were equally pleased with his magnificence.'[54] Wickaninish used foreigners to bolster his status among his kinfolk and neighbours, and would neither negotiate exchange rates nor trade with vessels until 'homage' had been paid.[55]

Traders ignored this prestation system at their peril. When the *Columbia* returned to the Sound in June 1791, loaded with muskets to sell, Wickaninish 'appear'd quite indifferent about trading; rather wishing to receive our articles of traffic as presents'.[56] Gray was reluctant to give over the muskets and other items as presents, however, because he thought that they 'would cost much dearer than if the skins were purchased', and he declined some of Wickaninish's invitations to attend some important events at Opitsat.[57] This evidently irritated the chief and tension mounted. In June 1791, a Hawaiian boy deserted the *Columbia* and Gray, suspecting the boy had been kidnapped, held one of Wickaninish's brothers hostage until he was returned.[58] Gray's actions seemed to be forgotten when the *Columbia* anchored near Opitsat for the winter, but in October 1791 one of Wickaninish's brothers tried to take

Gray's 'great coat' and there were other thefts.[59] Then, on 18 February 1792, Gray thought he had uncovered a native plot to capture his ship and massacre his crew. The Hawaiian boy admitted to his captain that one of Wickaninish's brothers promised to make him a great chief if he would wet the firearms, small cannon, swivel guns and powder on the *Columbia*. On 20 February, Wickaninish visited the vessel and presented Gray with a sea-otter cape and some skins. Gray took the cape and furs from Wickaninish and his attendants, it is recounted, 'and told them to go to Yethlure and Yeklan [two of Wickaninish's family] to whom a musket and cloth [coat] had been sent for their pay[ment.] [T]hese chiefs were then ordered to depart and never to return again on pain of death.' Gray's dismissal of Wickaninish 'effectively shut up our source of trade'.[60] Finally, Gray bombarded Opitsat as he was leaving the Sound at the end of March in retaliation for the insults he thought he had endured.[61] When Captain Magee of the American vessel *Jefferson* visited the Sound in 1793, Wickaninish's brothers told him that native frustration with Gray had been greatly heightened by Gray's 'loan of a coat of war' to Wickaninish (probably the transaction of 20 February mentioned above).[62] Gray viewed this loan as a transaction and complained about the number of furs he got for the coat.

This is a classic example of how native–Western relations could disintegrate, and it is one that was repeated many times along the coast. Mutual suspicion did not vanish as natives and traders grew familiar with each other. Contact relations often became more brittle the longer a trader stayed in one place. Cultural miscomprehension over a coat that was of little value to Gray in his grander commercial scheme of things diminished the American's ability to make a profit. And a copper kettle, again of trifling value to Meares but apparently prized by Wickaninish, facilitated trade. The point is that exchange relations were emblematic of power relations – of the facility to use objects to establish and hold together social relationships. The exchange of coats and kettles exemplified the power invested in trading captains to protect a vessel's cargo and crew, and the power invested in a chief by primogeniture, rank and a larger kin community to police interaction with foreigners and redistribute wealth.

These relations of power were also acutely spatialised. In times of calm, trade vessels and native houses and villages were congenial spaces of cultural exchange and performance. But in times of tension and conflict they became defensive spaces in unpredictable cross-cultural waters. Ships and native villages were transformed from spaces of mutual exploration into stark containers of power. Chiefs like Wickaninish looked to strike deals with 'King George men' and 'Boston men', but when these figures of 'authority and power' confounded native ambition and abused their protocol he was forced to think of them as a collective 'Other' – as unknown quantities.

THE NORTHWEST COAST OF NORTH AMERICA

SPACES OF CULTURAL EFFACEMENT

In turning to the processes of imperial appropriation that swirled around these contact relationships, I will be briefer because this type of story is well known to scholars and critics of imperialism. Even so, it is important to think about the specificity of this story in a northwest coast context.

At one level, the Nootka and Oregon disputes created a Western/Euro-centric space of empire that was premised on what Simon Ryan describes (with reference to Australia) as imperialism's self-legitimising view that space is 'a universal, mensurable and divisible entity'. The northwest American coast, like Australia, was constructed as a monolithic Cartesian space that allowed imperial strategists to hierarchise the use of space to their own advantage.[63] Among other things, British, Spanish and American politicians worked out of the polarity between civilisation and savagery, and assumed that Western nations had a legitimate right to native territory because they would better utilise the land. At another level, however, the northwest coast became a combative imperial space that was created at the intersection of competing, nation-centred imperial drives. Britain, Spain and the United States drew on different legal precepts, invoked different visions of empire, and mobilised different ideas and facts about the northwest coast to make their imperial case for sovereignty.

During the Nootka crisis, for example, Britain's call for satisfaction from Spain for the injuries incurred by British traders became rancorous in April 1790, when John Meares presented the Home Office with a detailed *Memorial* about the incident at Nootka Sound and the nature of the sea otter trade. British ministers were particularly struck by his revelation that he had pur-chased spots of land at Nootka Sound from native chiefs, erected a small building there, and 'hoisted the British Colours thereon', a year before the Spanish arrived.[64] This information allowed the British to push the legal precept that 'Discovery alone, not followed by Actual Possession and Estab-lishment, can never be admitted as giving any Right to the Exclusion of Other Nations'.[65] The British claimed that dominion over alien lands was rooted in building, cultivation and residence.[66]

The Spanish, by contrast, based their claim to exclusive sovereignty over the Pacific littoral of the Americas on treaties, conventions, royal cedulas and pre-emptory orders stretching back to the late fifteenth century. They invoked a body of texts and assumptions, which, they thought, proved that Spain had 'immemorial possession' of this part of the world and had 'pre-served her possession entire'.[67] The Spanish also questioned the veracity of Meares's *Memorial*, and it subsequently became apparent that Meares had lied to the British Cabinet about his activities. However, British politicians based their demand for satisfaction and diplomatic arguments on a fact that was undisputed by the Spanish: that Meares had occupied a patch of land at Nootka Sound before the Spanish staked their claim in 1789. Neither Britain nor Spain were interested in the nature of Meares's relationship with native people. All that Meares had to do to have an imperial effect was demonstrate that he had bought and occupied some land.[68] When he was interviewed by Britain's Privy Council in 1791, for instance, he recounted how he had given Chief 'Maquilla' of Nootka Sound 'considerable presents for leave to build a House' and pointed to the difficulties of the contact process. The notes that the Privy Councillors made in the margins of Meares's testimony only deal, however, with where he had erected buildings: they had no interest in the cultural dynamics of the sea otter trade.

The Nootka crisis was fuelled by the determination of British politicians (especially William Pitt, the Duke of Leeds and Henry Dundas) to protect Britain's international trading interests. As Linda Colley has spelled out, 'the claim that trade was the muscle and soul of [eighteenth-century] Great Britain, both the source of its greatness and the nursery of patriots, was clearly echoed in the poetry, drama, novels, newspapers, tracts, parliamentary speeches, private correspondence, and even the sermons of the day'.[69] This 'cult of trade', she notes, crossed political divisions and social boundaries, and I would add that it crossed the oceans with traders such as Meares. As Dundas declared in a Commons debate on the Nootka Convention, 'The spirit of the nation was roused' over Nootka because Britain 'would not be limited in its market'. Britain's wealth and greatness 'was founded upon the skill of our manufacturers, and the adventures of our merchants'.[70] Or, as one of Meares's associates wrote, 'the vigorous and tender shoots of diverging commerce should be fostered and protected, with the same scrupulous vigilance as its bank paper'.[71]

This was not trade as natives and traders on the coast knew it. The Nootka crisis brought the sea otter trade into realms of political and imperial calculation that lay at a great remove from native shores. Politicians drew on practices of counting and measuring that shaped the mercantilist policies of the Georgian state, and the crisis fed the public's fascination with colonial maps and the commodities of empire (see John Gascoigne's discussion of Banks in this respect: Chapter 8, pp. 151–73). The British had what we might call a 'ledger-book imperial mentality': Pitt, for example, kept a large collection of maps, trade gazetteers, and 'universal dictionaries' in his Downing Street office.[72] Inscription devices such as maps, commercial treatises, and narratives of exploration allowed ministers to peel away layers of complexity in the imperial archive and picture the world through more basic coordinates. Custodians of imperial knowledge such as Alexander Dalrymple supplied the British government with such texts, and they played an important role in the presentation of Britain's diplomatic case.[73]

We get a vivid sense of the synoptic quality of British commercial and imperial thinking in an interview that the Committee of Trade and Plantations conducted with Meares in May 1790 at the height of the dispute. The trader was asked a range of general questions. What was 'the highest and lowest latitude of successful commerce' in the North Pacific? Was the native population large enough to make the demand for British manufactures 'considerable'? Was the Asian market for furs likely to become overstocked in the near future?[74] The Committee wanted an assessment of the reach and value of the trade rather than a detailed account of how it was prosecuted. The intricacies of commercial interaction were reduced to simpler equations. The Nootka crisis illustrates how the British imperial impulse to create orderly systems of commerce and governance had come to rest on technologies of representation that had the capacity to transport information and knowledge over long distances without any significant loss of meaning. The ambit of empire was enhanced by projects of enumeration, classification and synthesis that made knowledge more mobile and seemingly immutable.

Cartography had a special place in these imperial proceedings. Cook's scanty map of the coast formed a baseline of British knowledge and understanding in ways echoed in Flinders's map of Terra Australis (see Figure 8.1, p. 156). More precisely, Cook brought the coast into commercial and imperial circulation with a bifocal system of representation. He recounted his dealings with native people in his journal, but there are few signs of native life on his map of the coast.[75] Between 1778 and 1790, explorers and traders gradually filled in Cook's map, but the rarefied, cartographic way of seeing that he brought to the coast lived on. Vancouver, who arrived on the coast in 1792 to negotiate with Spanish officials at Nootka Sound over the restoration of British property, and to conduct a more exhaustive survey of the coast than Cook had managed, was the principal preserver and developer of Cook's cartographic vision.

This vision with its imperial connotations is shown in Vancouver's *Chart Shewing Part of the Coast of N.W. America*, which was published with his journal in 1798 (Figure 2.3). This map rationalises the cartographic results of his survey in selective ways. Vancouver emphasised those aspects of his survey that he and the Admiralty deemed important.[76] Vancouver noted that his maps incorporated Spanish 'authorities' (including Spanish names), and he acknowledged the assistance he received from the Spanish explorers Galiano and Valdés, who also circumnavigated the island in the summer of 1792.[77] Yet his *Chart* retains few of the names that the Spanish bestowed, only a handful of native place names, and hardly any of the names bestowed by traders. It does not give us much indication of the fact that Vancouver's team had frequent dealings with traders and native people.[78] Vancouver discussed such dealings in his journal, yet proclaimed that most fur traders 'had neither the

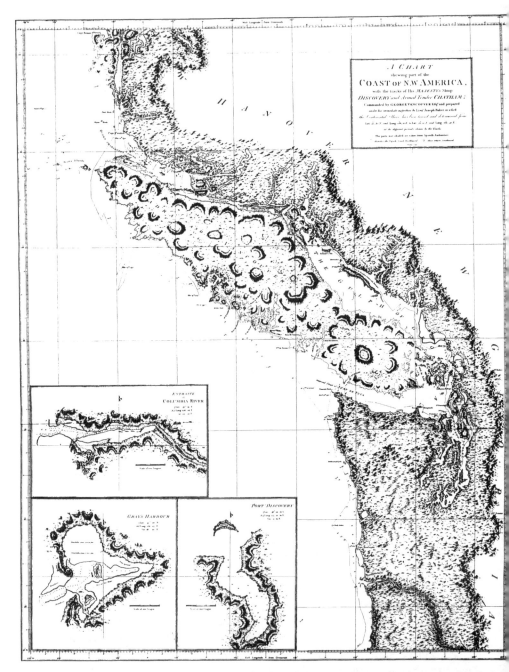

2.3 *A Chart Shewing Part of the Coast of N.W. America*, in George Vancouver, *A Voyage to the North Pacific Ocean* (1798). (Courtesy of the University of British Columbia Library, Archives and Special Collections Division)

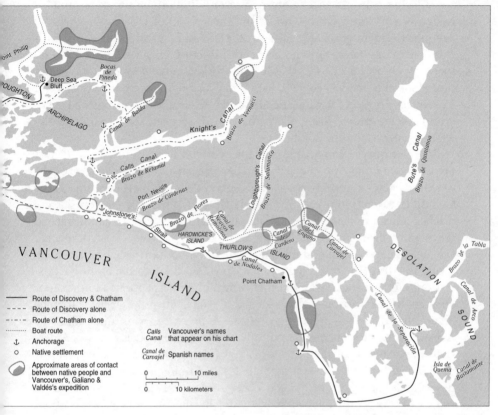

Cultural effacement and erasure in Vancouver's cartography. (Courtesy of Graeme Sandeman)

means, nor leisure . . . for amassing any certain geographical information', and that native testimony about geographical matters was untrustworthy.[79] His instructions and *Chart* compound these written asides about traders' and natives' 'inferior' grasp of geography.

Vancouver's cartography partly erases, and certainly effaces, the geographies of cultural engagement that in a circuitous way prompted his survey, and imposes British names (for example, 'the Gulph of Georgia', after the King) on the coast. Figure 2.4 illustrates the ways in which Vancouver's *Chart* rationalises his work around 'Johnstone Strait' (named after one of his hardest-working officers). The figure depicts the tracks of Vancouver's ships and boats, the names he bestowed, where his team and the Spanish encountered native people, and the broader pattern of native settlement around 1792 (as hypothesised by Bob Galois).[80] His published *Chart*, by contrast, does not depict the native villages, or indicate Spanish names.

Vancouver saw his cartography as a record of maritime surveying, and his charts, which were engraved under the supervision of Dalrymple (then the Admiralty's hydrographer), connote the technical prowess of the British Admiralty but efface prior and alternative inscriptions on the land. His cartography obfuscates the fact that he had worked in native waters and sometimes looked to native people to help him get along. There was little space in Vancouver's project for native people, and pitched as it was against the background of a territorial dispute, it perhaps made strategic sense to marginalise Spain's presence on the coast.

But Vancouver's imperial legacy does not end here. In the 1820s, British politicians arguing over the status of the Oregon territory appealed to the exactitude and authoritativeness of his survey to foil American claims to the Columbia River (discovered by Robert Gray).[81] When the Oregon dispute reached a head in 1845, the British insisted that Vancouver 'circumnavigated the island which now bears his name; and here we have ... as complete a case of discovery, exploration, and settlement, as can well be presented, giving to Great Britain ... the strongest possible claim to the exclusive possession of that island'.[82] The fact that British diplomats appealed to the tenor and texture of Vancouver's work, and sidelined maps (especially traders' maps) that depicted something of a native presence, again underlines the imperiousness of particular brands of knowledge and models of truth. American diplomats did not question the quality of Vancouver's cartography. Rather, they looked for facts and legal precedents that would give them a way around it. For their part, the British made Vancouver's survey and map amenable to translation into principles of sovereignty. By the mid-nineteenth century, politicians and diplomats had become accustomed to evaluating maps in terms of the cartographic codes and imagery that Vancouver's work exemplified, and did not question the ethnocentric assumptions that were built into his way of seeing.

There is barely any mention of native people in the official diplomatic correspondence over Oregon.[83] Britain and the United States claimed sovereignty over far-off lands with a few basic images and some propitious facts. The techniques of cartographic and political abstraction that emanated from London and Washington also made it easier for colonists and pioneers to forget about native people, and assume that non-native sovereignty over native land was secure. I have shown elsewhere that many British colonists viewed Vancouver Island as Vancouver represented it – as a cartographic shell awaiting colonial development, and one largely devoid of a native presence.[84] Cook, Vancouver and a string of politicians helped to create what Brian Harley has called an 'anticipatory geography of colonialism', a spatial context in which colonialism could take root.[85] Vancouver cannot be held personally responsible for the Oregon Treaty, or for the way colonists viewed and treated native people, but the imperial geography that politicians derived, in part, from his survey would not have taken the precise form it did without his map of the coast.

Stories about the links between exploration, trade and empire in the Pacific have never had single or simple meanings. They have been told from different perspectives, and, as I have tried to show here, work through a variety of spaces and geographies. The appearance of 'King George men' on the northwest coast led to the creation of local geographies of native–Western interaction that native people could manipulate, and can now be used to write an alternative native history of contact. Almost from the start of contact, however, these geographies were encompassed by a more abstract way of connecting with the coast that had effects of power that native people could not influence. Impulses and representations emanating from the imperial metropolis circumvented the connections that natives and Westerners made on the ground and started to push native people out of the territorial picture. For many years, this process of imperial appropriation and inscription taking place in imperial centres of calculation had little bearing on the contact process. In the longer run, however, there emerged an imperial space that formed the framework of colonial incursion.

There are echoes here of Nicholas Thomas's more general observation about material exchange and colonialism in the Pacific: that we need to specify the 'balance of forces' between natives and newcomers at particular times and in particular places. Like Thomas, I think that local forms and geographies of contact are never completely overdetermined by the epistemic violence of colonialism, and that we thus have a commitment to 'localise' our understanding of native–Western relations. Yet as Thomas also rightly acknowledges, 'there clearly are times when indigenous peoples cannot do much to shape the events which overtake them'.[86] In the present case, native people could not manipulate the dynamics of imperial aggrandisement that eventually reshaped their lives. All of this raises important questions about what constitutes the moment of colonialism, and about how academic work is implicated in the construction of pre-colonial, colonial and postcolonial divides. I will end with three implications of the story I have sketched for work on the northwest coast and its Georgian geographies.

First, I have tried to show that we cannot fully understand the sea-otter trade unless we root traders' activities and representations in local processes of cross-cultural exchange and consider the native side of the story (as best we can get at it through the filters of the ethnohistorical record). Work on what, to the imperial centre, were distant and peripheral processes of capitalist expansion brings an air of ambivalence to the assertive cult of commerce that many historians suggest lay at the heart of Georgian identity and well-being. Metropolitan commercial impulses were not imposed on the northwest coast in a mechanical fashion, but were actively fashioned on the coast in relation to native agendas. On the other hand, what I have said about native competition, warfare and territorial change brushes against the grain of commonly held ideas about native people. This story does not square with romanticised images of the timeless and 'ecological' Indian living in harmony with nature and his or her neighbours, which figure prominently in white sympathy for native causes. Nor does it conform to politically strategic representations of native groups living in traditional territories 'from time immemorial', which are prominent in native land claims in the courts. In other words, in the context of the northwest coast, scholarship that probes native histories and geographies can fracture and fragment the current balance of forces between natives and non-natives, and particularly those forces that centre on native land rights.[87] Pursuit of the well-intentioned view that we should get out of the imperial centre and pay more attention to 'the historical geographies of the colonised world' can have problematic effects in the (former) margins of empire.[88] In places like British Columbia, where legal proof of the authenticity of native title rests on the longevity and stability of occupation in particular places and areas, the recovery of native processes of colonisation and settlement instability may not be helpful.

Secondly, work on Georgian geographies that emphasises the plurality and diversity of centres and margins will inevitably be read in different ways in different places. Scholars of the pre-colonial period of contact on the northwest coast have tended to keep the local and global modes of connection that I have sketched apart, and to have downplayed the imperious sway and colonial implications of the latter. It is held that native groups did not start to lose control over the direction of change until the onset of formal colonialism, and that the causes of and reasons for colonial incursion in the late 1840s were only tangentially connected to the Nootka and Oregon disputes.[89] The story I have told goes against this model of change, in part by drawing attention to the imbrications of knowledge and power in a range of projects – scientific exploration, mapping, diplomacy – that have traditionally been seen as fairly innocuous from a colonial point of view. I suggest that Cook's and Vancouver's projects, and the imperial disputes that reinscribed the meaning and significance of their work, induced and supported colonial intervention. We should not underestimate the ideological import of this pre-colonial period of exploration and imperial aggrandisement in the formation of a body of imperial ideas and assumptions about land and sovereignty that diminished native agency and effaced the need to deal with native land issues. Furthermore, the Western models of truth that were given graphic and written form by explorers and politicians continue to frame the legal theories and practices of representation that British Columbian and Canadian judges use to adjudicate native land claims. Work on imperial events that happened centuries ago relates directly to the question of what it means to provincialise British and European systems of thought from and for margins like the northwest coast.

Finally, when the meaning of 'empire' is no longer so tightly controlled by the imperial centre, the margins are enjoined to specify how they want to insinuate themselves into the narratives of colonialism, modernity and empire. The question of what, in the wake of empire and colonialism, 'Britain', 'Europe' or 'Georgian geographies' means from different locations is central to the way in which any postcolonial historiographical operation gets going. For the native peoples of British Columbia and other parts of Britain's former settler empire, this question centres on land – on how natives and newcomers can accommodate their different attachments to land. From the perspective of the northwest coast, work on the geographies of empire that infused the Georgian geographies dealt with in this volume would be radically incomplete without this focus on land and an interest in the spatiality of power, knowledge and history.

NOTES

1 On how and why geographers have come to think about geography in this way, see D. N. Livingstone, 'Putting geography in its place', *Australian Geographical Studies*, 38 (2000), 1–9, and the Introduction to this volume.

2 See, for example, D. Armitage, *The Ideological Origins of the British Empire* (Cambridge: Cambridge University Press, 2000); J. Brewer, *The Sinews of Power: War, Money and the English State, 1688–1783* (London: Unwin Hyman, 1989); C. A. Bayly, *Imperial Meridian: The British Empire and the World, 1780–1830* (London and New York: Longman, 1989); L. Colley, *Britons: Forging the Nation, 1707–1837* (New Haven and London: Yale University Press, 1992); R. Porter, *Enlightenment: Britain and the Creation of the Modern World* (London: The Penguin Press, 2000); K. Wilson, *The Sense of the People: Politics, Culture and Imperialism in England, 1715–1785* (Cambridge: Cambridge University Press, 1995).

3 This phrase is taken from D. Chakrabarty, *Provincialising Europe: Postcolonial Thought and Historical Difference* (Princeton: Princeton University Press, 2000), 16. See also F. Cooper and A. L. Stoler (eds), *Tensions of Empire: Colonial Cultures in a Bourgeois World* (Berkeley and London: University of California Press, 1997).

4 This phrase is taken from M. L. Pratt's influential study, *Imperial Eyes: Travel Writing and Transculturation* (London and New York: Routledge, 1992), 7.

5 K. Wilson, 'The good, the bad, and the impotent: Imperialism and the politics of identity in Georgian England', in A. Bermingham and J. Brewer (eds), *The Consumption of Culture, 1600–1800* (London and New York: Routledge, 1995), 237–62, quote on p. 254.

6 See A. G. Hopkins, 'Back to the future: From national history to imperial history', *Past and Present*, 164 (1999), 198–220; D. Kennedy, 'Imperial history and post-colonial

theory', *Journal of Imperial and Commonwealth History*, 24 (1996), 345–63; S. Marks, 'History, the nation and empire: sniping from the periphery', *History Workshop Journal*, 29 (1990), 114–16; P. J. Marshall, 'Introduction', in P. J. Marshall (ed.), *The Oxford History of the British Empire. Volume 2: The Eighteenth Century* (Oxford: Oxford University Press, 1998), 1–27.

7 See C. A. Bayly, 'The first age of global imperialism', *Journal of Imperial and Commonwealth History*, 26 (1998), 28–47; H. V. Bowen, 'British conceptions of global empire, 1756–1783', *Journal of Imperial and Commonwealth History*, 26 (1998), 1–27.

8 See P. Miller, *Defining the Common Good: Empire, Religion and Philosophy in Eighteenth-Century Britain* (Cambridge: Cambridge University Press, 1994); A. Pagden, *Lords of all the World: Ideologies of Empire in Spain, Britain and France, c. 1500–c. 1800* (New Haven and London: Yale University Press, 1995).

9 On Burke, see U. S. Metha, *Liberalism and Empire: A Study of Nineteenth-Century Liberal Thought* (Chicago: University of Chicago Press, 1999).

10 D. Cannadine, *Ornamentalism: How the British saw their Empire* (London: The Penguin Press, 2001), xvii.

11 E. W. Said, *Culture and Imperialism* (New York: Alfred A. Knopf, 1993), 61.

12 P. D. Morgan, 'Encounters between British and "indigenous" peoples, c. 1500–c. 1800', in M. J. Daunton and R. Halpern (eds), *Empire and Others: British Encounters with Indigenous Peoples, 1600–1850* (Philadelphia: University of Pennsylvania Press, 1999), 42–78, quote on p. 68.

13 Chakrabarty, *Provincialising Europe*, 16 and *passim*.

14 For a full bibliography, see the Introduction to this volume, and, on geography, see D. N. Livingstone and C. W. J. Withers (eds), *Geography and Enlightenment* (Chicago: University of Chicago Press, 1999); R. J. Mayhew, *Enlightenment Geography: The Political Languages of British Geography, 1650–1850* (London and New York: Macmillan and St Martin's Press, 2000).

15 See D. P. Miller and P. H. Reill (eds), *Visions of Empire: Voyages, Botany, and Representations of Nature* (Cambridge: Cambridge University Press, 1996).

16 V. T. Harlow, *The Founding of the Second British Empire*, 2 volumes (London: Longmans, Green, 1953–64); B. Smith, *European Vision in the South Pacific, 1768–1850: A Study in the History of Art and Ideas* (Oxford: Clarendon Press, 1960). More recently, see J. Gascoigne, *Science in the Service of Empire: Joseph Banks, the British State and the Uses of Science in the Age of Revolution* (Cambridge: Cambridge University Press, 1998); D. Mackay, *In the Wake of Cook: Exploration, Science and Empire, 1780–1801* (London: Croom Helm, 1985); B. Smith, *Imagining the Pacific: In the Wake of Cook's Voyages* (New Haven and London: Yale University Press, 1992); J. Samson (ed.), *British Imperial Strategies in the Pacific* (Aldershot: Ashgate Publishing, 2002); G. Williams, 'The Pacific: exploration and exploitation', in Marshall (ed.), *The Oxford History of the British Empire. Volume 2*, 552–75.

17 Chakrabarty, *Provincialising Europe*, 16–17.

18 See N. Thomas, *Entangled Objects: Exchange, Material Culture and Colonialism in the Pacific* (Cambridge MA: Harvard University Press, 1991); M. Sahlins, 'Goodbye to tristes tropes: ethnography in the context of modern world history', *Journal of Modern History*, 65 (1993), 1–25.

19 For a more detailed account, see my *Islands of Truth: The Imperial Fashioning of Vancouver Island* (Vancouver: UBC Press, 2000).

20 For an overview of the native societies of the coast in pre-contact times, see W. Suttles (ed.), *Handbook of North American Indians: Northwest Coast*, 7 volumes (Washington: Smithsonian Institution, 1990), Vol. 7.

21 'Secret instructions for Capt. James Cook', in J. C. Beaglehole (ed.), *The Journals of Captain Cook on his Voyages of Discovery: The Voyage of the* Resolution *and* Discovery, *1776–1780*, 3 volumes (Cambridge: Cambridge University Press for The Hakluyt Society, 1967), Vol. 3, ccxxiii. La Perouse and Malaspina received similar instructions: see J. Dunmore, *French Explorers in the Pacific: The Eighteenth Century*, 2 volumes (Oxford: Clarendon Press, 1965), Vol. 1; D. C. Cutter, *Malaspina and Galiano: Spanish Voyages to the Northwest Coast, 1791 and 1792* (Seattle: University of Washington Press, 1991).

22 See, especially, R. Fisher, 'Contact and trade, 1774–1849', in H. Johnston (ed.), *The Pacific Province: A History of British Columbia* (Vancouver/Toronto: Douglas and McIntyre, 1996), 1–23. The official account of the voyage, commissioned by the Admiralty and based on Cook's journals, appeared in 1784: James Cook and James King, *A Voyage to the Pacific Ocean . . . In the years 1776, 1777, 1778, 1779, and 1780*, 3 volumes and an atlas (London: G. Nicol and T. Cadell, 1784), Vol. 2, 265–331. Cook's officers also kept logs and journals, and there are a number of native accounts of Cook's visit. See D. Clayton, 'Captain Cook and the spaces of contact at Nootka Sound', in J. Brown and E. Vibert (eds), *Reading Beyond Words: Contexts for Native History* (New York: Broadview Press, 2002), 95–123.

23 G. Williams, *Voyages of Delusion: The Search for the Northwest Passage in the Age of Reason* (New York: HarperCollins, 2001).

24 On the sea otter trade, see J. R. Gibson, *Otter Skins, Boston Ships and China Goods: The Maritime Fur Trade on the Northwest Coast, 1785–1841* (Montreal, Kingston, London: McGill-Queen's University Press, 1992). For Cook's remarks, see Cook and King, *Voyage to the Pacific Ocean*, Vol. 2, 437–40. News of Cook's transactions also spread to New England and India via a number of 'unofficial' accounts of Cook's voyages published by his officers.

25 See H. Appleton Lamb, 'Notes on trade with the northwest coast, 1790–1810', Houghton Library, Harvard University, photostat in UBC Library, Special Collections.

26 See, for example, F. W. Howay (ed.), *The Journal of Captain James Colnett aboard the 'Argonaut'* (Toronto: Champlain Society, 1940), 70; F. W. Howay (ed.), *The Voyages of the 'Columbia' to the Northwest Coast, 1787–1790 and 1790–1793* Orig. pub. 1941 *Massachusetts Historical Society Collections*, 79 (Portland: Oregon Historical Society, 1990), 111.

27 See W. R. Manning, 'The Nootka Sound controversy', *Annual Report of the American Historical Association*, 1904, 279–478. On the Spanish side of the story, see W. L. Cook, *Flood Tide of Empire: Spain and the Pacific Northwest, 1543–1819* (New Haven: Yale University Press, 1973).

28 See R. S. Mackie, *Trading Beyond the Mountains: The British Fur Trade on the Pacific, 1793–1843* (Vancouver: UBC Press, 1997).

29 The classic accounts of the Oregon dispute are F. Merk, *The Oregon Question: Essays in Anglo-American Diplomacy and Politics* (Cambridge MA: Harvard University Press, 1967), and D. M. Pletcher, *The Diplomacy of Annexation: Texas, Oregon, and the Mexican War* (Columbia, MO: University of Missouri Press, 1973). Many primary documents pertaining to the dispute can be found in W. R. Manning (ed.), *Diplomatic Correspondence of the United States: Canadian Relations*, 5 volumes (Washington: Carnegie Endowment for International Peace, 1945), and *British Parliamentary Papers. Colonies: Canadian Boundary* (Shannon: Irish University Press, 1969). For a contemporary overview of the story from an American perspective, see A. Gallatin, *The Oregon Question* (New York: Bartlett and Welford, 1846).

30 On early colonial developments north of the border, see C. Harris, *Making Native Space: Colonialism, Resistance, and Reserves in British Columbia* (Vancouver: UBC Press, 2002).

31 For ways into the ethnographic literature on native social organisation among Nuu-chah-nulth and other language groups, see P. Drucker, 'Rank, wealth and kinship in northwest coast society', in T. McFeat (ed.), *Indians of the Northwest Coast* (Seattle: University of Washington Press, 1967), 134–46; E. Sapir, 'The social organisation of the west coast tribes', in D. G. Mandelbaum (ed.), *Selected Writings of Edward Sapir in Language, Culture and Personality* (Berkeley: University of California Press, 1985), 468–87: E. Arima and J. Dewhirst, 'Nootkans of Vancouver Island', in W. Suttles (ed.), *Handbook of North American Indians*, Vol. 7, 391–411; W. Suttles, 'Variation in habitat and culture on the northwest coast', in his *Coast Salish Essays* (Seattle: University of Washington Press, 1987), 26–44.

32 See S. Golla, '"He has a name": History and social structure among the Indians of western Vancouver Island' (unpublished PhD thesis, Columbia University, 1987), 86, 99–111.

33 There were diverse motives for native warfare, but the links between scarcity and the cohesion of the kin group are often emphasised: see P. Drucker, 'Ecology and political organization on the northwest coast', in E. Tooker (ed.), *The Development of Political Organization in Native North America* (Washington DC: American Ethnological Society, 1983), 86–96; M. Swadesh, 'Motivations in Nootkan warfare', *Southwestern Journal of Anthropology*, 4 (1948), 76–93.

34 P. Drucker, *The Northern and Central Nootkan Tribes*, Smithsonian Institution Bureau of American Ethnology, Bulletin 144 (Washington DC: US Government Printing Office, 1951), 247; see also E. Sapir and M. Swadesh, *Native Accounts of Nootkan Ethnography* (New York: AMS Press, 1955), 111, 135, 346.

35 See R. Fisher, *Contact and Conflict: Indian-European Relations in British Columbia, 1774–1890* (Vancouver: UBC Press, 1977).

36 For an assessment of native and territorial change among the Nuu-chah-nulth groups, see Clayton, *Islands of Truth*, 150–61. For a broader coastal overview, see C. Harris, 'Social power and cultural change in pre-colonial British Columbia', *BC Studies*, 115–16 (1997/98), 45–82.

37 See F. W. Howay, 'Indian attacks upon maritime fur traders of the northwest coast, 1785–1805', *Canadian Historical Review*, 6 (1925), 287–309.

38 The natives of Nootka Sound massacred the crew of the American vessel *Boston* in 1803, and natives from the Clayoquot Sound/Barkley Sound region attacked another American vessel, *Tonkin*, in 1811. A survivor of the former attack, and later ethnographers, noted that native people had not forgotten the violence used by traders since 1785. While the causes of the attack on the *Tonkin* have conventionally been deemed to lie in the punishment meted out by a trader on a native chief, native testimony suggests that it was traders' abuse of the native prestation system that caused the attack: see J. R. Jewitt, *A Journal kept at Nootka Sound* (Boston: Printed for the author, 1807), 13; British Columbia Archives and Record Service (BCARS), Add. MSS 1077 Newcombe Family Papers, Vol. 16, file 16; E.W. Gisecke, 'Search for the *Tonkin*', *Cumtux: Proceedings of the Clatsop County Historical Society*, 10/11 (1990–91), 3–8, 23–40; Leicester University Library, CMS 2./o Church Missionary Society, North Pacific Mission, Banfield to Prevost, 30 October 1859.

39 G. M. Sproat, *The Nootka: Scenes and Studies of Savage Life* (London: Smith, Elder, 1868), 5.

40 J. Walbran, *British Columbia Coast Names, 1592–1906* (Ottawa: Government Printing Bureau, 1909), 205.

41 G. Dening, *Performances* (Chicago: University of Chicago Press, 1996), 109.

42 Argonaut [John Cadman Etches], *An Authentic Statement of the Facts Relative to Nootka Sound* (London: T. Beckett, 1790), 16.

43 S. W. Jackman (ed.), *The Journal of William Sturgis* (Victoria: Sono Nis Press, 1978), 121. 'The laws of supply and demand were frequently disregarded', Sturgis noted elsewhere: 'The northwest fur trade', *Hunt's Merchant's Magazine*, 14 (1846), 537.

44 Thomas, *Entangled Objects*, 27.

45 This was recognised most acutely by Vancouver, but the point was by no means lost on traders themselves. See British Library Add. MSS 17,552, f.13v, 'Papers relating to the voyage of the Discovery and Chatham 1790–1795'. For a flavour of traders' concerns, see W. D. Phelps, 'Solid men of Boston', Bancroft Library, Berkeley, MS P-C 31, 4; Ingraham to Martinez, May 1789, Mexico City, Archivo General de la Nacion, Ramo, Historia 65, in Freeman Tovell Collection, BCARS, Add. MSS 2826; William Sturgis, 'Ms. of 3 lectures dealing with his voyages', 1846, Massachusetts Historical Society. For an elaboration of this theme in other parts of the world, see A. Appadurai (ed.), *The Social Life of Things: Commodities in Cultural Perspective* (Cambridge: Cambridge University Press, 1986).

46 Again, explorers saw this as clearly as anyone. Dawson Turner Copies (DTC) of the Correspondence of Sir Joseph Banks in the Botany Library, British Museum (Natural History), 23 volumes, Vol. 8, 146, Menzies to Banks, 1 January 1793. On traders' competitive drives, see F. W. Howay (ed.), *The Dixon-Meares Controversy* (Toronto: The Ryerson Press, 1929).

47 R. Fisher and J. M. Bumstead (eds), *An Account of a Voyage to the Northwest Coast of North America in 1785 and 1786 by Alexander Walker* (Seattle: University of Washington Press, 1982), 188.

48 BCARS, Add. MSS 828, Ebenezer Dorr Papers, Dorr to Dorr, 16 August 1801.

49 J. Meares, *Voyages Made in the Years 1788 and 1789, from China to the North West Coast of America* (London: Logographic Press, 1790), 141–2.

50 H. K. Bhabha, *The Location of Culture* (London and New York, 1994), 72–82.

51 'Haswell's log of the first voyage of the "Columbia"', in Howay, *Voyages of the 'Columbia'*, 57.

52 Sturgis, 'Ms of 3 lectures'.

53 Meares, *Voyages*, 140.

54 *Ibid.*

55 When the Spanish visited Clayoquot Sound, they presented Wickaninish with shells and sheets of copper, and were treated well by the chief. See H. R. Wagner, *Spanish Explorations in the Strait of Juan de Fuca* (Santa Ana, CA: Fine Arts Press, 1933), 86, 186.

56 'Hoskins' narrative of the second voyage of the "Columbia"', in Howay, *Voyages of the 'Columbia'*, 183.

57 *Ibid.*, 265.

58 *Ibid.*, 186.

59 *Ibid.*, 250; for native memories of Gray, see UBC Library, Special Collections, 5/12, F. W. Howay Papers, Newcombe to Howay, 24 September 1921.

60 'Hoskins' narrative', 275.

61 'Boit's log of the second voyage of the "Columbia"', in Howay, *Voyages of the 'Columbia'*, 391. Boit lamented that 'This fine Village, the Work of Ages, was in a short time totally destroy'd'.

62 B. Magee, 'Log of the Jefferson', 13–14 June 1793, Massachusetts Historical Society.

63 S. Ryan, *The Cartographic Eye: How Explorers Saw Australia* (Cambridge: Cambridge University Press, 1996), 4–5.

64 J. Meares, *The Memorial of John Mears* (London: Published at the request of the British government, 1790).

65 This argument, echoed by numerous politicians and pamphleteers, is most clearly articulated in government correspondence: e.g., Public Record Office, London (PRO), 30/8/151, 57, Chatham Papers, Leeds to Pitt, 2 June 1790; PRO, FO 72/18, 22, 189, Leeds to Fitzherbert, 5 July and 17 August 1790.

66 See P. Seed, *Ceremonies of Possession in Europe's Conquest of the New World, 1492–1640* (Cambridge: Cambridge University Press, 1995).

67 PRO, FO 72/17, 239–61, Floridablanca to Merry, 4 June 1790; British Library, Add. MSS 28,066, 27–55, Leeds Papers, Floridablanca to Fitzherbert, 16 June 1790.

68 PRO, PC 2/135, 439–53, Meares interview, 8, 11, 13 February 1791; PRO, PC 1/63/B22, draft bundles.

69 Colley, *Britons*, 59–60.

70 W. Cobbett (ed.), *The Parliamentary History of England*, XXVII (London: Hansard, 1816), 979.

71 [John Cadman Etches], *Continuation of an Authentic Statement of the Facts Relative to Nootka Sound* (London: T. Beckett, 1790), 23.

72 See J. Ehrman, *The Younger Pitt. Volume 1: The Years of Acclaim* (London: Constable, 1969), 354.

73 PRO, FO 95/7/4, 339–40, 438, Dalrymple to Nepean, 3 July and 20 August 1790; BL Add. MSS 28,066, 27, Leeds Papers, Leeds to Fitzherbert, 16 August 1790.

74 PRO, BT 5/6, 113–19, 'Examination of Mr. Meares (fur trade)', 27 May 1790.

75 Cook depicted the coast with a thin line and left blank the vast area between the coast and Hudson Bay. His cartographic baseline was strengthened by the team that prepared his chart (which was drawn by Henry Roberts) for publication. Alexander Dalrymple and Sir Joseph Banks – the veritable custodians of geographical knowledge about the Pacific during this period (see Gascoigne on Banks in Chapter 8 here) – played an important role in the engraving of this chart. They persuaded the Admiralty to omit the Hudson's Bay Company's interior discoveries from this map and highlight only Cook's endeavours. They viewed Cook's chart as a record of maritime exploration and thus wanted to depict only what Cook had seen: see H. Wallis, 'Publication of Cook's journals: some new sources and assessments', *Pacific Studies*, 1 (1978), 163–94.

76 As far as we know, neither Vancouver not his map engravers received any specific instructions about what to include on the chart, but there are some hints in this regard in the Admiralty and Home Office records.

77 See W. K. Lamb, *The Voyage of George Vancouver, 1791–1795*, 4 volumes (London: The Hakluyt Society, 1984), Vol. 2, 591–2, 663. The activities of these Spanish explorers are recounted in J. Kendrick, *The Voyage of the Sutil and Mexicana, 1792: The Last Spanish Exploration of the Northwest Coast of North America* (Spokane: Clark Publishers, 1991).

78 On these dealings, see R. Fisher, *Vancouver's Voyage: Charting the Northwest Coast, 1791–95* (Vancouver/Toronto: Douglas and McIntyre, 1992).

79 For a selection of Vancouver's comments about native attitudes to 'geographical truth' (as he saw them), see Lamb, *Voyage of George Vancouver*, Vol. 1, 274–84; Vol. 2, 551, 597–8. On Vancouver's use of traders' charts, see *ibid.*, Vol. 2, 592; Vol. 3, 1069–71; Vol. 4, 1322–6. The importance of traders' discoveries was related to the Home Office by Alexander Dalrymple who collected copies of their journals, published a number of their charts, and was an important adviser to the British Cabinet during the Nootka crisis.

80 R. M. Galois, *Kwawaka'wakw Settlements, 1775–1920: A Geographical Analysis and Gazetteer* (Vancouver: UBC Press, 1994), appendices.

81 See Addington to Canning, 6 May 1826, in E. Stapleton (ed.), *Some Official Correspondence of George Canning*, 2 volumes (London: Longmans, Green and Co., 1887), Vol. 2, 110–15.

82 Packenham to Buchanan, 29 July 1845, *British Parliamentary Papers, Canadian Boundary*, 43.

83 When native issues did arise, usually in relation to the Hudson's Bay Company's monopoly, questions of territory and sovereignty were separated from issues of contact.

84 D. Clayton, 'On the colonial genealogy of George Vancouver's Chart of the northwest coast of North America', *Ecumene*, 7 (2000), 371–401.

85 J. B. Harley, 'Rereading the maps of the Columbian encounter', *Annals of the Association of American Geographers*, 83 (1992), 522–42.

86 Thomas, *Entangled Objects*, 35.

87 On these processes, see Harris, *Making Native Space*.

88 See B. Yeoh, 'Historical geographies of the colonised world', in B. Graham and C. Nash (eds), *Modern Historical Geographies* (London: Longman, 2000), 146–66.

89 I think especially of Fisher's influential *Contact and Conflict*.

3

Creole negotiations: white anti-Methodism in Barbados, 1823–26

ℰ

David Lambert

QUESTIONS ABOUT what constituted a British national identity in the Georgian period have focused on ideas of liberty, commercial success and Protestantism, particularly in the context of long-running conflict with Catholic France. According to Jack Greene, above all it was the notion of liberty, as traced to the Magna Carta, common law and the revolutionary settlement of 1688, which came to be seen as the hallmark of an English, and later British, national sense of self. Greene also argues that a concept of liberty was the foundation of a more expansive 'Imperial identity' that encompassed the British Empire.[1] As Peter Marshall contends, however, there was 'no . . . agreed interpretation as to what constituted British liberty. Opposing interpretations gained acceptance on either side of the Atlantic.'[2] These differing conceptions of liberty were most starkly manifest in the greatest crisis for the Georgian empire, namely, the American Revolution.

It is the tensions within 'Imperial identity' that is the subject of this chapter. My focus is not on Revolutionary America, however, but on the West Indies in the early nineteenth century. While not downplaying the significance of the revolt in the thirteen American colonies for British imperial culture, it is worth recalling that, as Andrew O'Shaughnessy points out, they represented only half the total number of Britain's American possessions in 1776.[3] The other thirteen colonies, the most important of which were the sugar islands of the West Indies such as Barbados and Jamaica, did not revolt.[4] The foundations of their 'loyalty' included strong social and cultural ties with Britain, military dependency, and reliance on protected markets.[5] Yet even in the 'loyal' part of the empire, tensions arose with

Britain over the issue of slavery. It is the contention of this chapter that the controversy over slavery had a significant impact on the constitution of 'Imperial identity'.

Aided by the American Revolution, which led to the isolation of the West Indian planters, the British anti-slavery movement emerged as a potent political force in the 1780s. Having campaigned for the cessation of British involvement in the transatlantic trade in enslaved people (achieved in 1807), its leaders became concerned with conditions in the plantation societies themselves. The Society for the Mitigation and Gradual Abolition of Slavery Throughout the British Dominions was founded in 1823 with Thomas Fowell Buxton as its president and anti-slavery campaigning took on an increasingly emancipationist direction.[6] Seeking to steer a course between such calls for immediate emancipation and the rearguard action of pro-slavery West Indian interests, the imperial government adopted a policy of 'amelioration'.[7] As a result, despatches were sent to the governors in each of the West Indian possessions in May 1823 with instructions about the reforms that were either to be enacted or, in the case of the self-legislating colonies such as Barbados or Jamaica, placed before the local political institutions. The reforms included limitations on physical punishment, and the promotion of Christianity and monogamous marriage among enslaved people.[8]

The adoption of amelioration as governmental policy was met with hostility and obstruction in the West Indies, especially in the self-legislating colonies. In a debate in Barbados's elected lower house, the Assembly, the arrival of the 1823 proposals was described as the most important event since the establishment of the colony in 1627. The Speaker, Cheesman Moe, argued that the reformist turn in imperial policy reflected the 'diabolical falsehoods and infamous aspersions' cast by 'a few interested and designing hypocrits [sic]'. He claimed that the aim of the instructions was to cast the West Indies 'headlong into the gulph of destruction'. Despite his strident tone, Moe called for moderation in the Barbadian response, so as to prevent their anti-slavery opponents from undermining the familial link between West Indians and their 'transatlantic brethren' in Britain.[9]

Moe's speech contains many of the features that would characterise white West Indian responses to the resurgent anti-slavery campaign in the late Georgian period. First, the contemporary ameliorative turn in imperial policy was placed in the context of two centuries of Barbados's colonial history. This would prefigure the importance attached during the resistance to anti-slavery to a foundational episode for local white identity – the island's mid-seventeenth-century opposition to the Cromwellian state. Secondly, there was the notion that the forces of anti-slavery and their realisation in imperial policy threatened to displace and dislocate Barbados from the material and ideological heartlands of the British Empire. Thirdly, Moe's call for caution signalled the ever-present concern that the adoption of an oppositional position would play into the hands of Barbados's enemies, especially in the anti-slavery campaign.

Moe's speech encapsulated the anxious attempts to negotiate a place for slave colonies in a changing late-Georgian empire. These changes were related to what Michael Craton has called a 'double switch in imperial focus' from Atlantic to Orient and from protectionism to laissez-faire economics, which had reduced the relative economic, political and cultural significance of the West Indian plantation societies. The rise of humanitarianism, particularly anti-slavery campaigning, occupied a crucial place in this switch and served to undermine the status of the West Indies. This switch also had profound implications for British imperial culture. By the early Victorian period, 'humanitarianism had become a vital component of Britain's national or Imperial identity'.[10]

This chapter is concerned with the question of whether, in the context of the controversy over enslavement, white West Indian identities could remain within this 'Imperial identity', and within the expansive sense of Britishness it represented. More specifically, it aims to explore the ambiguities of white West Indian identity by focusing on an intense period of white persecution of the Methodist community in Barbados, which coincided with the resurgence of the British anti-slavery campaign in the early 1820s. Encompassing popular and official forms, this anti-Methodism will be explored in terms of its rhetoric and mythology. It should be read as part of a broader reaction to anti-slavery and therefore connected to legislative obstruction to amelioration, as well as to other contemporary pro-slavery expressions. Yet it is also important to emphasise that anti-Methodism was not a coherent political and cultural project, but a locus of West Indian anxieties. For this reason, the modes of representation that accompanied and were directed toward this anti-Methodism will be read, first, as part of a strategy of 'negotiation' on the part of the white colonists that aimed at stabilising their place vis-à-vis metropolitan opinion, and, secondly, as a target for countervailing anti-West Indian efforts by British forces opposed to slavery. The relationship between the latter and the 'forging' of new, hegemonic forms of British identity in the late-Georgian period[11] – a process in which an anti-West Indian politics was far from coincidental – is discussed in the conclusions.

THE UNCERTAIN PLACE OF THE WEST INDIES

Although a crucial part of the first British Empire, with sugar plantations that produced wealth and highly desired consumer products, the West Indian colonies occupied an uncertain place in metropolitan culture. Located 'beyond the line' of European geopolitical certainties, with landscapes that were tropically 'other', and the source of wealth for *nouveaux riches* planters, the islands represented a 'different and disturbing culture'.[12] This sense of West Indian culture is at the heart of the ambiguous identity category of 'creole'. At its simplest, this refers to non-indigenous people, flora or fauna born in, or naturalised to, the Americas. The description of West Indians – of any 'race' – as 'creole' seeks to capture social, political, demographic, economic and cultural adaptations in the context of a tropical environment, plantation system and racialised slavery. Owing to these (perceived) adaptations, white West Indian creoles were not seen as 'English English' by many white metropolitans.[13]

The issue that brought the 'creole' status of the West Indies to the fore was slavery. The British imperial project became intertwined with the mass enslavement of African people from the mid-seventeenth century with the development of Barbados into the 'original and quintessential British sugar colony'.[14] Even at this stage, plantation slavery and the transatlantic trade that supplied it attracted opposition – not least from the enslaved people themselves. It was not, however, until the late eighteenth century that there was the development of what has been seen as 'a widespread conviction that New World slavery symbolized all the forces that threatened the true destiny of man [sic]'.[15] The emergence of such opinion and its institutionalisation in the anti-slavery campaign in the 1780s had profound implications for the white inhabitants of the West Indian slave societies, something that David Brion Davis captures in his reference to 'a profound change in the basic paradigm of social geography – a conceptual differentiation between what can only be termed a "slave world" aberration and the "free world" norm'.[16] The anti-slavery campaign sought to portray the West Indies as an 'un-English' place of white planter cruelty and black suffering.[17] In so doing, they inscribed an imaginative 'invidious demarcation' between the West Indies and Britain.[18] They also sought to have this cartography realised in imperial interventions that would reform and eventually terminate slavery, as well as in metropolitan public support for missionary activity and the boycott of West Indian sugar.[19]

This anti-slavery imaginative geography did not go uncontested. Catherine Hall has written of a 'war of representation' occurring between competing accounts of the West Indies.[20] Supporters of slavery in the region and in Britain affirmed the centrality of the colonies to the imperial project by emphasising their economic value, strategic importance, cultural legitimacy and loyalty, particularly during the American Revolution.[21] Nowhere were such discourses of shared identity and colonial loyalty more powerfully manifest than in the self-description of Barbados as 'Little England'.[22] Such a description not only symbolised the supposed political, social and cultural similarities between metropole and colony, but also their mutual dependence.

The imaginative geography this description sustained sought to maintain metropolitan support for West Indian institutions and rights – including the right to own slaves. Through such forms of representation, supporters of West Indian interests sought, as Keith Sandiford has it, to 'negotiate' a place for the colonies in the imaginative and material geographies of the British Empire. The term negotiation is used by Sandiford to describe attempts made to 'win a tenuous and elusive legitimacy for an evolving Creole civilization, conflicted by its central relation to slavery and its marginal relation to metropolitan cultures'.[23] Such negotiations sought to contest the construction of the West Indies as an aberrant and marginal 'slave world'.

As Sandiford's deconstruction suggests, negotiation was beset by anxiety and ambivalence.[24] The increasing influence of the anti-slavery campaign on imperial policy and the greater willingness of the metropolitan authorities to intervene in West Indian affairs engendered more hostile reactions from planters and their supporters. Often evoking Lockean notions of sovereign power and appropriating the rhetoric of Revolutionary America, these reactions bordered on the anti-imperial and, sometimes, anti-British.[25] At the same time, however, the threat of imperial intervention was itself portrayed as 'un-English' and resistance to it as evidence of colonial commitment to British liberty.[26] This portrayal of West Indian colonial resistance to imperial policy as thoroughly British is indicative of a white West Indian identity that was 'simultaneously assertive, defensive and loudly loyal', particularly in the context of the controversy over slavery.[27] This was exacerbated in Barbados because its white population defined itself in terms of ultra-loyalty, Anglicanism, indispensability to empire and adherence to liberty – in other words, the sameness of 'Little England'. In consequence, Barbados occupied an uncertain place on the imperial map. The vacillating nature of white Barbadian responses to anti-slavery and the attempts made to negotiate between ultra-loyalty (identity with Britain) and anti-imperialism (difference from Britain), points to the uncertain place of white West Indian identity – of creole identity – in the British Empire.

COLONIAL RESISTANCE

As shown, the reformist instructions placed before the Barbadian legislature in 1823 were angrily received. In January 1824 a bill to reform the local slave code was introduced in the Assembly and the resultant Consolidated Slave Act, which was passed in March 1825, was viewed in the metropole as an inadequate response to the imperial will.

Beyond the legislative realm, an illuminating manifestation of white responses to metropolitan-originating reformist impulses was apparent in the treatment of Barbados's Methodists in the period 1823–25. The Methodist presence on the island was largely the result of the activities of the Methodist Missionary Society (MMS) from the late eighteenth century. Unlike elsewhere in the West Indies, however, the MMS had had little success in Barbados and there were fewer than fifty members in the early nineteenth century. Methodism in Barbados was dominated by free people of colour and remained unpopular within Barbados's white population.[28] Older concerns about alleged links between the metropolitan Methodist church and Jacobinism were compounded by white West Indian suspicions that Methodist missionary activity was 'inextricably connected' to anti-slavery.[29] Leading proponents of anti-slavery were, indeed, key figures within missionary organisations and both groups shared evangelical concerns about the lack of religious instruction for enslaved people. At the same time, religious instruction remained controversial because many slaveholders believed it would undermine the socio-racial order.[30] Such beliefs were related to the entrenched and reactionary nature of the Anglican church in the island, which was deeply wedded to plantocratic dominance. As a result, anti-Methodist feeling was strong in Barbados and its missionaries were harassed by what has been described as the 'clergy-planter nexus', which included sections of the local press, the magistracy and the legislature.[31]

In the wake of news of the alleged role of missionary activity in inciting an enslaved revolt in the British South American colony of Demerara in August 1823, and in the broader context of resurgent anti-slavery, suspicions in Barbados centred on the resident Methodist missionary, William Shrewsbury. In early October, Methodist services were disrupted and Shrewsbury's attempts to seek the prosecution of his assailants failed. Shrewsbury was also ordered to appear before a magistrate for his failure to enrol in the militia. Anglican ministers were exempt from serving and Shrewsbury believed that, under the terms of the 1689 Toleration Act, this extended to non-Anglican clergy. Yet, as will become clear, Barbados's authorities argued that the Act did not apply to the West Indies and that Shrewsbury was liable for militia service. In this way, the actions of the judicial authorities paralleled broader perceptions that Methodism was a 'mock' religion and official harassment accompanied popular persecution.[32]

Whilst Shrewsbury was seeking protection from the governor, an anonymous handbill was circulated calling for the destruction of the Methodist chapel in the island's capital, Bridgetown.[33] Receiving warning of the plot, Shrewsbury fled to the nearby island of St Vincent. Meanwhile, on 19 October 1823, a crowd of up to two hundred white Barbadians began the demolition of the Bridgetown chapel. The persecution of the Methodist community continued for the next two years, intensifying around the anniversary of the chapel's destruction and when the MMS attempted to re-establish its presence. On such occasions, Methodist houses were attacked, and effigies of

Shrewsbury and leading opponents of slavery were burnt, a fact that indicates the connection between anti-Methodism and broader white opposition to reformism.

ANTI-METHODIST DISCOURSE

Following the destruction of the chapel, the anti-Methodists were at pains to portray their actions in a favourable light. This can be clearly seen in the anonymous proclamations that were disseminated over the next two years, the first appearing on the day after the chapel's destruction to celebrate a 'Great and signal triumph' over Methodism:

> The Inhabitants of this island are respectfully informed, that in consequence of the unmerited and unprovoked attacks which have repeatedly been made upon the Community by the Methodist Missionaries, (otherwise known as agents to the villainous African Society,) a party of respectable Gentlemen formed the resolution of closing the Methodist Concern altogether: with this view they commenced their labours on Sunday Evening; and they have the greatest satisfaction in announcing that by 12 o'clock last night they effected the TOTAL DESTRUCTION OF THE CHAPEL. It is hoped that as this Information will be circulated throughout the different Islands and Colonies; all persons who consider themselves true Lovers of Religion will follow the laudable example of the BARBADIANS, in putting an end to Methodism and Methodist Chapels throughout the West Indies.[34]

These decrees were the textual codification of the political and cultural project of anti-Methodism: to unify the white population against 'subversives', to protect the established Church against Dissenters, to purify Barbados of Methodism and to defend the colonial (and imperial) state against the forces of anti-slavery. The proclamations were linked to particular acts of persecution by seeking to mobilise popular support, by planning violence, and in challenging the authority of the British governor and terrorising the Methodists.

Such proclamations were anonymous. Nevertheless, despite their secrecy (no one was ever convicted for the chapel's destruction), a central theme of the proclamations was the attempt to establish a respectable and distinctive West Indian identity. The anti-Methodists portrayed themselves as a 'party of respectable Gentlemen', 'true Lovers of Religion' and, most emphatically, as 'BARBADIANS'. Other references to the 'patriotic and Loyal' motives of anti-Methodism evoked the discourse of 'Little England', defender of the established Church, Great Britain and its empire. Indeed, some of the anti-Methodists sought to realise this self-proclaimed leading role in 'putting an end to Methodism and Methodist Chapels throughout the West Indies' by travelling to neighbouring colonies to stir up trouble.[35] Such rhetoric was related to the Barbadian settler myth of Royalist, Anglican resistance to Cromwell's Puritanical 'Usurpation'.

The portrayal of anti-Methodism as an act of Anglican piety and colonial loyalty was not limited to these decrees. In 1825, the MMS sought to re-establish its presence on the island by sending a new missionary, Moses Rayner. Barbados's political establishment responded angrily, terming it an 'obnoxious' attempt to foist Methodism upon the population.[36] Meanwhile, a letter appeared in the press from 'Philo Ecclesiae'. Addressed to Bishop William Coleridge, the letter argued that allowing Rayner to land was an unnecessary 'Evil' given the increasingly active role played by the Anglican church on the island. Coleridge had been appointed in 1825 after the formalisa-tion of the established Church's presence in the region.[37] Highlighting the deeply-embedded nature of anti-Methodist feeling, Philo Ecclesiae's appeals to the Anglican Church portrayed anti-Methodism not as an act associated with an aberrant 'slave world' but with normal, Anglican societies.

WHITE ANXIETIES

At first sight, anti-Methodism would seem to be a locus for confident colo-nial assertions of a British 'Imperial identity'. Yet, anxieties were evident in letters sent by planters expressing concern that the events would 'tend to increase the prejudice so industriously (and so unjustly) excited against the West India proprietors' and be used to attack Barbados as a whole.[38]

Evidence of these anxieties can also be seen in the rhetoric of anti-Methodism itself. Nowhere is this clearer than in the proclamation produced in 1824 on the first anniversary of the chapel's destruction. The ostensible pur-pose of this proclamation was to call for renewed attacks on the Methodist community. The way in which the original destruction was commemorated is significant:

> [I]t is hereby made known to all whom it may concern, that for the avowed purpose of rooting *eternally* from their shores the damned doctrine, and public exhibition of Methodistical hypocrisy now again rearing its baleful head, and spreading its blasted and pestilential principles amongst us, we have decreed that from and after the said memorable, the blessed 21st October, more dear to firm and true Barbadians than Trafalgar to Britons, that we will, with fire and sword, root and out and destroy, all and every abettors of Methodism and Methodists.[39]

The 'blessed 21st October', the date on which the chapel's destruction was first celebrated, was also the anniversary of the Battle of Trafalgar, which had occurred on 21 October 1805. Trafalgar was an important victory for British West Indians because it marked a check to the French naval threat in the Caribbean. After news of the battle reached Barbados, white society engaged in celebrations and mourned the death of Admiral Horatio Nelson. An appeal was launched to commemorate the events 'WITH a view of testifying the high regard and veneration which the people of this ancient and loyal

Colony entertain of the transcendent services rendered to the BRITISH EMPIRE by the late heroic LORD NELSON', and a statue was unveiled in 1813 in a central part of Bridgetown named 'Trafalgar Square'.[40] For white West Indians, the commemoration of Nelson and Trafalgar was not only about thanksgiving: it was also crucial to forging a settler identity. It marked the loyalty of Barbados to Britain and the importance of the colony within the empire. As one visitor to the island put it: 'Barbadians pride themselves not a little' on the statue of Nelson.[41]

Despite the central place of Nelson in white Barbadian settler mythology, the evocation of Trafalgar in the 1824 proclamation was ambiguous.[42] It equated domestic conflict with foreign war in elevating the chapel's destruction to the status of a glorious triumph over a foreign foe. Yet by downgrading the commemoration of Trafalgar in favour of the 'Great and signal triumph' over Methodism ('the blessed 21st October, more dear to firm and true Barbadians than Trafalgar to Britons') a difference between the national mythologies of Barbados and Britain was posited. What was important to white Barbadians was not the imperial struggle against France, but a local struggle against 'Methodistical hypocrisy'.[43]

By suggesting that white Britons and white Barbadians did not share the same commemorative priorities, the decree implied that there *were* differences between West Indians and their transatlantic brethren. When it is also noted that the 1824 decree was circulated by the 'committee of public safety' but signed by the enigmatic 'ROCK', this ambivalence is more evident. The former title alluded to the reactionary organisations that had emerged in Britain in the 1790s in the context of fears about revolution, with abolitionism as one of their targets. In contrast, the appellation 'ROCK' was a reference to 'Captain Rock', a semi-mythical figure who was the supposed leader of 'the most notorious insurgent movement in nineteenth-century Ireland'.[44] The use of 'ROCK' to identify anti-Methodism – which led Buxton, the leading abolitionist, to describe the persecution as of an 'Irish model' – served to represent opposition to imperial reformism as an anti-colonial struggle.[45] Along with the uncertain place of Nelson and Trafalgar in anti-Methodism's collective memory, these two very different designations underline the ambivalence of white West Indian responses to anti-slavery as they oscillated between ultra-loyalty and anti-imperialism.

Other anti-Methodist texts betray similar anxieties. A decree produced in 1825 while the replacement missionary, Rayner, was anchored offshore called on the island's whites to 'hurl the thunder of their excited fury at the daring miscreant's head'. The decree represented the persecution of Methodism as a critical opportunity for Barbadians to 'prove that the proud blood of Englishmen yet flows uncontaminated in the remains of their West India progeny'.[46] That anti-Methodism was a proving ground suggested an anxiety about metropolitan perceptions of the religious persecution and West Indian culture more broadly. Indeed, the strenuous need to assert the 'English' nature of anti-Methodism throughout the period 1823–25 betrayed a lack of white colonial self-assurance and seemed to point to an awareness that a backlash was inevitable, particularly in the context of the increasing influence of anti-slavery politics in Britain.

NEGOTIATING A PLACE FOR BARBADOS

Much of the uncertainty in the articulation of white West Indian identity during the slavery controversy stemmed from fears that West Indian complaints would invite greater anti-creole hostility. In Barbados in the early 1820s, this uncertainty centred on white colonial concerns over how anti-Methodism would be interpreted in the metropole, particularly the destruction of the chapel and the opposition to the attempts made by the Governor – the embodiment of imperial authority – to protect religious freedom. Something of the response to this, or, rather, attempts to pre-empt it, can be seen in the efforts involving the colonial agent to relate the destruction of the chapel to the revolt in Demerara, Shrewsbury's allegedly disruptive behaviour and the broader context of anti-slavery campaigning. Such efforts to explain if not excuse anti-Methodism turned on an attempt to normalise white Barbadian responses, given that 'Human feelings' were the 'same in all countries and in all ages'.[47]

The efforts made through the colonial agent were part of the attempt to negotiate a place for white West Indian politics and culture – as articulated in anti-Methodism – in the metropolitan imagination. A prime example of this can be seen in the politico-judicial logic evoked to justify the official harassment of one Sarah Ann Gill. The settler mythology on which this logic was based is significant and the case repays examination. Gill was a relatively wealthy free woman of colour who became the leader of the Methodist community in the absence of a missionary. Meetings were held at her house, which, in consequence, became a target for attack. She was also harassed by the island's authorities, which included visits from magistrates and a summons to appear before the legislature.[48] The actions of the civil authorities were symptomatic of the entrenched nature of anti-Methodism: the forms taken by official harassment mirrored the anonymous threats made to her. The formal reason for much of the official persecution was that Gill was guilty of holding a 'conventicle'. The 1664 Conventicles Act had forbidden gatherings (conventicles) of more than five people for divine worship other than in a licensed meeting place and led by a licensed preacher.[49] Although it had been made obsolete in England by the 1689 Toleration Act, legal opinion in early nineteenth-century Barbados declared that the Toleration

Act did not extend to the island and that the Conventicles Act remained in force.[50]

The Conventicles Act had been passed during the reign of Charles II. To appreciate the significance of its enforcement in early nineteenth-century Barbados, it must be understood as part of the effort to suppress Dissenting religion after the restoration of the monarchy in 1660. During the English Civil War, many of the island's planters were keen to remain out of the conflict and Barbados was initially neutral.[51] Nevertheless, after the victory of Parliamentary forces and the 'Usurpation' of the monarchy, Royalist sympathisers in Barbados, swollen in their numbers by émigrés from England, moved in favour of independence from Cromwell's Commonwealth. Parliament responded in 1651 by dispatching a fleet to subordinate the colony. After a blockade, the colonists agreed to recognise Parliamentary rule in exchange for continued self-government as codified in a charter of 1652. For the plantocracy, this charter represented 'confirmation that propertied Englishmen overseas were also entitled to the same political freedoms that they enjoyed at home'.[52] As well as guaranteeing certain political rights as enshrined in the charter, opposition to the Cromwellian state and the constitutional concessions they had won became a symbol of white Barbadians' supposed commitment to liberty and was, as such, mythologised in the collective settler identity.[53] The notion that white Barbadians were the 'most faithful Subjects' of an 'ancient and loyal Colony' was an important aspect of the 'Little England' discourse. As one early nineteenth-century commentator put it:

> Many of the Colonies have been . . . colonized by the best blood of England, flyers from the invaders and usurpers of the church and state. In the Colonies last of all the King's dominions [was] . . . Barbados . . . [F]rom this honourable circumstance, and from priority of settlement, [it is] justly styled most ancient and most loyal.[54]

In the early nineteenth century, defenders of Barbadian slavery used the island's reputation for ancient loyalty (and the rights their ancestors had won) to forestall what they considered metropolitan 'interference'. Moreover, parallels were drawn between the 'Puritan' abolition of the monarchy and the contemporary threat posed by anti-slavery (which drew much of its support from Dissenters) to portray a renewed 'Usurpation'. Both were characterised as anti-Establishment forces, opposed to the Anglican church and a state that respected liberty.[55] According to Nathaniel Lucas, a Barbadian planter and commentator on local affairs, this could be seen in the 'malign influence' of 'puritanism' over the British Cabinet that had been realised in the adoption of the ameliorative policy in 1823.[56] The intensity (and violent manifestation) of anti-Methodism in Barbados was also related to the 'days of the Usurpation', which had 'only increased in their descendants their fixed

Attachment to the Church . . . and their destation [sic] of the Dissenters'.[57] In this way, the strength of colonial loyalty and 'zeal for Episcopacy', both rooted in events of the mid-seventeenth century, explained and justified the form that anti-Methodism had taken in the Barbados of the mid-1820s.

Drawing upon earlier opposition to Cromwell, white Barbadians claimed in the 1820s that it was possible to be loyal to British values while being opposed to the British state. The notion of 'loyal' resistance to renewed 'Usurpation' was a discursive strategy of negotiation. It paralleled those arguments that the resistance of the colonial legislatures to anti-slavery measures was a sign of the cultural sameness of white West Indian and white metropolitan, while a lack of resistance would have been 'unworthy to the name of Britons'.[58] Both the anti-Methodists' self-representation as defenders of 'Church and State', and the enforcement of the Conventicles Act by the island's authorities (as a means of suppressing contemporary Dissenters), served to locate Barbados in a post-Cromwellian, pre-Toleration era, in which Puritan 'enthusiasticks' – and therefore contemporary anti-slavery campaigning – could be forthrightly resisted by loyal, British Anglicans.

Nevertheless, the evocation of ancient loyalty during the 'Usurpation' was problematic because it was also an acknowledgement that the interests of Barbados's planters might not always coincide with those of the metropole. Evoking the 'Usurpation' left open the possibility of future colonial estrangement and was indicative of the anxiety-ridden nature of the negotiation process because it expressed an uncertainty about the Britishness of West Indian identity. Similar forms of anxiety can be seen in other arguments that sought to define a stable moment of origin to defend slavery. For example, Lucas was concerned to show that West Indian slavery was almost as old as the colonisation of the region and therefore a fully British institution: 'England has given every encouragement to the Slave Trade . . . By such assurances, our Ancestors, relying on the faith of England, invested their Capitals here on as firm a basis, as if the Colonies had been the Fifty Third County of that Kingdom.'[59]

By demonstrating that the imperial government had 'given every encouragement to the Slave Trade', Lucas claimed that it had to respect the current rights of slaveholders. He contested the 'free world'/'slave world' demarcation asserted by anti-slavery campaigners and placed Barbados firmly at the heart of metropolitan culture ('as if the Colonies had been the Fifty Third County of that Kingdom'). Nevertheless, Lucas was forced to acknowledge the novelty of West Indian slavery and the fact that it was Dutch capital and knowledge that had transformed Barbados into a sugar cane-growing slave society. Moreover, the fact that this occurred in the context of the Civil War and its aftermath – when 'The Mother Country forgot she had Colonies' – seemed to suggest that slavery was a foreign-financed, 'New World' innovation (and therefore creole), rather than the transference of something essentially British. Although Lucas was at pains to demonstrate that slavery had been 'anglicised' after the Restoration, his recognition that 'Negro Slavery was established here during the Anxiety and Confusion of the Civil Wars, without any authority whatsoever from the Parent State' weakened his arguments.[60]

Aware of the ambiguous nature of their position and fearing the implications of opposition to anti-slavery, white Barbadians sought to pre-empt metropolitan criticisms. Attempting to win 'tenuous legitimacy', particularly through the foundational and mythologised moment of the 'Usurpation', those involved in anti-Methodism and the broader defence of slavery sought to negotiate between the poles of anti-imperialism and ultra-loyalty.[61] This goal could never be achieved, however, and the very process of negotiation was beset by anxiety. Lucas, for example, sought to demonstrate the thoroughly 'English' nature of West Indian slavery, but in recognising that it had become established in Barbados during a period of rupture with the metropole, he was forced to acknowledge that slavery could be seen as a prime marker of creole difference.

METROPOLITAN CENSURE

The anxiety apparent in the representation of anti-Methodism seemed justified in the context of the opprobrium expressed in Britain. The anti-slavery campaign condemned the resistance to ameliorative reform as further evidence of planter intransigence.[62] Nevertheless, '[t]he issue that . . . evoked a massive and irrepressible outcry in Britain was not slavery per se but religious persecution'.[63] The events in Barbados had already been condemned, particularly in the publications of the MMS.[64] In June 1825, anti-Methodism came to the attention of a wider audience when Buxton introduced a motion in Parliament calling for the censure of the chapel's destruction and the protection of religious freedom on the island.[65] The events of the previous two years were described as 'a triumph not merely over Methodism . . . but a triumph over the Governor there, over the Parliament here, and over the feeling of the people of England'.[66] In so describing them, Buxton sought to mobilise a morally outraged metropolitan identity that would not tolerate such religious persecution, particularly given Barbados's place in humanitarian discourse as the ultimate site of planter conservatism.[67] As well as condemning the actual persecution and relating it to a broader context of West Indian opposition to amelioration, supporters of Buxton's motion challenged those representations that sought to portray anti-Methodism as proof of Britishness or an act of colonial loyalty. This was exemplified by the speech of William Smith, a vehement opponent of slavery who also argued that a strong response to the anti-Methodists was necessary if 'the honour of this country' was to be restored.[68] Smith ridiculed the Little England rhetoric deployed by Barbadian planters in their defence of slavery:

> There has always existed, on the part of the inhabitants of that Island, the most inordinate and ridiculous ideas of their own importance. They seemed, in this instance to be nearly on the same level with the poor simple Welchman [sic], who exclaimed, when he was about to leave the city of Bristol, 'Alas! What will become of thee, poor Bristol, when I am gone!'[69]

This deliberate, mocking reference to the white Barbadian aphorism 'What would poor old England do, were Barbados to forsake her?' encapsulated the anti-slavery reaction to West Indian opposition. Echoing Buxton's reference to the 'Irish extraction' of anti-Methodism, Smith compared Barbadian identity to a non-English form of white identity (Welshness) and marginalised white Barbadians to the peripheries of Britain. This represented a rejection of the notion that 'Little England' had a special relationship with Britain or deserved exceptional treatment with regard to amelioration. Instead of being either one of the 'props' of the 'Mother Country' or the linchpin of empire, Barbados was an ungovernable embarrassment whose politicians' dark allusions to the American Revolution were 'justly a subject of ridicule'.[70] Other supporters of the bill combined such dismissals of Barbados's imperial status with a reassertion of the need to enforce ameliorative measures.

At the end of the debate, although Buxton's motion was amended, the tone of censure remained: the demolition was condemned and religious freedom was to be protected. Parliament had been united in its denunciation of anti-Methodism. The metropolitan reaction was also manifest in imperial demands that the Barbadian legislature bring about substantive reforms to the local condition of slavery.[71] Nevertheless, while conflict between the Barbadian legislature and Colonial Office continued over the adoption of ameliorative reforms, it was religious persecution that served to focus anti-Barbadian feelings. The anger expressed in the parliamentary debate and motion, as well as the threat to step up anti-slavery campaigning, perturbed many white Barbadians and the years 1825 and 1826 saw attempts at accommodation that amounted to new forms of negotiation. But rather than drawing on historicised discourses of ancient loyalty and renewed 'Usurpation', these forms of negotiation revolved around the assertion of class division in the colony and were explicitly associated with Barbados's white elite. Much to the chagrin of the plantocracy, the post-demolition humanitarian attack on white Barbados had not acknowledged the divided nature of the society. Rather, anti-Methodism had been used to vilify white society as a whole. In an effort to resist this uncompromising representation of Barbados as an aberrant space by asserting a more nuanced account, a public meeting of over a hundred of the richest planters and merchants was held in December

1825 and a declaration was produced. Expressing disapproval for the chapel's destruction and accepting the parliamentary censure, the most striking aspect of the declaration was the internal division drawn between the 'respectable part of the community', which had always condemned the demolition, and the 'rabble'. The declaration was published in 1826 and set before Parliament by the colonial agent.[72]

Elite white attempts at 'negotiation' were manifest in other realms. The MMS was able to re-establish its presence in 1826 and by 1832 two new Methodist chapels had been officially registered. At the same time, a number of reforms to local slave codes were made and accepted by Parliament. With the lessening of anti-Methodism in Barbados, the site of missionary persecution in the 1830s was to be Jamaica.

CONCLUSIONS

For Linda Colley, the anti-slavery campaign of the late eighteenth and early nineteenth centuries served to validate a hegemonic British identity. This self-image was that of Britain as the 'friend of the negro' and it was crucial to how late Georgian and early Victorian Britain projected itself on the world stage.[73] The construction of such an identity must be seen as resting not only on the humanitarian possession of the enslaved subject, but also on the asserted otherness of the 'creole planter' as a manifestation of an 'off-white' identity.[74] The strength of what Gordon Lewis terms an 'anti-Caribbean animus' and its spatialisation in the 'invidious demarcation' drawn between 'slave world' and 'free world' was related to the changing geographies of the British Empire, including the declining importance of the West Indian colonies.[75] This 'slave'/'free' division became realised in the increasing imperial concern with, and legislative involvement in, slavery, which culminated in its formal abolition in 1834, the ending of apprenticeship in 1838 and the equalisation of sugar duties in 1846.

The expression and realisation of this 'anti-Caribbean animus' suggests one of the ways in which 'creole' can be understood as a form of identity in the Georgian imperial world: a negatively-represented figure within metropolitan discourse and a marker of white West Indian difference. Central to metropolitan claims about the 'un-English' nature of white creoles was their involvement in slavery. Yet 'creole' refers to more than this. Lewis describes white West Indian identities as 'Anglo-Saxon and anti-English', signalling the ambivalent responses that metropolitan attacks engendered amongst the West Indian slaveholders, their supporters, agents and institutions.[76] Here, 'creole' is understood as a peripheral manifestation of the 'tensions of empire' as Barbados's whites were 'trapped in a dilemma of discovering themselves to be at once the same, and yet not the same, as the country of their origin'.[77]

Colonial responses in Barbados were manifested in the vacillation between ultra-loyalty and anti-imperialism. In the former, white Barbadians claimed their rights as 'free-born Englishmen' within an expansive sense of British 'Imperial identity', and denied their 'creole-ness' through a Little Englandist rhetoric of loyalty and indispensability to the empire. Nevertheless, the institutionalisation of the 'problem of slavery' in the British anti-slavery campaign also engendered assertions of West Indian difference that paralleled those 'subaltern English nationalisms and countercultural patriotisms . . . generated in a complex pattern of antagonistic relationships with the supra-national and imperial world'.[78]

Anti-Methodism in Barbados in the 1820s was a locus of such creole complexities. It was an articulation of a strident colonial project of identification that engendered metropolitan projections of otherness *and* it was characterised by attempts to resolve West Indian difference through what Sandiford terms 'negotiation'. In the context of the latter, the significance of the evocation of the Conventicles Act has been stressed. This Act and its contemporary mobilisation in Barbados spanned the 'long' eighteenth century, connecting a mythologised past to a then contested present in the 1820s. That the 'Usurpation' was afforded such symbolic importance in Barbados underscores the significance of anti-humanitarianism to white colonial identity and politics in the Caribbean of the late Georgian period.

John Barrell's notion of 'this/that/the other' seems particularly useful for capturing the interplay of tensions and anxieties within the constitution of an 'Imperial identity' during the controversy over slavery. It suggests how metropolitan identity could be constituted both in relation to the enslaved victim ('that') and the white creole victimiser ('the other').[79] It must be emphasised, however, that this logic was associated with a particular historical-geographical context in which humanitarian discourse was ascendant. From the mid-nineteenth century, the non-white colonised subject, particularly the 'free' black subject, would move firmly into the position of the absolute 'other' and white West Indians would no longer occupy a central role in the constitution of British identity.

NOTES

1 L. Colley, *Britons: Forging the Nation, 1707–1837* (New Haven and London: Yale University Press, 1992); J. P. Greene, 'Empire and identity from the Glorious Revolution to the American Revolution', in P. J. Marshall (ed.), *The Oxford History of the British Empire. Volume 2: The Eighteenth Century* (Oxford: Oxford University Press, 1998), 208–30, quote on p. 208.

2 P. J. Marshall, 'Britain without America – a second empire?', in Marshall, *The Oxford History of the British Empire. Volume 2*, 576–95, quote on p. 590.

3 A. J. O'Shaughnessy, *An Empire Divided: The American Revolution and the British Caribbean* (Philadelphia: University of Pennsylvania Press, 2000).

4 With some exceptions, the term 'West Indies' refers to the islands of the Caribbean, including the Greater and Lesser Antilles. In this chapter, the term will be used to refer to those Caribbean islands under British control.

5 R. B. Sheridan, 'The formation of Caribbean plantation society, 1689–1748', in Marshall (ed.), *The Oxford History of the British Empire. Volume 2*, 394–414; O'Shaughnessy, *An Empire Divided.*

6 See, for example, T. Clarkson, *Thoughts on the Necessity for Improving the Condition of the Slaves in the British Colonies, with a View to their Ultimate Emancipation* (London: Richard Taylor, 1823).

7 J. R. Ward, *British West Indian Slavery, 1750–1834* (Oxford: Clarendon Press, 1998).

8 H. McD. Beckles, *A History of Barbados: From Amerindian Settlement to Nation-State* (Cambridge: Cambridge University Press, 1990).

9 PRO, CO 31/49, Minutes of Barbados Assembly, 23 September 1823.

10 M. Craton, *Sinews of Empire: A Short History of British Slavery* (London: Temple Smith, 1974), 239; Marshall, 'Britain without America'; A. Porter, 'Trusteeship, anti-slavery, and humanitarianism', in A. Porter (ed.), *The Oxford History of the British Empire. Volume 3: The Nineteenth Century* (Oxford: Oxford University Press), 198–221, quote on p. 198.

11 Colley, *Britons, passim.*

12 D. Arnold, *The Problem of Nature: Environment, Culture and European Expansion* (Oxford: Blackwell, 1996); A. L. Stoler, 'Rethinking colonial categories: European communities and the boundaries of rule', in N. B. Dirks (ed.), *Colonialism and Culture* (Ann Arbor: University of Michigan Press, 1992), 319–52; C. Hall, *Civilising Subjects: Metropole and Colony in the English Imagination, 1830–1867* (Cambridge: Polity, 2002), 70.

13 B. Anderson, *Imagined Communities: Reflections on the Origin and Spread of Nationalism* (London: Verso, 1991), 93.

14 M. Craton, *Testing the Chains: Resistance to Slavery in the British West Indies* (London: Cornell University Press, 1982), 105; Sheridan, 'The formation of Caribbean plantation society', *passim.*

15 D. B. Davis, *The Problem of Slavery in the Age of Revolution, 1770–1823* (London: Cornell University Press, 1975), 41.

16 D. B. Davis, *Slavery and Human Progress* (Oxford: Oxford University Press, 1984), 81.

17 J. P. Greene, 'Changing identity in the British Caribbean: Barbados as a case study', in N. Canny and A. Pagden (eds), *Colonial Identity in the Atlantic World, 1500–1800* (Princeton: Princeton University Press, 1987), 213–66.

18 Davis, *Slavery and Human Progress*, 81.

19 K. A. Sandiford, *The Cultural Politics of Sugar: Caribbean Slavery and Narratives of Colonialism* (Cambridge: Cambridge University Press, 2000); Hall, *Civilising Subjects, passim.*

20 Hall, *Civilising Subjects*, 107.

21 Sandiford, *Cultural Politics of Sugar, passim.*

22 This term first appears in D. McKinnen, *A Tour Through the British West Indies, in the Years 1802 and 1803* (London: J. White, 1804). It has very different connotations to the way 'Little Englander' is used in the metropolitan context. For example, Richard Gott notes that 'Little Englander' first appears in print in Britain in the 1890s as a pejorative term to describe those opposed to the Anglo-Boer War. Interestingly, one of the

best-known examples that established Barbados's reputation as 'Little England' was also bound up with an imperial war. This is the oft-repeated story of the communication sent from the colony at the outbreak of hostilities with the encouraging message 'Go ahead England, Barbados is behind you', although the details of which war remain unclear. While Gott traces the genealogy of 'Little Englander' back to anti-colonial and anti-slavery thought, 'Barbados-as-Little England' carried diametrically opposite connotations. See R. Gott, 'Little Englanders', in R. Samuel (ed.), *Patriotism: The Making and Unmaking of British National Identity. Volume 1: History and Politics* (London: Routledge, 1989), 90–102; R. B. Potter and G. M. S. Dann, *Barbados, World Bibliographic Series – Volume 76* (Oxford, Clio Press, 1987), xix.

23 Sandiford, *Cultural Politics of Sugar*, 3.

24 Sandiford draws attention to the etymological dichotomy and antagonism rooted in the Latin term *negotium*, which he splits into *neg-* (not) and *otium* (ease, quiet).

25 G. K. Lewis, *Main Currents in Caribbean Thought: The Historical Evolution of Caribbean Society in its Ideological Aspects, 1492–1900* (Baltimore: Johns Hopkins University Press, 1983).

26 J. P. Greene, 'Liberty, slavery and the transformation of British identity in the eighteenth-century West Indies', *Slavery and Abolition*, 21 (2000), 1–31; S. H. Carrington, 'West Indian opposition to British policy: Barbadian politics, 1774–82', *Journal of Caribbean History*, 17 (1982), 26–49.

27 A. Lester, 'Reformulating identities: British settlers in early nineteenth-century South Africa', *Transactions of the Institute of British Geographers*, 23 (1998), 515–31, quote on p. 525.

28 N. F. Titus, *The Development of Methodism in Barbados, 1823–1883* (Berne: Peter Lang, 1994); K. Lewis, *The Moravian Mission in Barbados, 1816–1886* (Frankfurt am Main: Peter Lang, 1985).

29 D. Hempton, *Methodism and Politics in British Society, 1750–1850* (London: Hutchinson, 1984); M. Turner, *Slaves and Missionaries: The Disintegration of Jamaican Slave Society, 1787–1834* (London: University of Illinois Press, 1982).

30 Hall, *Civilising Subjects*, 104–5.

31 Titus, *Development of Methodism*, passim.

32 School of Oriental and African Studies, University of London (SOAS), Methodist Missionary Society Archives, Box 3, No. 121, Letter from W. Shrewsbury to Methodist Missionary Society, 20 June 1820.

33 [Anonymous], *An Authentic Report of the Debate in the House of Commons, June the 23rd, 1825, on Mr. Buxton's Motion Relative to the Demolition of the Methodist Chapel and Mission House in Barbadoes, and the Expulsion of Mr. Shrewsbury, a Wesleyan Missionary, from That Island* (London: J. Hatchard and Son, 1825).

34 This 1823 Proclamation is reproduced in Methodist Missionary Society, *The Late Insurrection in Demerara, and Riot in Barbados* (London: Methodist Missionary Society, 1823).

35 *Ibid.*

36 PRO, CO 28/95, Address of the Barbados Assembly to H. Warde, 5 April 1825.

37 Bridgetown Public Library, Barbados (BPL), Reel UF12, Letter from Philo Ecclesiae in *The Barbadian*, 8 April 1825.

38 Methodist Missionary Society, *The Late Insurrection*, 2.

39 This 1824 Decree is reproduced in J. V. B. Shrewsbury, *Memorials of the Rev. William J. Shrewsbury* (London: 1868), 174.

40 [Anonymous], 'Some Nelson statues', *Journal of the Barbados Museum and Historical Society*, 18 (1951), 4–17, quote on p. 7.

41 F. Bayley, *Four Years' Residence in the West Indies, During the Years 1826, 7, 8 and 9* (London: W. Kidd, 1830), 30.

42 Nelson himself had been suspicious about West Indian loyalty in the aftermath of the American Revolution, and whilst stationed in Barbados in the late 1780s he had described it as the 'Barbarous Island' and a 'detestable spot'. See B. Dyde, *A History of Antigua: The Unsuspected Isle* (London: Macmillan, 2000), 98; [Anonymous], 'Some Nelson statues', 6.

43 Shrewsbury, *Memorials*, 174.

44 L. Gibbons, 'Between Captain Rock and a hard place: art and agrarian insurgency', in T. Foley and S. Ryder (eds), *Ideology and Ireland in the Nineteenth Century* (Dublin: Four Courts Press, 1998), 23–44, quote on p. 24.

45 [Anonymous], *An Authentic Report*, 42.

46 The 1825 Decree is reproduced in Shrewsbury, *Memorials*, on pages 178–9.

47 Barbados Department of Archives, Agents' Letter Books, Reel Bs. 9, Letter of Committee of Correspondence of the Barbados Assembly to G. Carrington, 28 June 1824.

48 Information on Gill's harassment can be found in Box 5 of the Methodist Missionary Society Archives at SOAS.

49 F. W. Blackman, *National Heroine of Barbados: Sarah Ann Gill* (Barbados: Methodist Church in Barbados, 1998), 26.

50 See the letter from the Attorney General and Solicitor General to Governor Henry Warde, dated March 1825, reproduced in *Journal of the Barbados Museum and Historical Society*, 21 (1953–54), 13.

51 G. A. Puckrein, *Little England: Plantation Society and Anglo-Barbadian Politics, 1627–1700* (New York: New York University Press, 1984).

52 Beckles, *History of Barbados*, 26.

53 O'Shaughnessy, *An Empire Divided, passim*.

54 G. W. Jordan, *An Examination of the Principles of the Slave Registry Bill, and of the Means of Emancipation, Proposed by the Authors of the Bill* (London: Printed for T. Cadell and W. Davies, 1816), 13–14.

55 J. MacQueen, *The West India Colonies. The Calumnies and Misrepresentations Circulated Against Them by the* Edinburgh Review, *Mr Clarkson, Mr Crupper, Etc. Etc.* (London: Baldwin, Cradock and Joy, 1824).

56 BPL, Lucas MSS, Miscellanous items, Volume 1: N. Lucas, 'Methodists', *c.* 1823, 417.

57 *Ibid.*, 388.

58 MacQueen, *West India Colonies*, xviii.

59 BPL, Lucas MSS, Miscellaneous items, Volume 1: N. Lucas, 'The introduction of the Negro and other slaves in Barbados', *c.* 1823, 46.

60 *Ibid.*, 44, 47; Hall, *Civilising Subjects*, 102.

61 Sandiford, *Cultural Politics of Sugar*, 3.

62 Society for the Mitigation and Gradual Abolition of Slavery, *The Slave Colonies of Great Britain; or A Picture of Negro Slavery Drawn by the Colonists Themselves; Being an Abstract of the Various Papers Recently Laid before Parliament on That Subject* (London: Printed for the Society, 1825).

63 Davis, *Slavery and Human Progress*, 195.

64 Methodist Missionary Society, *Late Insurrection, passim*; J. Walvin, *Black Ivory: A History of British Slavery* (London: HarperCollins, 1992).

65 [Anonymous], *An Authentic Report, passim*.

66 *Ibid.*, 40–1.

67 Hall, *Civilising Subjects*, 114; C. Levy, 'Slavery and the emancipation movement in Barbados, 1650–1833', *Journal of Negro History*, 55 (1979), 1–14.

68 [Anonymous], *An Authentic Report*, 62.

69 *Ibid.*, 66.

70 *Ibid.*, 66, 90.

71 PRO, CO 29/31, Letter from Bathurst to the Officer Administering the Government of Barbados, 25 August 1825.

72 J. Barrow, *A Declaration of Inhabitants of Barbados, Respecting the Demolition of the Methodists Chapel, With an Appendix* (Barbados: The Barbadian, 1826).

73 Colley, *Britons, passim*; Hall, *Civilising Subjects*; Davis, *Slavery and Human Progress*; Greene, 'Empire and identity'.

74 M. Wood, *Blind Memory: Visual Representations of Slavery in England and America, 1780–1865* (Manchester: Manchester University Press, 2000); Hall, *Civilising Subjects, passim*.

75 Lewis, *Main Currents*, 23.

76 *Ibid.*, 75.

77 Canny and Pagden, *Colonial Identity in the Atlantic World*, 9.

78 D. B. Davis, *The Problem of Slavery in Western Culture* (Ithaca: Cornell University Press, 1966); P. Gilroy, *The Black Atlantic: Modernity and Double Consciousness* (London: Verso, 1993), 11.

79 Quoted in Hall, *Civilising Subjects*, 19.

4

The art of tropical travel,
1768–1830

ℓ̃

Luciana Martins

'WHAT A PLACE for an artist! I do most fervently hope that I may once more visit it, and have more time to revel in such delicious scenes . . . I shall not attempt a description of the place here; I am indeed but ill qualified to describe any thing but the scenery, and I am certainly better able to do with the pencil than the pen.' So wrote the artist Conrad Martens on his arrival in the bay of Rio de Janeiro on 5 July 1833.[1] Well aware of the picturesque qualities of the Brazilian harbour ('a rare place as I am told, for sketching'), Martens had little time to appreciate the scenery.[2] Having learned news from the *Beagle* that Captain Fitzroy had unexpectedly dispensed with the services of the artist originally appointed to the expedition, he immediately set off for Montevideo to offer his services. But his short stay in Rio provided material for works finished during his subsequent Australian career.

The picturesque appropriation of Rio de Janeiro by European voyagers formed part of an imaginative geography of tropical travel whose outlines are registered in a large and heterogeneous archive of sketches, paintings, charts, maps, diaries and letters.[3] A common feature of these images was the view of harbours such as Rio from the sea; a long-anticipated vision of a secure haven for travellers across the ocean, though at a comfortably safe distance from the hectic life of the city. Significantly, however, British artists produced relatively few major finished works depicting the Rio landscape, in comparison with the output of their French, German, Austrian and North American counterparts.[4] The visual representation of the bay and its surrounding topography was left for much of the late eighteenth and early nineteenth centuries in the hands of maritime surveyors: midshipmen, officers, chart makers, hydrographers.[5] Although beyond the formal reach of the British empire, Rio de Janeiro was a much-frequented port of call for Royal Navy ships bound for Australia, the Indian Ocean and the Far East. In 1808 it became the headquarters of the Admiralty's South American station.

The relative paucity of depictions of the Brazilian landscape produced by British professional artists prompts broader questions about the cultures of landscape art and the place of tropical travel in Georgian culture. In addressing such questions, we need to attend to the multiple ways in which landscapes may be rendered and made available to wider publics. In fact, with few exceptions, the majority of Brazilian landscapes produced by travelling British artists remained in their sketchbooks, unfinished and largely unseen. While it is possible to trace the historical geography of taste in terms of changing artistic preferences for particular places as subjects appropriate for landscape painting,[6] it is important to note that the work of professional painters depended not merely on their own preferences but also upon those of their audiences. Their works were intended to be exhibited in picture galleries or displayed within private houses in Britain and elsewhere.[7] The production of painted landscapes was thus a complex process in which philosophical debates, academic theories and art criticism were combined with wider processes of cultural consumption (see also Dias's discussion of the audience for art in Chapter 5).[8]

Art historians have conventionally identified a broad shift in the Georgian period from the classical ideal of landscape to a new model of picturesque taste, a model which was itself increasingly challenged by a tendency to naturalistic landscape painting.[9] The latter tendency is frequently said to have favoured the practice of open-air sketching, a development which ought in principle to have privileged the travelling artist, who had until then occupied a liminal position in the hierarchy of conventional taste. In contrast to the academic painter who regarded nature as the means by which he could display his art and afford amusement, the travelling artist in the era of naturalism was said (in the words of the naturalist William Burchell, himself an accomplished draughtsman) to consider art as a 'means of exhibiting nature, and of conveying information'.[10] Given such claims, one might expect to see, from the late eighteenth century and especially after the end of the Napoleonic wars, the appearance of an increasing number of finished paintings of landscape scenery from around the globe. Yet, with the notable exception of Italian scenery, the 'nature' depicted in British landscape art of the early nineteenth century was represented principally by landscapes of the mother country which, as Stephen Daniels and others have shown, helped to construct a powerful visual identity for the nation.[11] The relative rarity of tropical landscapes may be due to some extent (until 1815) to the restrictions on travel which accompanied the French revolutionary and Napoleonic Wars. Yet this context is insufficient to explain the formation of a particular taste for domestic landscape. Furthermore, even when overseas landscapes were admired on aesthetic grounds, their qualities were attributed less to their intrinsic content than to the opportunity they afforded for British imaginative genius to show its talent, as in the case of Turner's Swiss views exhibited to much acclaim in 1819.[12]

In recent years, the visual arts have proved fertile ground for critical studies of relationships between culture, travel and empire.[13] Yet the traveller's gaze has in this work perhaps too easily been associated with the figure of the 'monarch-of-all-I-survey', and the experience of novelty too readily reduced to repetition. The 'imperial eyes' of the European observer do not simply 'passively look out and possess', a formulation which leaves little room for the unexpected, for surprises and disappointments which demand an active reconfiguration of travellers' intentions and preconceptions.[14] The depiction of the colours, scale, atmosphere and light of the tropics in the work of travelling artists, for example, required a series of difficult negotiations between European aesthetic conventions and the experience of traversing the field, especially under tropical skies. Merely being in the tropics was sometimes said by European travellers to induce a sense of unease – affecting not only the eyes, but the whole of the body.[15] As it was translated into the finished products of artists, this unease was not well calculated to meet with the approval of the metropolitan artistic community. Moreover, it was common for travellers to complain of the difficulty of giving any visual form to what was experienced 'on the spot'.[16] Seeing and knowing the tropics was far from easy. As Leonard Bell has argued in his study of the work of the travelling artist Augustus Earle, 'rather than being unproblematic constituents of projects of domination' such images may often be 'pluralistic in their meanings and modes of operation'.[17]

This chapter focuses specifically on the art of tropical travel, set within the context of a broader visual archive of voyaging during the late eighteenth and early nineteenth centuries. I begin with an account of the relationship between open-air painting and the representation of nature in British landscape art during this period, before moving on to consider the shifting relations between science and art in Georgian Britain, particularly in relation to practices of observation in the field and visualisation more generally. There follows a case study of the tropical landscapes of William Havell, a professional artist who travelled in both Brazil and India in the years after 1815. At the end of the chapter, I return briefly to the more general issue of the relationship between the uneasiness of tropical landscapes and British landscape art in order to qualify the account of absence with which I began. While tropical subjects were rarely to be found in British art galleries, the work of travelling artists could provide a pictorial identity for colonial elites across the empire.

OPEN-AIR PAINTING AND THE STUDY OF NATURE

The reconciliation of art and nature in a unified aesthetic system was a major challenge for British landscape painters in the Georgian period. Although not a novelty in itself, having been a recurrent challenge in Western art since the ancient Greeks, the issue generated heated debate at this time because a new conception of 'nature' was in the making. Both the classical ideal of Italianate landscapes and the more modern aesthetic of the picturesque were increasingly being modified or undermined by a novel approach to landscape art, in which nature 'unvarnished' provided the inspiration. For artists like Cornelius Varley, the picturesque aesthetic was as selective and artificial as the classical: 'less a new look at nature than a new idea of what could make a picture'.[18] Even though it had played a pivotal role in the development of landscape aesthetics, the picturesque was to be transformed or even abandoned by a new generation of artists wedded to a new ethos of naturalism.

Linked with this critical attitude to earlier pictorial conventions was a radical commitment to improvisation and experiment *sur le motif*. This in some respects reflected the increasing influence of new methods and approaches in natural philosophy and, in particular, the burgeoning 'iconographic inventory of the world' provided by the voyages of navigators such as Cook and Bougainville (see also Clayton's discussion of scientific exploration in Chapter 2, pp. 27–43).[19] By itself, of course, empirical observation in the field could not guarantee the production of a work of art.[20] Indeed, throughout the Georgian period, the spontaneity of outdoor sketching continued to be sufficient to disqualify its immediate products from being considered as elevated works of art. The direct study of nature was still on the margins of artistic activity; it was merely part of the artist's training, the results of which were conceived as raw materials, available to the painters themselves, their friends, and perhaps students.[21] As Charlotte Klonk suggests, the phrase 'sketch from nature' present in many of the titles of pictures displayed at the Royal Academy from the 1790s implied simply that they were derived from observations (particularly sketches) in the field, rather than necessarily being painted on the spot.[22]

As Philip Conisbee has shown, the practice of open-air painting itself can be traced back to pictures of seventeenth-century Rome.[23] Beginning with an account of Claude Lorrain's experiments during the early 1630s, Conisbee traces the possible evidence for the continuation of this practice in some of Velázquez's Villa Medici paintings, sketches by Salvator Rosa, Gaspar Dughet and Alexander-François Desportes, and subsequently in the practice of Claude-Joseph Vernet and Pierre-Henri de Valenciennes. Such techniques of open-air painting eventually filtered into the work of English landscape artists, such as Alexander Cozens, who was one of the earliest British artists to study in Rome. During his stay in Italy in 1746, when he worked in the studio of Vernet, Cozens noted in his sketchbook that he had been sketching from nature both in watercolours and oils. Back in England, however, he worked almost exclusively in monochrome washes. From 1750 to 1754, Cozens occupied the position of Drawing Master at the Royal School of Mathematics, Christ's Hospital, where he was involved in the training of naval surveyors. Marine views and coastal profiles were prominent in his own work, and it is possible to discern a correspondence between Cozens's role as a teacher of the art of drawing coastal profiles and his elaboration of a perceptive theory of landscape forms. Cozens's theory of landscape was based on recognition of forms through individualisation and instant interpretation of their essential characters, precisely the visual skills that were also demanded in the art of navigation.[24] Significantly, Anne Lyles attributes Cozens's preference for working in monochrome to his developing interest in landscape theory, especially his idea of composing imaginary landscapes using ink blots.[25] Gradually, Cozens's emphasis on tone and mass led him away from open-air painting, as he became more and more concerned with the representation of idealised rather than actual landscapes. His methods, however, exerted an important influence on the following generation of British landscape painters, especially his son, John Robert Cozens, as well as upon John Constable. It was left to these artists to narrow the gap between the imaginary landscape and the topographical view.

Another British artist who came under Vernet's influence was Richard Wilson. Although there is no direct evidence that Wilson painted in oils out of doors (his preferred medium was drawing), one of his Italian paintings shows an artist seated on a folded stool working at a portable easel, perhaps implying an endorsement of the practice.[26] Wilson also taught open-air painting techniques to his pupils, Thomas Jones and William Hodges. As Bernard Smith suggests, the work of Hodges was pioneering in the sense that he made the first tentative efforts in British art to fuse the qualities of the open-air oil sketch with that of his finished work.[27] Smith emphasises, however, that 'what we have in Hodges is not the beginnings of a tradition but an important anticipation of naturalistic landscape painting'.[28]

Hodges accompanied James Cook on his second voyage to the South Pacific from 1772 to 1775, and, five years later, made a four-year tour in India. It is in Hodges's landscapes of the South Pacific that significant innovations in painterly practice may be discerned. Some of Hodges' paintings during this voyage have the freshness and directness of a work composed in the light of the day, and they suggest a considerable shift in his technique since his days as a pupil of Richard Wilson. Significantly, it is clear that Hodges was under pressure to produce works which would satisfy the demands of quite different but overlapping metropolitan communities of *curiosi*, *virtuosi* and savants.[29] Indeed, when he exhibited his Pacific landscapes at the Royal Academy in 1777, they met with some scepticism. As one critic put it, 'his pictures all appear as if they were unfinished, and as if the colours were laid on the canvas with a skewer'.[30]

Although it was widely practised by oil painters and watercolour draughts-men, the presentation of accurate information in the form of topographical views was regarded as a lowly specialism for much of the eighteenth century. Henry Fuseli, Professor at the Royal Academy Schools, once described topography as mere 'map-work', contrasting with the higher ideals expressed in landscapes by such masters as Poussin and Lorrain.[31] In his influential *Discourses* on art delivered to the Royal Academy between 1769 and 1790, Joshua Reynolds similarly urged artists to rise above the 'particular' in order to produce a 'general' representation of the natural world through a process of idealisation. The academic debate over the status of landscape art which arose in the era of Hodges and Varley centred not only upon questions of composition or subject matter, but also upon assumptions about the relative merits of particular media and techniques, such as the use of colour or monochrome, outlines or shades, watercolour or oil. As Anne Lyles explains:

> in theories about art, colour had often been associated with verisimilitude and lifelike imitation. In particular, there had been a long-running debate, originating in Italy in the sixteenth century, about the relative merits of drawing and design (*disegno*) on the one hand, and colour (*colore*) on the other. According to this debate, *disegno* was associated with invention, with the concept or idea originating in the artist's mind, whereas *colore* was equated with nature and the real world, its diversity, variety and above all its particularity.[32]

Colore therefore signified more than simply colouring: it implied a particular artistic skill which required accurate observation, dexterity and precision in delineating the contours of nature. Such practices linked the 'art of colouring' to the empirical, experimental sciences. On the other hand, *disegno* demanded an intellectual, theoretical way of seeing the world, an approach closer to the Platonic idealism and the intellectual speculation of the abstract sciences. Charlotte Klonk has argued that, in the period between 1790 and 1830, changes in the scientific conception of nature increasingly led artists to 'abandon conventional pictorial formulae, such as the sublime, the picturesque and the beautiful, in favour of a more "naturalistic" representation, giving priority to detailed observation of particular cases'.[33] It is important to note, however, that in continuing to privilege the use of colour and shade, this new generation of landscape painters still owed much to classical pictorial conventions. This apparent contradiction sheds some light on the dilemma faced by these artists: on the one hand, inspired by a philosophical curiosity consistent with the spirit of the Enlightenment, they aimed to reproduce nature as it was presented to their eyes; on the other hand, their audiences did not consider the results of their experiments to be works of art in themselves.[34] It is to this 'scientific' way of seeing nature that I now turn.

THE ARTS OF SEEING AND KNOWING

'Seeing is an art which must be learnt': thus wrote William Herschel, the natural philosopher who designed many of the telescopes used in eighteenth-century maritime expeditions.[35] Following in his father's footsteps, the astronomer John Herschel mapped the stars of the southern hemisphere, incidentally becoming one of the pioneers in the development of the modern techniques of photography.[36] As Jonathan Crary suggests, a tangible shift in the 'techniques of the observer' and, indeed, in the epistemological conditions of observation can be identified in the opening decades of the nineteenth century:

> Vision, rather than a privileged form of knowing, becomes itself an object of knowledge, of observation. From the beginning of the nineteenth century a science of vision will tend to mean increasingly an interrogation of the physiological makeup of the human subject, rather than the mechanics of light and optical transmission. It is a moment when the visible escapes from the timeless order of the camera obscura and become lodged in another apparatus, within the unstable physiology and temporality of the human body.[37]

Central to this shift, argues Crary, 'was the discovery that knowledge was conditioned by the physical and anatomical functioning of the body, and perhaps most importantly, of the eyes'.[38] Such a development is especially significant in the present context because it implies a new attitude towards the repertoire of visual practices available to the observer and hence the legitimacy of scientific observation itself. For the observer who leaves the darkened room of the camera obscura and experiences the world through direct sense impressions, the locus of truth and power becomes his or her physical body.[39] The increasing relevance of both observing 'in the field' and the reflexive character of embodied experience in the making of science both attest to the emergence of this new (ideal) figure of the observer.

The emergence of these new observational practices can be traced in the visual archive of philosophical travel.[40] The work of the naturalist William Burchell provides a case in point. Among the numerous drawings which he produced on St Helena between 1805 and 1810, when he was employed as a botanist for the East India Company, there is a small but remarkable sketch entitled a 'Group of Plantains from Nature', dated 20 February 1807 (Figure 4.1). Upon this sketch, now in the archives of the Royal Botanic Gardens, Kew, are drops of the plantain's own juice, which have fallen on the page either by accident or by design. These drops are themselves used as a sort of evidence – 'not blood but drops of Plantain juice', writes Burchell in annotating his sketch.[41] In this way, the visual image becomes something more than mere representation: stained red by the specimen itself, the very scrap of paper itself acquires scientific value. No longer just an 'illustration',

4.1 *A Group of Plantains from Nature*, by William Burchell. Pencil and watercolour, 1812. (Courtesy of the Royal Botanic Gardens, Kew)

Burchell's sketch provides confirmation of the authentic presence of the observer in the field, thereby affirming his credibility as a faithful witness.

Burchell's vast body of work, arising from his travels in South Africa (1810–15) and Brazil (1815–30), provides a clear instance of a naturalist using his artistic skills in tandem with his scientific expertise in order to provide what he regarded as an accurate record of the features of landscapes, peoples, flora and fauna he encountered.[42] In a broader context, it signals the extent to which the boundaries between science and art were being redefined within this new field of vision. The practice of drawing in the field was not merely a way of illustrating, or of decorating, texts: it was becoming a mode of scientific expression in itself. In this sense, Goethe provided a paradigm: in response to Schiller's suggestion that he write a novel based on eighteenth-century Pacific travel literature, he lamented that he lacked the first-hand visual experience (*'das unmittelbare Anschauen'*) that came with being on the spot.[43] Indeed, words alone were inadequate to such a task. As Goethe put it, philosophers 'ought to talk less and draw more. I, personally, should like to renounce speech altogether and, like organic nature, communicate everything I have to say in sketches.'[44]

Goethe's concerns are echoed in Alexander von Humboldt's account of the 'expression of tropical scenery' in the work of travelling artists:

> Sketches drawn from Nature, can alone, after the return from the voyage, enable us to represent in more elaborate landscapes the peculiarities of distant regions; they will be all the more perfect if the artist has, at the same time, drawn or painted from Nature in the open air a great number of separate studies of the top of trees, leafy branches well covered with blossoms of fruit . . . The possession of these studies from Nature, accurately designed and sketched, can alone prevent the artist, upon his return, from being misled by the assistance which he obtains from hot-house plants and the so-called botanical pictures.[45]

Humboldt was intrigued by the new techniques of visual projection emerging in the late eighteenth and early nineteenth centuries, especially dioramas and panoramas, which could, he argued, play a useful role in conveying the 'magical effect' of tropical nature ('those prospects in which Nature abounds in the wild luxuriance and fullness of life') to European audiences. In a well-designed panorama, 'removed from all the disturbances of realities', the spectator would feel 'himself surrounded with strange scenery'.[46] William Burchell also experimented with panoramas on a smaller scale, producing topographical panoramas of Belém do Pará and Rio de Janeiro in the 1820s. The fashion for panoramas provided another link between spectacle, mapping and landscape and eventually had a distinct influence on the scale and colour of landscapes exhibited at the Royal Academy.[47]

In his own narratives of tropical travel, Humboldt was actively engaged in the construction of the figure of the 'observer-in-transit', to whom the voyage presented the occasion for reflecting not only about points of view for landscape prospects but also for enquiring about the observer's own capacity to observe.[48] The reputation of the explorer's knowledge depended ultimately on establishing credibility, on building trust in observation at a distance.[49] As Dorinda Outram argues, 'such trust could be built up by means of authorship, and it is not surprising that many explorers, most notoriously Alexander von Humboldt, invested perhaps as much in writing the narrative of travel as they did in travelling itself'.[50] Humboldt's penchant for experimentation with graphic representations in the form of thematic maps, isolines and graphs, among other devices, also suggests that he was constantly 'looking for a language at once highly descriptive but also analytical'.[51] At the same time, his use of images and words was conceived as a way of conveying emotions, of evoking the sensibility of the cultivated European mind seeking to comprehend the pattern of nature.[52]

It should now be clear that far from being entirely discrete, practices of visual representation in the spheres of aesthetics and natural science in the Georgian period were in many respects intermingled. We have briefly considered some aspects of the skills and techniques common to both, and some of the available philosophical foundations for uniting, or at least connecting, aesthetic and scientific concerns. Yet these philosophical systems, notably that of Humboldt himself, were precisely that – philosophies of nature – and it would be wrong to assume that somehow the actual practices of the artist and the natural philosopher simply became one and the same. In this context, it becomes important to consider the institutional regulation of the art market and the evolving profession of the artist. How could the travelling artist reconcile the new philosophies of naturalism with existing aesthetic conventions? To what extent could the tropical view acquire the status of landscape art?

'STRANGE COLOURING': WILLIAM HAVELL'S TROPICAL LANDSCAPES

On 9 February 1816, the painter William Havell departed from England on board HMS *Alceste* employed as a draughtsman in Lord Amherst's diplomatic mission to China. After calling at Madeira, the ship made for Rio de Janeiro, following the usual transatlantic route, where she remained for ten days before proceeding to the East Indies via the Cape of Good Hope. On its return voyage from Macao, on 26 January 1817, the *Alceste* was wrecked off the coast of Sumatra, with the loss of most of the embassy's possessions.[53] Having escaped the wreck, William Havell took a passage to India on the *Lyra* under Captain Basil Hall. During his nine-year stay in India Havell made his living by painting portraits of East India Company officials and Army officers, as well as landscapes.[54]

It has been suggested that Havell's decision to leave England at the age of thirty-four and in the middle of a promising career was a reaction to the British Institution's refusal to exhibit his largest and most ambitious oil painting – *Walnut Gathering at Petersham* – (a picture now known only by an engraving).[55] According to Roget, who wrote what has now become the standard history of the Society of Painters in Watercolour, Havell boasted that his skill in executing this picture surpassed even that of Turner.[56] But the authorities at the British Institution Committee dismissed it as mere experiment: the painting was 'nothing but light!'[57] While Havell's disappointment may have influenced his decision to travel abroad, the foregoing discussion of relationships between art, science, nature and travel suggests other interpretations. Following the wreck of the *Alceste* in the Gaspar Straits, Havell could well have returned to England with other members of the diplomatic mission. In the event, he stayed in India for nine years, only returning to

England in the wake of a cholera epidemic. Two years later, in 1828, he travelled again to southern climes, spending two fruitful years in Italy.[58] Even though he complained about the heat – saying that it was as bad as in Bombay – southern skies continued to have their attractions.[59]

The tropical landscapes produced by Havell in Brazil and in India are of particular interest here in so far as they provide evidence of his 'experimental' approach to painting.[60] Rather than understanding his journey south as a matter of the moment, an impulsive response to disappointment, Havell's change of direction could rather be understood as the search for a laboratory where he could carry out his graphic experiments with light and colour with a greater degree of freedom. The impulse to travel among Havell and his contemporaries cannot of course be reduced merely to intellectual aspirations or artistic pursuits. A depressed metropolitan economy in the aftermath of Waterloo heightened competition between artists. At the same time, a new wave of old masters from continental collections was on the market. Travelling abroad was thus an appropriate project for an artist in his mid-thirties who considered his chosen profession under threat of failure. My concern here, however, is less with the artistic merits of Havell's work in itself than with its contribution to the understanding of the methods of the 'observer-in-transit', and, specifically, to the problem of translating the experience of travelling in the tropics into a pictorial language.

It was probably through his connection with his uncle Robert Havell, an engraver and printer in London, that William Havell first became acquainted with the methods of Turner and Thomas Girtin, as well as with the exotic landscapes by Thomas Daniell and his nephew, William.[61] At the age of twenty, Havell had travelled through North Wales in the company of John and Cornelius Varley, Joshua Cristall and Thomas Webster (a geologist and architect). This pioneering group was later to be dubbed the 'Varley circle', a group that, as Charlotte Klonk points out, 'modified the practice of sketching in two important respects: first, they sketched extensively in colour on the spot rather than just preparing pencil outlines; and, second, they elevated the status of the sketch done outdoors to a work in its own right which was worthy of exhibition'.[62] Although Klonk is right to emphasise the role of the Varley circle in the development of naturalistic painting, we might note here that while two of Cornelius Varley's sketches were exhibited as finished paintings, this does not mean that the status of the open-air sketch was universally held to have been elevated.[63]

In the present context, what deserves attention is Klonk's emphasis on the importance of open-air sketching to Cornelius Varley's later development as both scientist and artist. She argues that Varley's inability to translate natural phenomena into finished paintings gave direction to his scientific activity, which materialised in the development in 1805 of his graphic telescope, a drawing instrument. Klonk focuses her analysis on the degree to which the artist departed from compositional formulae. For Cornelius Varley, the accurate visual depiction of a particular phenomenon seems to have been more important than the construction of a defined pictorial space. Open-air sketching was certainly relevant for Havell's work as well, especially given that he too applied his technical knowledge to the development of photogenic drawings. In order to explore this further, we may consider Havell's oil sketch of the Braganza shore in Rio, a place now called Niterói, made on his visit in the *Alceste* in 1816 (Figure 4.2). In view of its small size (about 8 cm by 11 cm), this was surely a sketch made 'on the spot'. This image is very much a matter of brushwork, a study in light and colour. We can, however, see Havell laying the foundations for a more finished picture in that it is a composed view. The problem with oil in the open air was that its wet pigments reflected light, altering one's sense of sense. Many landscape painters had faced similar problems: in Italy, for example, some of them chose to paint from a window, or to employ a parasol.[64] Havell, however, had concocted a recipe to avoid such effects: 'Copal varnish mixed with sugar of lead to make all the colours dry immediately'.[65] By such means, Havell hoped to combine landscape as perceived with his creative artistic sensibility.

4.2 *The Braganza Shore, Rio de Janeiro*, by William Havell. Oil on card, 1816. (Copyright Reading Museum Service, Reading Borough Council. All rights reserved)

A watercolour from the same date testifies to Havell's wanderings in the neighbourhood of the city of Rio de Janeiro (Figure 4.3).[66] This picture should be seen in the context of what we know of Havell's earlier participation in the meetings of the London Sketching Society.[67] Rather than drawing inspiration from the classics, Havell's prime source for this study was the landscape of Rio itself. Although its composition is in accordance with basic picturesque rules, this study offers a richer range of tones and a greater subtlety in the description of light and shade, due to the combination of coloured washes and white bodycolour. It is in his 1821 oil painting of the Coromandel Coast, however, that the brilliancy of light and colours is at its most impressive (see Figure 4.4). In trying to depict tropical atmosphere as presented to his eyes, Havell was creating a visual language that proved to be profoundly anti-academic. If Havell subsequently reworked some of his studies to compose finished paintings, as in the *Garden Scene on the Braganza Shore* (1827) (Figure 4.5), his way of colouring defied academic rules. When it was exhibited at the Watercolour Society, this work was subjected to severe criticism for its use of bodycolour.[68]

4.3 *Near Rio de Janeiro*, by William Havell. Watercolour, 1816. (© Copyright The British Museum)

4.4 *On the Coromandel Coast, South India,* by William Havell. Oil on canvas, 1821. (Copyright Reading Museum Service, Reading Borough Council.)

Garden Scene on the Braganza Shore, Rio de Janeiro, by William Havell. Gouache, 1827. (Courtesy of Trustees of the Victoria & Albert Museum)

85

The fact that some of these images are likely to have been open-air sketches, together with the variety of media employed (watercolour, bodycolour and oil), highlights Havell's experimental approach to painting. If southern skies encouraged a new approach to colour and light, the experience of observation in the field also presented a challenge to the artist's métier. The fact that Havell exhibited so few of his tropical landscapes indicates the sheer difficulty of reconciling the two.[69] In this respect, the ambivalent response to a selection of Havell's work from Italy and elsewhere exhibited in 1842 is telling: 'Havell still retains his strange colouring which renders most of his subjects unpleasing. We well remember the scenery around San Cosimeto, but cannot recognise it in the effect of colouring of Mr Havell. His method unpoetises nature.'[70]

The suggestion that Havell's method 'unpoetises nature' coincided, significantly, with his experiments in photogeny, in partnership with his brother Frederick James. Having learned Henry Fox Talbot's secret of fixing the image in 1839, the Havells worked out a process 'for the delineation of the work of the artist's pencil', a process they claimed to be exactly the reverse of Talbot's, in which 'you make the powers of nature work for you'.[71] What might be noted in this context is that what is under development is a process involving the instrumentalisation of sight comparable to that identified by Svetlana Alpers for seventeenth-century Dutch art.[72] Be that as it may, there is a fundamental difference from the techniques of the camera obscura: as Jonathan Crary suggests, the observer now leaves the protected dark room in which the exterior world is reflected in order to make sensory observations out of doors.[73] The idea of an 'unpoetised nature' dramatised the divide between art and science: at the moment of transition between Georgian and Victorian tastes, the battle between accurate depiction and artistic inspiration was once again at stake.

CONCLUSION

Through the materiality of paint on canvas or pencil on card, the tropical landscapes of William Havell testify to the interactive character of art. Rather than being products of pure subjectivity, these landscapes highlight the intermingled effects of contemporary innovations in techniques of scientific and artistic observation. They also express part of what Havell knew, part of what he saw, part of what he learned by voyaging, and part of what he had forgotten. These tropical landscapes are, above all, the result of a constant negotiation between the actual and the ideal, a process that required Havell to reconcile the representation of landscapes in situ with the demands of his metropolitan audience.

While Havell found it difficult to adjust his painterly style when returning home, other travelling artists, such as Conrad Martens and Augustus

Earle, were reluctant even to return from their travels abroad.[74] Earle was eventually compelled to do so due to poor health, while Martens remained for the rest of his life in New South Wales following the *Beagle* voyage. The colonial élite provided a ready market for their views and visions which they could not find in the metropolis. This market depended on the elevation of the colonial landscape itself as appropriate subject matter for the production of a work of art, as well as upon the development of a visual grammar appropriate to the distinctive light, colour and landscapes of the southern hemisphere. Such works of art helped to provide colonial communities in Australia and elsewhere with a distinct identity from the metropolis, yet one authenticated by metropolitan pictorial conventions and techniques.

In this chapter I have chosen to emphasise the unsettling consequences of the art of tropical travel. In comparison with the idea of the observer as 'the monarch-of-all-I-survey', the 'observer-in-transit' is an altogether less triumphal figure, although, of course, it was one encumbered by all sorts of cultural baggage. We have got so used to thinking of the imperial eye of European travellers in and beyond the tropics that we have paid less attention to the problems which voyaging could pose both for individual travellers and for metropolitan conventions. As Greg Dening puts it, perhaps travellers' eyes 'sometimes see things that they did not expect to see'.[75] My reading of Havell's tropical landscapes suggests one way of getting closer to the visual worlds which those travellers had to negotiate in order to make sense of their experience. There are many others still to be explored.

NOTES

This chapter forms part of a research project funded by the Arts and Humanities Research Board: 'Knowing the Tropics: British Visions of the Tropical World, 1750–1850'. My thanks to Felix Driver, Miles Ogborn, Charles Withers and Denis Cosgrove for comments on an earlier version.

1 C. Martens, *Journal of a Voyage from England to Australia, 1833–35* (Sydney: State Library of New South Wales Press, 1994), 9.

2 *Ibid.*, 8.

3 L. Martins, *O Rio de Janeiro dos Viajantes: O Olhar Britânico, 1800–1850* (Rio de Janeiro: Jorge Zahar, 2001).

4 On which, see P. Berger, H. G. Mathias, D. Mello Júnior (eds), *Pinturas e Pintores do Rio Antigo* (Rio de Janeiro: Livraria Kosmos, 1990); A. M. M. Beluzzo, *The Voyager's Brazil* (São Paulo: Metalivros, 1995); K. E. Manthorne, *Tropical Renaissance: North American Artists Exploring Latin America, 1839–1879* (Washington and London: Smithsonian Institution Press, 1989); R. Wagner and J. Bandeira, *Viagem ao Brasil nas Aquarelas de Thomas Ender, 1817–1818*, 3 volumes (Petrópolis: Kapa Editorial, 2000); M. L. P. Horta (ed.), *Visões do Rio na Coleção Geyer* (Petrópolis: Museum Imperial e Centro Cultural Banco do Brasil, 2000); G. Ferrez, *Iconografia do Rio de Janeiro, 1530–1890*, 2 volumes (Rio de Janeiro: Casa Jorge Editorial, 2000).

5   See L. Martins, 'Mapping tropical waters: British views and visions of Rio de Janeiro',
    in D. Cosgrove (ed.), *Mappings* (London: Reaktion Books, 1999), 148–68; and F. Driver
    and L. Martins, 'John Septimus Roe and the art of navigation, *c.* 1815–1830', *History
    Workshop Journal*, 54 (2002), 148–65.

6   P. Howard, 'Painters' preferred places', *Journal of Historical Geography*, 11 (1985), 138–
    54; S. Faunce, 'Rome and its environs: painters, travelers, and sites', in P. Conisbee,
    S. Faunce and J. Strick (eds), *In the Light of Italy: Corot and Early Open-Air Painting*
    (New Haven and London: Yale University Press, 1996), 49–77.

7   D. H. Solkin (ed.), *Art on the Line: The Royal Academy Exhibitions at Somerset House,
    1780–1836* (New Haven and London: Yale University Press, 2001); B. F. Tobin, *Picturing
    Imperial Power: Colonial Subjects in Eighteenth-Century British Painting* (Durham and
    London: Duke University Press, 1999).

8   For a detailed account of these categories, see A. Hemingway, *Landscape Imagery and
    Urban Culture in Early Nineteenth-Century Britain* (Cambridge: Cambridge University
    Press, 1992).

9   See A. Lyles, 'The transformation of the British landscape watercolour *c.* 1750–1805', in
    A. Lyles and R. Hamley (eds), *British Watercolours from the Oppé Collection* (London:
    Tate Gallery, 1997), 19–31; K. D. Kriz, *The Idea of the English Landscape Painter: Genius
    as Alibi in the Early Nineteenth Century* (New Haven and London: Yale University
    Press, 1997), 57–79; C. Klonk, *Science and the Perception of Nature: British Landscape
    Art in the Late Eighteenth and Early Nineteenth Centuries* (New Haven and London:
    Yale University Press, 1996); and Hemingway, *Landscape Imagery*, 79–104.

10 W. Burchell, *Travels in the Interior of Southern Africa*, 2 volumes (1824) (London:
    Batchworth Press, 1953), 396. The use of printed images to convey empirical data in
    the same period is considered in S. Smiles, *Eye Witness: Artists and Visual Documenta-
    tion in Britain, 1770–1830* (Aldershot: Ashgate, 2000).

11 S. J. Daniels, *Fields of Vision: Landscape Imagery and National Identity in England and
    the United States* (Cambridge: Polity Press, 1994); Hemingway, *Landscape Imagery*;
    W. J. T. Mitchell (ed.), *Landscape and Power* (Chicago and London: University of
    Chicago Press, 1994).

12 Kriz, *The Idea of the English Landscape Painter*, 109.

13 See M. L. Pratt, *Imperial Eyes: Travel Writing and Transculturation* (London: Routledge,
    1992); Mitchell, *Landscape and Power*; S. Ryan, *The Cartographic Eye: How Explorers
    Saw Australia* (Cambridge: Cambridge University Press, 1996).

14 D. Ferrer, 'The interaction of verbal and pictorial elements in the genesis of Eugène
    Delacroix's Sultan of Morocco', *Word and Image*, 13 (1997), 183–91.

15 A similar discomfort was experienced by British travellers in Italy: see C. Powell, *Italy
    in the Age of Turner: 'the Garden of the World'* (London, Dulwich Picture Gallery,
    1998), 68–89.

16 L. Martins, 'A naturalist's vision of the tropics: Charles Darwin and the Brazilian
    landscape', *Singapore Journal of Tropical Geography*, 21 (2000), 19–33.

17 L. Bell, 'To see or not to see: conflicting eyes in the travel art of Augustus Earle',
    in J. F. Codell and D. S. Macleod (eds), *Orientalism Transposed: The Impact of the
    Colonies on British Culture* (Aldershot: Ashgate, 1998), 117–39, quote on p. 130.

18 D. B. Brown, *Oil Sketches from Nature: Turner and his Contemporaries* (London, Tate
    Gallery, 1991), 17.

19 See C. Greppi, 'On the spot: l'artista viaggiatore e l'inventario iconografico del mondo
    (1772–1859)', *Geotema*, (1997) 137–49; Hemingway, *Landscape Imagery*, 19–23. It is
    important to emphasise, however, that an increasing interest in the empirical
    observation of nature does not necessarily entail a direct confrontation with nature.

In seventeenth-century Dutch art, Svetlana Alpers argues, this interest led to an increasing trust in optical devices such as the camera obscura and the microscope. See S. Alpers, *The Art of Describing: Dutch Art in the Seventeenth Century* (London: Penguin Books, 1989), 32–3.

20 Brown, *Oil Sketches from Nature*, 23–4.

21 Conisbee, Faunce and Strick, 'Introduction', in Conisbee, Faunce and Strick (eds), *In the Light of Italy*, 15.

22 Klonk, *Science and the Perception of Nature*, 107.

23 P. Conisbee, 'The early history of open-air painting', in Conisbee, Faunce and Strick (eds), *In the Light of Italy*, 29–47.

24 K. Sloan, *Alexander and John Robert Cozens: The Poetry of Landscape* (New Haven and London: Yale University Press, 1986), 22, 26; On Christ's Hospital and the training of naval surveyors, see Driver and Martins, 'John Septimus Roe and the art of navigation'. Cozens's appointment was far from unique: the Royal Military College at Great Marlow, Buckinghamshire opened in May 1802 with the artist William Alexander as the first Master of Landscape Drawing: see *William Alexander: An English Artist in Imperial China* (Brighton: Royal Pavilion Art Gallery and Museums, 1981), 8. On the links between landscape painting, military draughtsmanship and cartography, see N. Alfrey, 'Landscape and the Ordnance Survey, 1795–1829', in N. Alfrey and S. J. Daniels (eds), *Mapping the Landscape: Essays on Art and Cartography* (Nottingham: Nottingham University Art Gallery, 1990), 23.

25 Lyles, 'The transformation of the British landscape watercolour', 22.

26 Conisbee, Faunce and Strick (eds), *In the Light of Italy*, 110–11.

27 B. Smith, 'William Hodges and English *plein-air* painting', *Art History*, 6 (1983), 143–52.

28 *Ibid.*, 144.

29 It is worth noting that on Cook's first voyage, the challenge of satisfying diverse audiences resulted in the appointment of two artists to accompany Banks, Alexander Buchan (whose work was directed at the dilettanti) and Sydney Parkinson (who was hired to provide sketches of new species): S. Schaffer, 'Visions of empire: afterword', in D. P. Miller and P. H. Reill (eds), *Visions of Empire: Voyages, Botany, and Representations of Nature* (Cambridge: Cambridge University Press, 1996), 335–52.

30 Smith, 'William Hodges and English *plein-air* painting', 151.

31 Lyles, 'The transformation of the British landscape watercolour', 20.

32 *Ibid.*, 21.

33 Klonk, *Science and the Perception of Nature*, 67.

34 The popularity of topographical engravings beyond academic artistic circles guaranteed the living of many artists in this period; see Lyles, 'The transformation of the British landscape watercolour', 20.

35 Quoted in G. Dening, *Readings/Writings* (Melbourne: Melbourne University Press, 1998), 8.

36 J. Hamilton, *Turner and the Scientists* (London: Tate Gallery, 1998).

37 J. Crary, *Techniques of the Observer: On Vision and Modernity in the Nineteenth Century* (Cambridge MA and London: MIT Press, 1995), 70.

38 *Ibid.*, 79.

39 See also D. Poole, *Vision, Race, and Modernity: A Visual Economy of the Andean Image World* (Princeton: Princeton University Press, 1997), 81–4.

40 B. M. Stafford, *Voyage into Substance: Art, Science, Nature, and the Illustrated Travel Account, 1760–1840* (Cambridge MA: MIT Press, 1984); B. Smith, *European Vision and the South Pacific* (New Haven and London: Yale University Press, 1988).

41 W. Burchell, *St Helena Plants* (Kew Archives, n. d.).

42 On Burchell, see Martins, *O Rio de Janeiro dos Viajantes*, 115–24; F. Driver, *Geography Militant: Cultures of Exploration and Empire* (Oxford: Blackwell, 2001), 17–19.

43 L. Bodi, 'Captain Cook in German imaginative literature', in W. Veit (ed.), *Captain James Cook: Image and Impact. South Sea Discoveries and the World of Letters* (Melbourne: Hawthorn Press, 1972), 129–30.

44 W. H. Auden and E. Mayer, 'Introduction', in J. W. Goethe, *Italian Journey [1786–8]* (London: Penguin Books, 1970), 9.

45 A. von Humboldt, *Kosmos: A General Study of the Physical Phenomena of the Universe*, 5 volumes (London: Hippolyte Baillière, 1848), Vol. 2, 85–6.

46 *Ibid.*, 91.

47 A. Bermingham, 'Landscape-o-rama: the exhibition landscape at Somerset House and the rise of popular landscape entertainments', in Solkin (ed.), *Art on the Line*, 127–43.

48 F. Süssekind, *O Brasil Não é Longe Daqui: O Narrador, A Viagem* (São Paulo: Companhia das Letras, 1990), 122.

49 Driver, *Geography Militant*, 50–6; C. W. J. Withers, 'Voyages et crédibilité: vers une géographie de la confiance', *Géographie et Cultures*, 33 (2000), 3–19.

50 D. Outram, 'On being Perseus: new knowledge, dislocation and Enlightenment exploration', in D. N. Livingstone and C. W. J. Withers (eds), *Geography and Enlightenment* (Chicago: Chicago University Press, 1999), 281–94, quote on pp. 283–4.

51 A. M. C. Godlewska, 'From Enlightenment vision to modern science? Humboldt's visual thinking', in Livingstone and Withers (eds), *Geography and Enlightenment*, 236–75, quote on p. 267.

52 M. Dettelbach, 'The face of nature: precise measurement, mapping and sensibility in the work of Alexander von Humboldt', *Studies in History and Philosophy of Biological and Biomedical Sciences*, 30 (1999), 473–504.

53 PRO, Adm 37/5730, HMS *Alceste*, Muster Book.

54 F. Owen, 'Life and work of William Havell', in *William Havell, 1782–1857* (Reading: Reading Museum and Art Gallery, 1981), 14–15.

55 *Ibid.*, 14; Lyles and Hamley, *British Watercolours*, 208.

56 J. L. Roget, *A History of the Old Watercolour Society*, 2 volumes (London: Longman, 1891), Vol. 1, 296.

57 *Examiner*, 7 May 1815, 302.

58 Havell travelled through India, from east to west, visiting Calcutta (1817), Madras (1819–20), Hyderabad (1822), Ellora (1825) and Bombay (1826). His Asian and European travels are discussed in Owen, 'Life and work of William Havell', 15–16.

59 Roget, *History of the Old Watercolour Society*, 450.

60 L. Martins, 'A pintura inquieta da paisagem tropical: William Havell (1782–1857)', in H. A. Salgueiro (ed.), *Paisagem e Arte* (São Paulo: São Paulo University Press, 2000), 121–8.

61 Owen, 'Life and work of William Havell', 17. Robert Havell later published panoramic views of various sites around the world, including (in 1820) an aquatint panoramic view of Madras, in which William Havell may have had a hand.

62 Klonk, *Science and the Perception of Nature*, 101.

63 The works mentioned by Klonk – *Ross Market Place, Herefordshire* and *S. E. View of St Albans* – were exhibited in 1805 at the newly-established Watercolour Society: *Science and the Perception of Nature*, 107–9.

64 Powell, *Italy in the Age of Turner*, 73; Conisbee, 'The early history of open-air painting', 44–6.

65 Brown, *Oil Sketches from Nature*, 24.

66 This is one of the two watercolours of Rio de Janeiro by William Havell now held by the British Museum.

67 J. Hamilton, *The Sketching Society, 1799–1851* (London: Victoria & Albert Museum, 1971), 7.

68 Owen, 'Life and work of William Havell', 14–15.

69 Havell kept the sketches of his voyages, some of which were used to illustrate B. Hall, *Account of a Voyage of Discovery to the West Coast of Corea, and the Great Loo-Choo Island* (London: J. Murray, 1818). The Christie and Mason sale catalogue of his remaining works listed four sketchbooks of the *Alceste* voyage, twenty-three volumes of Chinese drawings and a finished watercolour drawing of Rio. See *Catalogue of the Whole of the Remaining Works of that Talented and Respected Artist, William Havell, Esq., deceased* (London: Christie and Mason, 1858).

70 'Exhibition – Royal Academy', *Blackwood's Edinburgh Magazine*, 52 (1842), 30. Havell's painting *Olevans* was earlier characterised as 'one of the disagreeably hot school', while his *Temple of Vesta* was dismissed as 'another of Mr Havell's yolk-of-egg pictures': 'Royal Academy Exhibition', *Blackwood's Edinburgh Magazine*, 48 (1840), 376–7.

71 *Blackwood's Edinburgh Magazine*, 45 (1839), 382–91.

72 Alpers, *The Art of Describing, passim*.

73 Crary, *Techniques of the Observer*, 38–9, 138–41.

74 M. Rosenthal, 'The extraordinary Mr Earle', in *The World Upside Down: Australia, 1788–1830* (Canberra: National Library of Australia, 2000), 35–41.

75 Dening, *Readings/Writings*, 76.

5

'A world of pictures': Pall Mall and the topography of display, 1780–99

ℰ

Rosie Dias

NEW SPACES FOR ART

AT THE BEGINNING of April 1794, the *Morning Post* gave its readers a preview of what the coming exhibition season had in store. It held out little hope that the Royal Academy could show anything of value, suggesting that three galleries in particular had siphoned the artistic talent away from the walls of Somerset House:

> The Historic Gallery is again open to the public, and boasts multiplied productions, and encreased effect. Such are the additional works this year, that we tremble for the splendour of The Exhibition; as many eminent RA.s, by contributing highly finished performances to this Gallery, must have abridged the time necessary to produce Pictures worthy of Somerset Place. If this should prove a real statement of the case, an eternal round of mawkish portraits, with feeble imitations of Claud, Salvator, and Cannaletti will mark the progress of an institution patronized by Royalty; and the Man of Taste, the Foreigner of Discrimination, will resort to the Shakespear; the Poets, and to the Historic Gallery, to form a just estimation of the genius of our artists, and the influence of encouragement by the People.[1]

Immersing its art criticism in the political discourse of the 1790s, the *Morning Post* – an opposition newspaper – was keen to mark out a distinction between two kinds of artistic spaces that had emerged by the end of the eighteenth century. One was an enclave of royalty, the other was patronised by the people. The three galleries to which the critic refers – Thomas Macklin's Poets' Gallery, John Boydell's Shakespeare Gallery and Robert Bowyer's

Historic Gallery – had opened between 1788 and 1793, and together they represented an effort to revive the flagging fortunes of history painting in England by fusing grand exhibition schemes with equally ambitious engraving and book projects. As the *Morning Post* suggests, however, it was not only questions of artistic genre which separated this new kind of gallery from the more established exhibitions at the Royal Academy. The difference was also a matter of political ideology.

Operating throughout the 1790s, the new galleries benefited from some extremely fortuitous timing, not least because a number of problems had arisen at the Academy during the 1780s. Escalating criticisms directed at an over-abundance of portraiture, discriminatory hanging, slavish artistic imitation and a disregard for the interests of its public, its students and indeed some of its members had been channelled into accusations of institutional tyranny by the press. A certain amount of ambiguity surrounded the notion of what it meant to be a royal institution: was this really a 'public' institution, or was it simply serving the interests of an aristocratic few? By the time the new galleries opened, the political climate in Britain had given these questions new impetus and this allowed Boydell's and Bowyer's ventures in particular to assume a natural place in the political discourse which pervaded almost every aspect of public life in the 1790s. These new spaces, the press was eager to claim, were spaces of a truly public art. Suffused with an air of liberty and patriotism, operating through a system of artistic meritocracy and acknowledging the patronage and the interest of the public, they allowed the political concerns of the 1790s to operate discursively within the art world.[2]

If the timing of the establishment of these galleries was fortuitous, there was one factor which seemed altogether more calculated to offer a challenge to the hegemony of the Academy, and that was their location (Figure 5.1). Four weeks after the *Morning Post*'s attempt to discriminate between the merits and ideologies of the Royal Academy and the new galleries, *The Times* noted that one particular stretch of the metropolis was offering the discerning viewer an extended aesthetic experience:

> The fashionable pedestrians have now enough to engage their attention in Pall-Mall, exclusive of the constant Auctions at Christie's . . . [T]he old Shakespeare on the North side, the Historical Gallery, the New Shakespeare, with the Polygraphic Pictures, on the South Side . . . are all so well worth notice, it would be doing discredit to the National taste and curiosity to suppose almost any person should leave town without seeing them.[3]

The Times was not the first publication to note the proliferation of artistic sites along Pall Mall. A number of contemporary London guidebooks also mapped out for their readers an itinerary of visual consumption across Pall Mall and the surrounding streets that took in the elegant architecture of

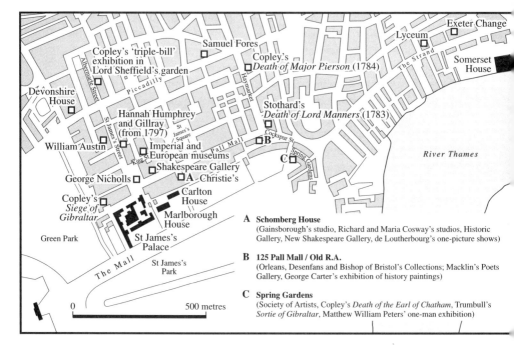

Exeter Change
Lyceum
Somerset House

Copley's 'triple-bill'
exhibition in
Lord Sheffield's garden

Samuel Fores

Copley's
Death of Major Pierson (1784)

Devonshire
House

The Strand

Hannah Humphrey
and Gillray
(from 1797)

Stothard's
Death of Lord Manners (1783)

William Austin

Imperial and
European museums
Shakespeare Gallery

George Nicholls

A   Christie's

Copley's
*Siege of
Gibraltar*

Carlton
House

Marlborough
House

St James's
Palace

Green Park

The Mall

St James's
Park

0   500 metres

River Thames

A   Schomberg House
(Gainsborough's studio, Richard and Maria Cosway's studios, Historic Gallery, New Shakespeare Gallery, de Loutherbourg's one-picture shows)

B   125 Pall Mall / Old R.A.
(Orleans, Desenfans and Bishop of Bristol's Collections; Macklin's Poets Gallery, George Carter's exhibition of history paintings)

C   Spring Gardens
(Society of Artists, Copley's *Death of the Earl of Chatham*, Trumbull's *Sortie of Gibraltar*, Matthew William Peters' one-man exhibition)

5.1 Art exhibitions and studios on and around Pall Mall, 1780–99

St James's and the fashionable exhibitions that many of these buildings housed.[4] Collectively, these texts promoted the Pall Mall area as the artistic nucleus of the capital, and as a space which could claim a distinct advantage over the now geographically distanced Royal Academy.

This chapter will examine the importance of the construction of urban and interior space in the forging of the elevated artistic identity of these new galleries. It will argue that this identity hinged upon a clear distinction between the aesthetic experience offered by the Pall Mall exhibitions and the more established exhibitions at the Royal Academy, and that this distinction can be accounted for as much in spatial terms as by the distinct modes of artistic production which these spaces generated. As we shall see, the identities of both the Pall Mall exhibitions and Somerset House were constructed through a series of discourses and representational strategies that contributed to the process of spatial formation. Here – although the list could clearly be more extensive – I limit myself to discussing representations of contrasting gallery-visiting publics in the 1780s and 1790s, to examining the intersection of the discourses of art and politics in this period, and to suggesting ways in which the spaces of the city shaped the interpretation of gallery spaces.[5]

ARTISTIC TOPOGRAPHIES

The schemes of Boydell, Macklin and Bowyer, along with Henry Fuseli's Milton Gallery which opened in 1799, may have been the most ambitious exhibition projects mounted in Pall Mall during the 1790s, but, as *The Times* suggested, they were by no means the only artistic attractions which the area had to offer. The Academy's move to Somerset House in 1780, from its earliest premises at 125 Pall Mall, was met, almost immediately, with a profusion of exhibitory activity in the very space which it had left behind. The vacated building continued in its function as an exhibition space housing not only Macklin's Poets' Gallery and Fuseli's Milton Gallery, but also a number of prestigious collections that were put up for sale, including the Orleans', Desenfans' and Bishop of Bristol's collections. The best known of the Pall Mall galleries was the Boydell Shakespeare Gallery, which opened in 1789 in specially-designed premises that offered a spectacular addition to the architectural splendour of Pall Mall. Schomberg House meanwhile, home to the Historic Gallery, was an illustrious and fashionable artistic site. During the 1780s and 1790s, the building accommodated the studios and apartments of Thomas Gainsborough and of Richard and Maria Cosway and the exhibition rooms of the Polygraphic Society. In 1794 the Irish entrepreneur James Woodmason opened his New Shakespeare Gallery in this building, across the road from the original version, and featured works by many of the artists that Boydell had employed. Next door to Schomberg House were James Christie's auction rooms, through which a number of important European collections passed, particularly during the political upheavals of the 1790s.

The streets surrounding St James's extended the artistic topography of Pall Mall. On King Street, off St James's Square, was the Imperial Museum – housing, until 1787, a collection of Old Master paintings – and, from 1789, the European Museum which initially exhibited works for sale by English artists at the same time as it displayed continental collections. The Great Room at Spring Gardens, situated just to the east of Pall Mall, was the main exhibition venue for the Society of Artists, and also housed a number of one-man shows and other exhibitions during the 1780s. Meanwhile, several aristocratic and royal residences housed picture galleries which could be viewed on application. The most notable of these were Devonshire House, on Piccadilly, and St James's Palace. A number of fashionable printsellers were also located in Pall Mall and the surrounding streets, the best known of which were Samuel Fores (based on Piccadilly) and Hannah Humphrey whose business (and her most significant asset, James Gillray) moved to the highly fashionable St James's Street in 1797.

The significance of these exhibitions and displays should not be underestimated. Some of the collections put up for sale at 125 Pall Mall and at Christie's formed large-scale exhibitions lasting for several weeks, often running concurrently with the Royal Academy's show. The Bishop of Bristol's collection, for example, which closed just before the RA's 1788 exhibition opened, contained over 450 paintings (certainly more than the Academy showed at the time), and was widely promoted in the press as a favourite resort for people of fashion and taste. Such collections offered many viewers their first opportunity to see Old Master paintings, and to view them alongside the works of native artists. William Hazlitt, for example, was to date his initiation into 'the pleasures of painting' to his visit to the Orleans collection in 1798, where he saw works by Titian, Raphael and Guido for the first time:

> [I]t was there I formed my taste, such as it is . . . I was staggered when I saw the works there collected, and looked at them with wondering and with longing eyes. A mist passed away from my sight; the scales fell off. A new sense came upon me, a new heaven and a new earth stood before . . . We had all heard the names of Titian, Raphael, Guido, Domenichino, the Caracci – but to see them face to face, to be in the same room with their deathless productions, was like breaking some mighty spell – was almost an effect of necromancy! From that time I lived in a world of pictures . . . This was the more remarkable, as it was but a short time before that I was not only totally ignorant of, but insensible to the beauties of art.[6]

Hazlitt may have entered an imaginative 'world of pictures' at this point, but he had also stumbled across a literal, geographical one which had been energetically cultivated in Pall Mall during the past two decades. The illustrious roll-call of contemporary artists and entrepreneurs working and exhibiting in these streets amounted to nothing less than a vibrant and competitive arena of artistic production and display which had sprung up in the aftermath of the Academy's move to Somerset House.[7]

This move had not gone entirely smoothly. Although William Chambers's new building was widely admired, the splendour of the edifice could not deflect from the criticisms directed at the Academy during the course of the 1780s. The new building brought together the schools, administration and exhibition space of the Academy for the first time, but far from consolidating the institution, it appeared rather to expose tensions and contradictions between these segments by bringing them into close proximity. Some academicians waged covert press wars against each other, others ceased to exhibit there, and students felt that the institution was failing to honour its obligations to aspiring artists. Meanwhile, the press was keen to point out that Somerset House was not a space for the promotion of history painting but that it offered, rather, a bizarre spectacle which placed abundant portraiture and its narcissistic viewers in uncomfortable juxtaposition.[8] Here, critics claimed, could be found the kind of gaudy, glittering wares that were symptomatic of the debasement of art through its contaminating contact with an unenlightened commercial public. More eager to flaunt its social credibility than actively to patronise the arts, the new art-viewing public typically found itself mirrored on the walls of the exhibition space, its 'profusion of rosy cheeks, cherry lips, and black eyebrows [thrusting themselves]', one critic observed, 'on our notice the moment we enter a modern exhibition room'. The artists themselves, naturally eager for their works to be noticed in the crowded exhibition space, colluded with their sitters' desire for social self-promotion, fashioning 'the highest coloured pictures' and framing them obtrusively with 'the fiery glare of burnished gold'.[9]

For the viewers themselves, the introduction of a shilling charge to discourage the presence of 'improper persons' and the display of nude male statuary at the opening of the new exhibition space at Somerset House in 1780 were disconcerting and brought the problematic issues of class and gender to the forefront of the aesthetic agenda. Charges of greed and indecency were levelled at the Academy, but it was hard to avoid the imputations that were, by default, being simultaneously levelled at the public. The suggestion that a proportion of the public who had, it was pointed out, all contributed 'to produce and support this royal institution', might be deemed socially 'improper' was not easily ignored.[10] It was also hard to avoid the implication that female viewers, even those of the most elevated rank, lacked the aesthetic education to appreciate the most celebrated forms of antique sculpture. Indeed, it was argued that they would find themselves confronted with an apparently shocking display of 'Apollos, Gladiators, Jupiters and Hercules all as *naked* and as *natural* as if they were alive', a sight which apparently guaranteed that any woman must instantly 'forfeit her claim to delicacy'.[11] As attention focused increasingly on the audience itself, and on the Academy's troubled relationship with that audience, a host of other issues and concerns appeared to have been left behind.

Indeed, these had been left behind quite literally in the move from Pall Mall to Somerset House. After 1780, a variety of artists, collectors and entrepreneurs took up the urgent concerns of patronage, aesthetic education, history painting and the prospect of an English School, and attempted to negotiate the problems between the art world and the public sphere that the Academy was spectacularly failing to resolve. They did so in a variety of spaces on and around Pall Mall, where their collective attempts to construct a viable relationship between historical painting and the public mounted a serious challenge to the hegemony of the Academy. Conflict between the Academy and other spaces of contemporary artistic production has traditionally been identified by art historians as beginning in earnest around the mid-nineteenth century, and as forming a key part in the narrative of European Modernism. I will demonstrate here that the challenge to the ideological space of the Academy began far earlier than has hitherto been recognised. Although some of the artists and entrepreneurs involved may not have ostensibly set out to challenge or disparage the Academy, their exhibitions were certainly represented in the press as offering such a contest.[12] These exhibitions fuelled discussion at a far more public level than had hitherto been experienced, demanding a reassessment of how patronage, artistic production and spaces of display might operate beyond the institutional enclave of the Academy, and within a more inclusive public sphere.

ARTISTS, ENTREPRENEURS AND AUDIENCES

The initial challenges to the Academy came from within its own ranks. They came from a number of artists who were either disillusioned by the institutional politics and discriminatory hanging of paintings at Somerset House, or simply felt that the Academy was no longer, if it ever had been, the place to show ambitious historical works. The first to do so was John Singleton Copley. In the spring of 1781, having completed his commemorative painting of the death of the Earl of Chatham, Copley decided to take advantage of the recently vacated premises in Pall Mall to exhibit his work. The Academy's treasurer, William Chambers, thwarted Copley's plans, preventing his use of 125 Pall Mall and accusing him of self-interest. Nevertheless, Copley's show went ahead in nearby Spring Gardens. Copley made no secret of the dispute between himself and Chambers, quoting from their acrimonious correspondence in his advertising for the show, and the eventual exhibition of the Chatham painting would no doubt have benefited from the added anticipation and publicity which the whole episode engendered. After this, Copley proceeded to exhibit his most ambitious canvases in a variety of locations on and around Pall Mall. *The Death of Major Pierson* was exhibited in rooms on the Haymarket in 1784, while *The Death of Chatham* was exhibited again at various times and locations along Pall Mall. In 1791, stuck for a venue large enough to house the enormous *Siege of Gibraltar*, Copley erected an 84-ft long tent in Green Park, close to St James's Palace. In 1799 he displayed his latest historical work depicting *Admiral Duncan's Victory at Camperdown* in another tent, this time in Lord Sheffield's garden on Albemarle Street, as part of a triple-bill exhibition of his works.

Copley's example was swiftly followed by other artists, most notably by Thomas Gainsborough in 1784. After a dispute with the RA's hanging committee, Gainsborough displayed his latest works in his studio at Schomberg House, and was never to exhibit at the Academy again. By now, the press was beginning to comment upon the numerous secessions from the Academy. The majority of these absent artists had begun to exhibit independently, and many chose to exhibit in the same geographical space within which Copley had immersed himself. What was particularly notable about the activities of Copley and many of his imitators was that they sought to cultivate, on and around Pall Mall, a space for the display of ambitious historical painting, the most prestigious genre in the academic hierarchy. Thomas Stothard, for example, who exhibited mainly literary and mythological drawings at the Academy, showed one of his few contemporary history paintings, *The Death of Lord Manners*, at a Mr Haynes's on the corner of Cockspur Street, facing Pall Mall in 1783. George Trumbull and George Carter, more rigorous than Stothard in their attempts to forge careers as history painters, both held exhibitions in the area in the second half of the 1780s, depicting, like Copley, key military moments in the Gibraltar campaign of 1782.

The exhibition of work by Carter, Copley and Trumbull focusing on this one military campaign formed a substantial and competitive project to real-ise new subjects, styles and spaces for history painting. While the Academy's avowed intention was to nurture an English School of history painting, the results it achieved could not have been more distant from its ambitions. A comparison between the exactly contemporaneous exhibitions at Somerset House and the French Salon in 1787 (Figures 5.2 and 5.3) shows that while artists exhibiting at the *Académie Royale de Peinture et Sculpture* produced and displayed predominantly large-scale history painting, the Royal Academy in England was far from fulfilling its ideological goals. At Somerset House, history painting mingled indiscriminately with the lesser genres, which tended, by their sheer quantity, to prohibit the sustained contemplation of more elevated art. Particularly troubling was the abundance of celebrity portrai-ture, easily the most intriguing component of the exhibitions for the crowd, which was visiting the Academy towards the end of the London Season and came fuelled with the latest gossip surrounding the figures portrayed.[13]

Ramberg's print (Figure 5.2) has been used widely by art and cultural historians seeking to capture and recreate the specific atmosphere of the Somerset House exhibitions.[14] In such circumstances, this image tends to be viewed either as merely illustrative of a range of viewing practices adopted by contemporary audiences or at most as offering a mild dose of satire dealt out in response to the frivolity of the new art-viewing public.[15] What has largely been ignored in relation to Ramberg's print is the extent to which it holds in tension a number of coexisting perspectives – regulatory and fluid, satirical and flattering, confused and integrated – whose sheer range surely contrib-uted to the contemporary popularity of this image. It was also this variety of simultaneous perspectives that would have allowed later artists and entre-preneurs simultaneously to draw upon and reject this dominant iconography of the gallery space when they set out to define their own exhibition spaces. Art historians have tended to ignore the relationship between Ramberg's print and other images of contemporary exhibitions, instead isolating the image of the Academy exhibition as befits the discipline's privileging of that institution as the only significant artistic locus of the late eighteenth century.

Yet a comparison of the representative strategies which pertain to a variety of contemporary exhibition spaces demonstrates that images of galleries and audiences, and the construction of their identity, hinged upon a distinction between the Academy and new sites of display, while at the same time continuing to draw upon the regulatory and propagandistic function of the exhibition print.

In contrast to the confusing mix of genres that covered the walls of Somerset House, the history paintings exhibited near Pall Mall allowed, and actively encouraged, an extended viewing of individual works. Although this harked back to an aristocratic ideal of art viewing, such a practice had hitherto been prevented from becoming widespread – initially by the absence of public exhibitions before 1760, and subsequently by the crowded conditions and avid sociability of the Royal Academy's exhibition space. Bartolozzi's engraved ticket for Copley's *Siege of Gibraltar* exhibition (Figure 5.4) suggests not only that Copley was engaged in the production and display of epic history painting of an unprecedented scale and effect, but also that he and his

5.2 *The Exhibition of the Royal Academy*, by Pietro Martini after J. H. Ramberg. Engraving, 1787. (© Copyright The British Museum)

contemporaries sought to reconstruct the relationship between the work of art and its public. This, Copley realised, was something that might be achieved by new modes of display, through the creation of an exhibition space in which the painting itself was of primary significance. In his exhibitions, history painting was no longer part of the disorientating mix of canvases, genres, colours and scales which had hitherto surrounded it and prevented sustained viewing.

In contrast to Bartolozzi's image of Copley's holistic exhibition space, Ramberg's representation of the 1787 Academy exhibition depicted a jostling, posing, flirting, easily-distracted crowd, as numerous as the paintings and requiring the aid of catalogues, glasses and male companions in order to view the exhibits, which tended to encompass the crowd itself as much as the works on display. Moreover, Ramberg's staged perspective worked to frame the spectators themselves as part of the spectacle, reflecting the preoccupations of the press with the behaviour of visitors to Somerset House. Bartolozzi's image, designed in advance of the exhibition's opening, would have functioned,

The Salon of 1787, by Pietro Martini. Engraving, 1787. (© Copyright The British Museum)

101

Mr Copley's Picture of the SIEGE OF GIBRALTAR *as Exhibited in the Green Park near St James's Palace.*

5.4 Engraved admission ticket to the exhibition of Copley's *Siege of Gibraltar*, by Francesco Bartolozzi, 1791. (© Copyright The British Museum)

however, as a kind of laconic guide to behaviour in the exhibition space. Clutching these tickets as they entered the tent, Copley's viewers would have seen themselves defined as informed and reflective members of a discerning public. Bartolozzi's perspective and the sheer scale of Copley's canvas force the painting itself to centre stage, while the visitors stand with their backs to us. They no longer compete with each other and with the exhibits for notice, but appear to converse comfortably on the painting's merit and on the events it depicts as instinctive participants in the spheres of art and nationhood. Ostensibly functional in its status as an admittance ticket – unlike Ramberg's larger and more clearly commodified print – Bartolozzi's image concealed its regulatory function, while neatly guaranteeing that every viewer entering Copley's exhibition came under its effect.

Like Bartolozzi's ticket, the only surviving depiction of viewers at the Shakespeare Gallery – a watercolour by Francis Wheatley, another of Boydell's exhibitors – may also have functioned as a blueprint for the exhibition space,

The Opening of the Shakespeare Gallery, 1790, by Francis Wheatley. Watercolour, 1790. (Courtesy of Trustees of the Victoria & Albert Museum)

albeit a rather less interventionist one (Figure 5.5).[16] Clearly drawing upon an established genre of exhibition scenes, Wheatley's depiction of the Shakespeare Gallery nonetheless departs from an image such as Ramberg's in a number of ways. Most obviously, Wheatley's image was produced as a single watercolour, resisting the commodification, dissemination and display which Ramberg's image became subject to as an engraving, a process which reinforced the narcissistic aspects of the Academy's exhibition and public. Thus, at the same time as Wheatley sought to depict and define an audience at the Shakespeare Gallery, the very absence of his image from the public gaze suggests the lack of either a desire or need to display, regulate or flatter the viewers visiting Boydell's exhibition.

Of course the absence, or, at least, the partial sequestration of the image from the public view can itself be seen as a regulatory strategy. Accustomed and encouraged to view itself through the lenses of the numerous graphic representations and printed commentaries that dealt with the exhibition space – representations which spanned the entire spectrum from the satirical to the polite – the Academy's audience was a highly self-conscious one. The overwhelming absence of such imagery and commentary in relation to the Shakespeare Gallery, which, unlike the Academy exhibition, elicited extended reviews of each painting with no observations on the behaviour or composition of the audience, suggests a desire to direct the public's attention away from its own body, and on to the artworks themselves. Avoiding Ramberg's perspective of the exhibition space and its audience as incorporated spectacle, Wheatley's image provides an intimate close-up of a fashionable public, self-assured rather than self-conscious, and engaging comfortably in the viewing and discussion of the paintings on display. Unlike the spectators in Ramberg's print who, as has recently been pointed out, fail to observe the large-scale historical works on display in the Great Room, the audience at the Shakespeare Gallery is represented as self-confident members of a visually literate public which enjoys a comfortable relationship with history painting.[17] Here, female viewers – a problematic component of the Academy's audience – are able to scrutinise and comprehend the exhibits, their presence legitimated within a public that is consolidated rather than divided by the act of viewing 'high' art. Dispensing with the male companions with whom they are invariably linked in various depictions of the Royal Academy exhibition, and who fulfil a dubious pedagogic function, Boydell's female spectators are defined as visually literate and exuding cultural self-confidence.[18]

ART AND THE POLITICS OF THE STREET

Wheatley's indication of the aesthetic and literary proficiency of Boydell's audience was no incidental gesture, but can be seen as part of a broader project to reformulate the dynamics of the exhibition space. Boydell was keen to acknowledge the patronage of the public and to provide exposure for younger artists. He actively invited 'candid criticism', and, in the permanency of this exhibition, the press saw an opportunity to justify its precarious existence in the exhibition space. *The Gazetteer* announced that:

> The papers teem with remarks upon the paintings in the Gallery of Shakespeare, and among these remarks there will doubtless be many which are well worth attending to . . . [I]t is undoubtedly the interest of the Proprietors, to have [the pictures] as perfect as possible, and should any errors which can be amended be pointed out, we may fairly rely upon their being done away by [the] next exhibition.[19]

Wheatley's image depicts the reopening of the Gallery, with the addition of a third room, in 1790, its second year of existence. On this reopening, and indeed in subsequent years, the critics were gratified to find that many of the criticisms made the previous year had been taken into account. As more paintings were added each year, it became clear that the dynamics of this exhibition venture were offering something quite new to the public. The addition of new canvases necessitated a shifting hang, with existing works benefiting from new lighting, perspectives and juxtapositions. Not only were canvases altered, improved and, in one case, removed altogether, but initial concerns about gaudy colour were allayed in subsequent years as it was noted that time had mellowed the tone of the paintings. Wheatley's watercolour, then, may be read as imaging a harmonious interaction between viewers and paintings, where the critical interventions of the public and the artworks' susceptibility to commentary and exchange operate as a kind of discursive dynamic through which the function, status and identity of both the public and art are informed, reciprocally played out and consolidated through a mutually-enhancing relationship.

The Shakespeare Gallery could, therefore, be seen as a site for rational critical debate in which artistic merit might be discussed and style itself might be constituted through discussion. Significantly, the newspapers were hostile to the work of Rome-trained artists such as James Durno, James Barry, Henry Tresham and Gavin Hamilton, criticising them either for their coldness and foreign flavour, or ignoring them altogether. These manifestations of a 'foreign' art seemed to the critics to be more at home in the Academy which theoretically privileged the Grand Style, while the Shakespeare Gallery came to be seen as a space of artistic freedom, of an originality that was peculiarly English. Among the many criticisms of Joshua Reynolds's *Death of Cardinal Beaufort* (1789), for example, were the observations that its composition was 'too like that of Germanicus by Poussin to claim the distinction of an original composition', and that it amounted to 'a jargon of Rembrandt-hues, gold, flesh and magic'.[20] Clearly the feeling was that an English school of painting could not be founded upon the slavish emulation of the work of continental artists which the Academy and its President appeared to advocate. There was, moreover, a sense that the public was better equipped than the 'aristocratic hangmen at Somerset House' to recognise what might constitute an English school. 'The publick will judge', stated the *St James's Chronicle*, 'and the works of Fuseli, Hamilton, Northcote, Rigaud, and Smirke, will be ranked with those which have hitherto engrossed the general attention'.[21] The writer proved to be correct. Over the following years these artists in particular were singled out by the press, and their stylistic attributes proved to be vital components in the attempt to form an English School.

As the press, no doubt fuelled by Boydell, worked hard to promote a conception of the Shakespeare Gallery as a public space which might offer a way forward for English art, it became increasingly difficult to detach the gallery's aesthetic agenda from the political agenda of the press.[22] Here is the *Morning Chronicle*, another opposition newspaper, writing in the spring of 1792, just when Fox's Libel Bill had provoked discussion in Parliament and in the press on the constitutional right of the people to freedom of speech:

In England, and England only, every man thinks as he will, speaks as he will, and writes as he will. In the Gallery, every picture *carries an air of freedom* – every Painter gives *his own* idea of a character without any the smallest reference to that drawn by his contemporary . . . [T]o the exertions of genius the constitution of England is in the highest degree favourable. Every man feels himself at liberty to express *what* he feels in the *manner* he feels it ought to be.[23]

These comments demonstrate how easy it was to slip from consideration of the politics of the art world into political discourse itself. Although they appear in a column specifically dedicated to an examination of the latest additions and changes to the Shakespeare Gallery, it is hard to separate such statements from the political concerns apparent elsewhere in the newspaper. What is significant here, however, is not that there might be a relationship between aesthetics and politics – this would have been nothing new at all – but that, for the first time, the art world might offer an exemplum which could justify broader political claims. This embryonic English school of painting is noted not only for the aesthetic liberty granted to its artists, it also represents in microcosm the English constitution in its perfection. The individual energies and discursive dynamic between artists and public function in a cohesive manner, with a palatable blend of liberty and consensus, and can be used by the press to remind its readers of their constitutional rights. Of course the language of politics also legitimated the Shakespeare Gallery. If there was any doubt that such diverse and, occasionally, idiosyncratic artistic practice could be presented as a collective school, then the English constitution could put those doubts to rest.

While the *Morning Chronicle* insisted that the Shakespeare Gallery neatly reflected and embodied its own views on the liberty of the press and the constitution of the people, it was a necessary consequence of this argument that the gallery therefore represented every other conceivable point of view. At the same time as the opposition press was keen to make claims for the democratic nature of the Shakespeare Gallery, the ministerial press were almost as quick to sanction it with its own appellation of patriotism. As might be expected, however, the Shakespeare Gallery's status as a microcosmic public sphere made it difficult for it to become wholly identifiable with any particular political interest. While the artist Joseph Farington – a supporter of Pitt's administration – used the gallery during the 1796 election to canvass votes for his preferred candidates, to catch up with news and to meet with colleagues on their way to the hustings, it is equally possible to detect a Whig presence there as well. Wheatley's watercolour contains portraits of several figures associated with the Prince of Wales's circle and the Opposition, including Richard Sheridan, the Duchess of Devonshire, Lady Jersey, and the Dukes of York and of Cumberland. The coexistence of Whig and Tory figures – each equally at home in the Shakespeare Gallery – suggests that it may have offered a moderating, discursive space, independent from the perceived autocracy of the Academy, where political concerns might be discussed, debated and played out, and various interests brought together.

What further substantiated the gallery's incursions into the discourse of politics was its inclusion, along with other artistic sites in the area, in another kind of urban topography which networked St James's, namely, a political geography. The area was home to a number of royal and aristocratic residences, gentlemen's clubs, coffee houses, print publishers and bookshops, spaces in which existing and emerging ideas of the public sphere were debated and performed in the course of the eighteenth century.[24] The artistic spaces in St James's – like the clubs and coffee-houses with which they were interspersed – seemed to occupy varying positions in relation to the political public sphere. Woven into the politically fluid topography of St James's and Westminster, they made the art world's relationship with the public sphere appear seamless in comparison with the Academy's inability to support political discourse. William Austin, for example, an artist known for republican views, found himself a victim of 'illiberal and oppressive proceedings' by the Academy when election fever gripped the metropolis in 1784. Ordered to remove his exhibits shortly before the exhibition commenced, he opened his 'Patriotic Print Rooms' on St James's Street the following year, displaying busts of the Prince of Wales and various members of the Opposition.[25] The graphic satirist James Gillray and his publisher Hannah Humphrey, who moved to this street in 1797, generally took a equivocal stance towards party politics, but their business relished, played upon, fuelled and profited from the confusion and discord which political conflict engendered.

Bowyer's Historic Gallery was generally incorporated into a loyalist discourse by the press when it opened in 1793, the same year, significantly, in which war broke out with France. But Bowyer's subject matter was more ambivalent and unstable than this suggests. Although it took a particular kind of history as its source – the Tory *History of England* by David Hume – Bowyer himself maintained a certain scepticism towards Hume and his partialities (see also the discussion of Hume by Wall in Chapter 6, pp. 114–29). By the 1790s, the retelling of history had become a key component of political discourse, with loyalists and radicals both eager to justify and consolidate their claims through the invocation of the past, each side conferring opposing ideologies and status upon identical events. The semiotic play to which the images became susceptible as they hung on the gallery wall, detached from the words of Hume and in a continually changing political climate, would have invited a variety of readings and may even have worked to destabilise further the textual foundations of history, making its hermeneutic aspects clearly visible. Filled with images of regicide, insurrection, faction and corruption, the Historic Gallery would have operated as a space which allowed for the exercising (and, perhaps, the exorcising) of the political imagination at a time when the articulation, and even the possession, of certain thoughts – to be found in abundance on the walls of Bowyer's Gallery – came to be prohibited by law.[26]

This political and semiotic dynamic, I have been trying to suggest, was facilitated by the literal and imaginative geography in which the various spaces on and around Pall Mall participated. The Pall Mall galleries often sought quite self-consciously to merge themselves with the discursive space of the street, something which the Royal Academy attempted to avoid for a number of reasons. The Academy's new site hovered ambiguously between the City and the 'polite' end of town. Visiting Somerset House in 1786, the German novelist Sophie von la Roche was quick to note the site's geographical disadvantage, admiring the building itself but observing that if it were 'situated on St James's Square it would merit a visit from all quarters of the globe'.[27] The commercial thoroughfare of the Strand with its dizzying array of shop windows and modish consumers offered a spectacle of luxury for passers-by such as Sophie von la Roche, who was something of an early *flâneuse*. She spoke of the seductive 'lure' of the 'new exhibits' that the shop windows offered, adopting terms which were alarmingly similar to those employed by critics surveying the paintings in nearby Somerset House.

In moving away from Pall Mall, the Academy found itself alongside a number of weird and wonderful spectacles which also went under the name of 'exhibitions', many of which advertised themselves as being situated near Somerset House. Exhibitions of shellwork, needlework and automaton figures; the menagerie and life-size puppet show at Exeter Change; and Lunardi's hydrogen balloon, Astley's equestrian amphitheatre and the waxworks at the Lyceum each took place within a stone's throw of the Academy's exhibitions. At the turn of the century, Charles Lamb likened the crowd which thronged the Strand to a 'multitudinous moving picture . . . like the scenes of a shifting pantomime', thus tying the entire locale, its visitors and inhabitants into a geography of spectacle, novelty and entertainment.[28] Unsurprisingly perhaps, the Academy attempted to deal with its troublesome neighbours through the organisation of space. As visitors entered Somerset House from the Strand and paid their shilling at the door – much as they would for any of the neighbouring shows which levied a similar charge – they would begin their ascent to the exhibition room, which was located at the top of the building so that it could be lit from above. But as they ascended the three flights of stairs that took them to the top of Somerset House, visitors were encouraged to believe that they were being drawn away from the level of the street to a more rarified space. As they entered the exhibition room they were confronted with a Greek inscription that instructed 'none but men of taste [to] enter here', a statement which neatly converted the literal elevation of the Great

Room into a figurative one. Yet the arduous climb to the apparently more cerebral exhibition room of Somerset House did not, in the end, prevent viewers from drawing unflattering analogies between the exhibition space and the street. In particular, the primary subject matter of the Academy's exhibitions – its overabundant portraiture with its 'gaudy', 'glittering' sitters – allowed viewers all too easily to slip into a mental geography which associated the Academy with its troublesome neighbours, among them the notorious bagnios and theatres of Covent Garden and Drury Lane. 'Such is the impression of vice [in the metropolis]', one newspaper reported, that:

> no disguise can conceal its effects, and in proof of his assertion [our correspondent] calls the attention of the public to the portraits of the females exhibited in Somerset House, in which a speculative eye may easily distinguish the vicious courtesan from the modest maiden or chaste wife.
>
> Some dozens of prostitutes parade in the front [of Somerset House] every evening, to the disgrace of humanity and scandal of police.[29]

It was not only the subject matter of the exhibits which allowed for this disturbing continuity between the exhibition space and the street. The Academy's decision to levy an admission charge following its move to a new building which had been provided for with public funds was deemed ill-judged by the press. Accusations of 'mercenary views' abounded, and charges of being involved in 'low traffic' and 'extortion' made the Academy sound as if it were joining the nearby shopkeepers and City stockjobbers in dealing in commodities rather than displaying art.[30]

William Chambers's attempts in his design for Somerset House to draw visitors away from the excess and carnality of the street, and towards an elevated sphere of artistic contemplation, were clearly evaded by visitors. They saw the artistic subject matter and administrative practices of the Academy as falling all too readily into a ready-made locale of scandal and spectacle, corporeality and commerce. By contrast, and to return again to Pall Mall, the exhibitions mounted in the St James's area made no attempt to define themselves apart from the social geography of their surroundings – quite the opposite in fact. The Shakespeare Gallery announced its presence and its subject matter at the level of the street, featuring an innovative façade by George Dance with a relief sculpture by Thomas Banks (Figure 5.6). Depicting Shakespeare seated between the Dramatic Muse and the Genius of Painting, the sculpture was inscribed with a quotation from *Hamlet*, 'He was a man, take him for all in all, I shall not look upon his like again.' Although ambiguous, the inscription differed from the Academy's inscription in two vital ways. First, it was not in Greek but was taken from the works of the national poet. Secondly, it focused attention on the subject of the exhibition rather than on the audience itself and thus offered an invitation rather than a prohibition.

5.6 *View of the Shakespeare Gallery*, by Samuel Rawle.
Engraving, 1804. (Courtesy of the Trustees of Sir John
Soane's Museum)

While the Academy attempted, then, to equip its visitors for the viewing
experience by emphasising their ascent from the level of the street, the Shakespeare Gallery's façade seemed prepared to deal with the viewer at that very
level. Boydell's confidence in putting high art literally out on the street, by
signalling its availability to the public suggests an anticipation of a certain
kind of viewer, one practised in the reading of a complex urban visuality.
Celebrated as Banks's sculpture was as an ambitious aesthetic object, it also
would have participated in a broader visual topography of shop and inn
signs, themselves often utilising the name and iconography of Shakespeare.
Moreover, the figures of Shakespeare, Poetry and Painting would have participated in a wider dialogue along this stretch of St James's, linking the
Shakespeare Gallery not only with other artistic sites, but also with the literary public sphere, through the numerous bookshops which the street housed,
such as the premises belonging to George Nichols, the publisher of the book
edition of Boydell's Shakespeare. Boydell thus sought to make the viewing of
history painting not a hermetically-sealed, temporally-limited experience,

as was the case with the Academy's isolation of its exhibitions from the spectacular consumerism of the Strand, but to offer high art as an everyday aspect of the life of the metropolitan public through a process permitted by the rather more rarefied commercial character of Pall Mall.

While the subject matter of Boydell's Gallery, and those of his imitators on Pall Mall, facilitated the kinds of dialogues between politics and art to which I have pointed in this chapter, the discursive enterprise which they collectively formed could only be sustained through a spatial process, by exploiting the possibilities of both the exhibition space and the street. The Royal Academy, indeed, eagerly took up the subjects which Boydell's and Bowyer's projects had proposed, but, after the closure of these galleries, these subjects were never to work in quite the same way again. They operated instead in an Academy which was faced with conflict and irreconcilable hetero-geneity, and which seemed to deal with these problems with various abort-ive attempts at regulation and coercion. In any case, James Barry's expulsion from the Academy in 1799 for the art world's equivalent of seditious libel had made it clear that this could never be an open discursive space, aesthetically or politically. An admirer of William Godwin, Mary Wollstonecraft and Jacques-Louis David, Barry was accused of using one of his lectures to make 'long digressions from the subjects on which he is bound exclusively to dis-course, in order to utter the most virulent abuse on the established laws, the arts and government of the Academy, and calumniating its actual and even its deceased members'.[31] Some of the students cheered, but the Academy was incensed and quickly closed ranks. The subjects of art, its rules, its ideology, its production and its administration were simply not open for discussion. Although Bowyer's and Boydell's ventures collapsed at the beginning of the nineteenth century as European war sealed off their vital export market, many more artistic sites sprang up on and around Pall Mall in their after-math. The promise of an artistic and ideological space beyond the Academy would remain with artists and the public for some time to come.

NOTES

1 *Morning Post*, 1 April 1794, 3.
2 Space does not permit extended discussion of the term 'discourse'. In brief, I am sug-gesting here that the artistic spaces in the vicinity of Pall Mall sustained and energised a network of people, images, texts, histories, ideologies and viewing practices that spanned the entire spectrum of political thought and behaviour.
3 *The Times*, 30 April 1794, 3.
4 See, for example, T. Malton, *A Picturesque Tour through the Cities of London and Westminster* (London: Tho. Malton, 1792); Sir J. Fielding Junior, R. King Esq. and Others [pseuds.], *The New London Spy; or a Modern Twenty-Four Hours Ramble through the Great British Metropolis* (London: Alex. Hogg, 1793); and [John Feltham], *The Picture of London for 1802* (London: Printed by Lewis and Co. for R. Phillips, 1802).

5 More detailed discussion of the distinction between the Pall Mall galleries and Somerset House can be found in my PhD thesis, 'John Boydell's Shakespeare Gallery and the Promotion of a National Aesthetic' (University of York).

6 W. Hazlitt, '[On the pleasures of painting] The same subject continued', in P. Howe (ed.), *The Complete Works of William Hazlitt*, 21 volumes (London and Toronto: Dent, 1932), Vol. 8, 14–15.

7 On the Academy's residence at Somerset House, see the essays in D. H. Solkin (ed.), *Art on the Line: The Royal Academy Exhibitions at Somerset House, 1780–1836* (New Haven and London: Yale University Press, 2001).

8 Comparing portraits to the 'originals' was a popular activity for visitors to the annual exhibition. On occasion, the 'originals' would court public celebrity by sitting close to their portraits and inviting recognition.

9 *Morning Chronicle*, 2 May 1781, 2.

10 *London Courant*, 15 May 1780, 2.

11 *Morning Post*, 15 May 1780, 4. On the problems of women viewing antique sculpture, see C. Chard, 'Effeminacy, pleasure and the classical body', in G. Perry and M. Rossington (eds), *Femininity and Masculinity in Eighteenth-Century Art and Culture* (Manchester: Manchester University Press, 1994), 142–61.

12 It must be remembered that a significant amount of press criticism and reporting relating to the art world was, in fact, paid 'puffery' inserted by these artists and entrepreneurs. This suggests a greater degree of agency on their part than has hitherto been recognised: see also note 22 below.

13 For an example of the kind of associations and gossip which the medley of (often scandalously interrelated) portraits may have invited, see G. Perry, 'The spectacle of the muse: exhibiting the actress at the Royal Academy', in Solkin (ed.), *Art on the Line*, 111–25.

14 See, for example, J. Brewer, *The Pleasures of the Imagination: English Culture in the Eighteenth Century* (London: HarperCollins, 1997), 277–8; M. Hallett, 'Painting', in I. McCalman (ed.), *An Oxford Companion to the Romantic Age: British Culture, 1776–1832* (Oxford: Oxford University Press, 1999), 250–9, and the essays in Solkin (ed.), *Art on the Line*.

15 One recent exception is C. S. Matheson, '"A shilling well laid out": The Royal Academy's early public', in Solkin (ed.), *Art on the Line*, 39–53. Matheson makes a case for the exhibition print and catalogue constituting the main disciplinary apparatus of the exhibition space, thus adding another dimension to the latter's representational strategies and motives.

16 *Ibid.* As Matheson suggests, Ramberg's print clearly had a regulatory function. What I am suggesting here is that, by the end of the 1780s, many viewers, commentators, critics and artists had identified certain problems in the way the Academy envisaged, and sought to regulate and define, its public.

17 *Ibid.*, 48.

18 This is the case not only with the Ramberg image, but also with depictions of the Academy's 1771 exhibition by Charles Brandoin and the 1784 exhibition by Daniel Dodd: both reproduced in Solkin (ed.), *Art on the Line*, 41 and 45.

19 *Gazetteer and New Daily Advertiser*, 8 May 1789, 2.

20 *St James's Chronicle*, 9–12 May 1789, 4 and *Analytical Review*, 4 (1789), 111.

21 *St James's Chronicle*, 5–7 May 1789, 4.

22 The 'puff' (a paid advertisement disguised as journalistic praise) was a common phenomenon in late eighteenth-century art criticism. It is likely that a significant number of the reviews for the Shakespeare Gallery were paid for by Boydell. Much of

the press criticism of the Gallery is indistinguishable from the critical catalogue of the paintings that Boydell commissioned from Humphry Repton. At any rate, press coverage of the Shakespeare Gallery seems to have dwindled after 1793, the year in which Boydell's financial difficulties began.

23 *Morning Chronicle*, 28 March 1792, 3.

24 The emergence of a public sphere in the eighteenth century has been the subject of much debate among historians, art historians and literary scholars following the publication in English of Jürgen Habermas, *The Structural Transformation of the Public Sphere* (Cambridge: Polity Press, 1989): see the Introduction here, pp. 9–11. Many scholars have pronounced themselves wary of the conceptual framework which Habermas offers: see, for example, T. Broman, 'The Habermasian public sphere and "science *in* the Enlightenment"', *History of Science*, 36 (1998), 123–49 and B. Cowan, 'What was masculine about the public sphere? Gender and the coffeehouse milieu in post-Restoration England', *History Workshop Journal*, 51 (2001), 127–57, who states that 'the term ["public sphere"] has become so fluid that with a little imagination it can be applied to almost any time and any place' (p. 128). Nonetheless, the fact remains that the eighteenth century witnessed an unprecedented number of writings and debates about the nature of 'the public' and, as far as the art world is concerned, witnessed not only the first public exhibitions of art in England but also a veritable 'rage for exhibitions' by the end of the century. The assumption behind discussions of the public sphere in this chapter has been that the audience for art is a complex phenomenon made up not only of actual visitors to exhibitions whom we can account for empirically, but also its construction through artistic discourses and practices. In this sense, the 'public sphere' identifiable in the environs of Pall Mall is as much a construction of various political, social and cultural interests as it is an empirically verifiable entity. For a discussion of the congruence or otherwise of the art audience with the public, see T. Crow, *Painters and Public Life in Eighteenth-Century Paris* (New Haven and London: Yale University Press, 1985).

25 This episode is mentioned in the *Morning Chronicle*, 17 April 1784, 2 and the *Gazetteer and New Daily Advertiser*, 27 April 1784, 2. The *Gazetteer* alludes to 'other gentlemen' as well as Austin being excluded from the Academy because of their political persuasion. During the 1790s, the Academy was perceived as becoming increasingly authoritarian.

26 On the treasonable status of imaginative regicide, see J. Barrell, *Imagining the King's Death: Figurative Treason, Fantasies of Regicide, 1793–1796* (Oxford: Oxford University Press, 2000). Among the images on display in Bowyer's gallery which depicted either episodes of insurrection or regicide, or evidence of anti-monarchical sentiment, were Francis Wheatley's *Death of Richard II*, Thomas Stothard's *Charles I taking leave of his Children*, Francis Rigaud's *The Collector of the Poll Tax Murder'd by Wat Tyler*, and sentimental images of the reign and death of Mary Queen of Scots by Robert Smirke and John Opie.

27 S. von la Roche, *Sophie in London, being the Diary of Sophie von la Roche*, trans. Clare Williams (London: Jonathan Cape, 1933), 154.

28 C. Lamb, 'The Londoner', in E. V. Lucas (ed.), *The Works of Charles and Mary Lamb*, 6 volumes (London: Methuen, 1903), Vol. 1, 39 (originally published in the *Morning Post*, 1 February 1802).

29 *Daily Universal Register*, 10 May 1786, 2.

30 *Gazetteer and New Daily Advertiser*, 16 May 1780, 3; *Gazetteer and New Daily Advertiser*, 27 April 1784, 2; *London Courant and Westminster Chronicle*, 15 May 1780, 3.

31 'Minutes of the Council of the Royal Academy of Arts', 2 March 1799, quoted in W. T. Whitley, *Artists and their Friends in England, 1700–1799*, 2 volumes (New York and London: Benjamin Bloom, 1968), Vol. 2, 228.

6

A geography of Georgian narrative space

ẽ

Cynthia Wall

> To call up our ancestors before us with all their peculiarities of language, manners, and garb, to show us over their houses, to seat us at their tables, to rummage their old-fashioned wardrobes, to explain the uses of their ponderous furniture, these parts of the duty which properly belongs to the historian have been appropriated by the historical novelist. (T. B. Macaulay, 1850)[1]

ACTUALLY, MACAULAY – that great Victorian voice of authority – has it slightly wrong. Historians had almost never considered the visualisation of space, particularly interior space, to be high on their list of duties. Until the time of the 'historical novelist', neither had novelists. In fact, the descriptions of clothes and houses, tables and wardrobes that readers of the novel have come to expect since the nineteenth century simply did not exist as a narrative category for most fictional prose of the seventeenth and early eighteenth centuries. (Poetry – in the epic catalogue, the blazon, the description of tapestries, the elaboration of landscapes, the satirical distortion – has a different descriptive tradition.)[2] For early novelists, characters and events – the elements of history writing – were the essential elements of fiction, precisely because they dealt with essentials rather than accidentals. Houses might be described as venerable or magnificent or showy or modest or inadequate, but all (and only) as they represented the true nature of their owners. That is all we know because it is all we need to know. Details emerge only in response to narrative need: in novels, windows and staircases appear only at the very moment the character needs a window to jump out of or a staircase to climb; in history writing, terrain is described to contextualise battle strategies, Star Chambers are cited as sites of political decisions. But by the end of the eighteenth century,

Ann Radcliffe's gothic novels would set the pattern for the nineteenth-century practice of unrolling a fully visualised setting for the characters to enter and act upon. Novelistic space gets filled in over the eighteenth century, and by the middle of the nineteenth century, Lord Macaulay is calling for the same from history writing, as if those spaces had somehow been stolen away, 'appropriated' by the historical novelist from the proper duty of the historian.

What happened to the status of narrative space such that in fiction it began to be filled, and in history began to seem empty? This essay will examine the eighteenth-century intersections between fictional and historical prose to map a geography of Georgian narrative interiors. In a 1737 translation of Lenglet du Fresnoy's *The Geography of Children*, the interlocutor asks, 'WHAT IS Geography?' The child's correct response is: 'Geography is a description of the terrestrial globe, or a division of the surface of the earth into its different parts.'³ Geography describes and divides surfaces. This geography of narrative space will show how surface itself changed in cultural and literary significance, to create (and respond to) new perceptions of space. As it is the job of description to make things, people and spaces visible, so it is novelistic and historical description that this chapter will address. Attitudes towards description changed across the eighteenth century. Trade brought in new things from all over the world and growing prosperity made acquiring those things possible. The quantity of goods created more individualised spaces. Travel and wider literacy meant readers were more diverse. Philosophically, the individual began to assume more importance. What differentiated people and things became more interesting than what might be universal or essential about them. And what was different could not be assumed, and therefore must be described. This chapter will, then, be a kind of geography of description itself, sorting its business with the novelist and the historian to outline the ascension of the particular and a new creation of space in Georgian narrative texts that, in its attention to 'accidental' details, found new psychological, social and narrative importance in the spaces and objects of interiors – in the 'accidentals' of surfaces.

THE GEOGRAPHY OF DESCRIPTION

The classical history of description is rather unimpressive. Until the middle of the eighteenth century, description was primarily a workhorse in the service of geography and topography, in city guides, military site locations, antiquarian enterprises, or as marginal commentaries on architectural drawings or allegories or paintings – a 'textual praxis'.⁴ Henry Peacham's *Garden of Eloquence* (1577), for example, defines 'pragmatographia' as 'a description of thinges, wherby we do as plainly describe any thing by gathering togeather all the circumstances belonging unto it, as if it were moste liuely paynted out in colloures, and set forth to be seene'.[5] It is indeed circumstances – the particular details of a person, place, or thing – that, on the one hand, essentially constitute description (what does this place, this thing, that person look like? How is it, how is she, different from something else?), and, on the other, cause all its problems.

Critics from Horace and Aristotle to Thomas Rymer, Peter Whalley, René Rapin and Nicolas Boileau had catechised against ornament and superfluity in all kinds of narrative, poetic, and historical writing. History in particular was territory severely circumscribed. A 1680 translation of Rapin's *Instructions pour l'histoire* (1677) enquires rhetorically: 'What Discernment and Recollection is there not requisite . . . to expose things at large or minutely, according as necessity or *decorum* require . . . and never to tire out the Reader by an excessive Uniformity?'[6] The 'grand Secret' of the historian, according to Rapin, is:

> to know how to make a prudent and judicious choice of the Circumstances, fit to give a great *Idea* of the thing . . . and by that minute dissection to render them capable of fastening on the Mind. A Collection of great and small Circumstances methodically intermix'd one with another, is of that nature when they are well chosen . . . It is 'mean, frivolous, and minute Particularities, which debase a Subject; for he becomes childish, and indeed ridiculous, who insists too much on small things'.[7]

No descriptions of kings' vests or emperors' bucklers were to be allowed. 'Of what concern is it to me, to know whether *Hannibal* had a fair Sett of Teeth, provided his Historian discover to me the Grandeur of his *Genius*[?]'[8]

One of the main objections to description, apart from its 'childishness' (a point to which I return) is that, as Beaujour writes, 'it lies athwart the thread of narrative time'.[9] Or, as Peter Whalley put it in 1744: 'When they are too numerous, the Narration is embarrassed, and the Thread of the Story is unnaturally torn asunder.'[10] Rapin cites the 'frigidity' of 'impertinent' descriptions, and Beaujour their 'stable, frozen, crystalline structures'. Samuel Johnson confirms that 'the mind is refrigerated by interruption'.[11] Description gets in the way, interrupting the linear movement of narrative, and the reader, losing plot or linearity in digression, just gets bored. 'For what Art is there not requisite to prevent the distraction of the Reader, and to keep him in a continual posture of Attention?'[12]

So descriptions in all the best models were kept, as Rapin had it, 'necessary, exact, succinct, elegant'.[13] One of the favourites that both Rapin and Whalley cite is from Tacitus's *Annals* (which I return to below as a template for change in history writing). Tiberius retires to Capri:

> an Island disjoin'd from the point of the Cape of Surrentum by a channel of three miles. I should chiefly believe that he was taken with its solitude, as the sea above

it is void of havens, as the stations for the smallest vessels are few and difficult, and as none could put in unperceiv'd by the guards. The genius of the climate is mild in winter, from the shelter of a mountain which intercepts the rigour of the winds: its summers are refresh'd by gales from the West; and the sea open all round it, makes a delightful view: from thence too was beheld a most lovely landskip, before the eruptions of Mount Vesuvius had chang'd the face of the prospect.[14]

Such a description draws the political lines: the open shoreline protected from secret invasions. It remarks on the climate, on the inhabitant's general experience; it offers a quick, undetailed bird's-eye view: mountains, open sea, lovely (now vanished) landskip. In short, it 'specifies the Reasons which *Tiberius* had to retire thither, toward the end of his days, which makes it necessary: and being short, elegant, polite, as it is, having nothing super-fluous, it may be said, that it is as it should be'.[15] It is a sketch.

In a sense, for the 'polite' reader there was perhaps less need for anything other than what was descriptively short, elegant and necessary, because much of what was 'necessary' was always already immanent in the basic vocabulary itself, in well-known allusions and common experiences. As Philippe Hamon claims: 'The word "description" is often used, as early as the sixteenth century . . . as a memory storehouse[,] a stock of learning to be reactualized.'[16] Michel Beaujour argues that there was a tradition of 'word pictures' in which 'the spheres of poetic culture and iconography are seemingly one world . . . [and] the reader's store of cultural images . . . [comes] from [works] which all educated men have learned by heart'.[17] Such was the force behind the early eighteenth-century poetic traditions of compound epithets, periphrasis, and abstract nouns. The words themselves acted as sort of freeze-dried descrip-tions, rehydrating in the reader's mind into the visual.

But gradually over the eighteenth century, although the language of class-ical recommendation did not appear to change much, the practice did, and as Hamon says, 'description begins to reach a "normal" literary status at the turning point of the eighteenth and nineteenth centuries'.[18] This 'normal' literary status itself turns on the change in attitude towards the particular, the 'minute circumstances'. The idea of individual, idiosyncratic detail moves from the dubious status of Aristotelian 'accidental' to something intrinsically interesting and empowering. In the middle of the eighteenth century, literary criticism was firmly on the side of the universal. Samuel Johnson articulated the well-known requirements for 'the business of a poet': the description must capture the essential, not 'number the streaks of the tulip, [nor] describe the different shades of verdure in the forest', but rather supply 'just representations of general nature'.[19] But overlapping and eventually voicing over Johnson is, for example, Thomas Gray: 'Circumstance ever was, and ever will be, the life and the essence both of nature and of poetry.'[20] Hugh

Blair argued that 'description is the great test of a Poet's imagination', and it is in the 'selection of circumstances' that characterises 'the great art of Picturesque Description'. The circumstances chosen must 'particularise the object described, and mark it strongly. No description, that rests in generals, can be good'.[21]

Marmontel had complained: 'What we call today, in Poetry, the descriptive genre was not known by the Ancients. It is a modern invention, of which, it seems to me, neither reason nor taste approve.'[22] This modern invention, unapproved by reason and taste, is precisely the old 'childish' preoccupation with the small things, with the minute particulars, with surfaces. Boileau had used the example of a poet-historian describing a child 'who, with his little hand, / Picked up the shining pebbles from the sand' as the perfect emblematic instance of overcircumstantiating, of poetic entrancement with shiny pebbles.[23] Roland Barthes makes a similar accusation against Dutch still-life painting and its celebration of surfaces, of objects, of its own well-fed, well-upholstered *empire des marchandises*.[24]

Early modern Europe in general has been characterised as a 'world of goods'. The intersections of trade and consumerism in Britain and the new passion for empirical scientific investigation, together with the lingering Puritan influence of 'reading' the small things of the world, have each been identified as factors in the development of the novel – that genre that first implicitly defined itself by its attention to ordinary people, ordinary things, the surfaces of this world.[25] And the worlds within novels became increasingly interested in not only the events of their characters' lives but also in the spaces they inhabited and the things that filled those spaces. Trade and consumerism meant more individuation of household interiors. Travel meant more experience of difference. Increasing literacy meant a more disparate readership. What was formerly taken for granted – the memory storehouse, the stock of cultural images, the shared elite experience of great houses and grand buildings, not to mention the assumed superiority of the universal or essential quality over the accidental or individuating particular – now needed re-evaluating, restocking, redrawing, revisualising. Descriptions of houses, of clothes, of rooms, of wardrobes and heavy furniture began to be valuable because, as Edward Casey puts it, for later writers 'essential features, and not accidents only, are to be found on surfaces'.[26]

THE SPACES OF THE NOVELIST

Until the mid-eighteenth century, most British novelistic space is firmly part of the *terra cognita* of classical rhetoric, where description remains as poetical ornament. Recall the description of Paradise Hall in Fielding's *Tom Jones* (1749), where the chapter heading warns: *'The Reader's Neck [is] brought into*

Danger by a Description.' But the description proves classically untreacherous: 'The *Gothick* Stile of Building could produce nothing nobler than Mr *Allworthy*'s House. There was an Air of Grandeur in it, that struck you with Awe, and rival'd the Beauties of the best *Grecian* Architecture; and it was as commodious within, as venerable without.'[27] The essential moral qualities of the Squire are worthily dimensioned in the essential architectural qualities of his house – the standard 'inside answerable to the outside' theory that architectural theory and country house poems had always propagated.[28] But the actual interior remains implicit. The rest of the description records the position of the house and the view 'seen from every Room in the Front'.[29] Rachel Trickett claims: '[The] self-consciousness itself warns us that Fielding is thinking of such description as a convention, but a high poetic convention, like the epic battle, not a convention of simple narrative. His attempt at it is clumsy and confusing; he is ill at ease with description, with any attempt to depict natural beauty.'[30] Yet that criticism itself forgets conceptual history. Fielding is 'ill at ease with description' in so far as he is a good classical scholar (or rather, the classically trained gentleman) in which the vocabulary as well as the conceptual space for spatial detail is prescriptively and consciously limited.

Early novelistic description tended to be emblematically concrete, serving up isolated objects or bits of architectural structure (windows, wainscottings, doors) as events – as narrative – called for them.[31] Rarely do we find connected visual space. Defoe is known for his things – Moll's stolen bolts of cloth and necklaces, Crusoe's large earthenware pot, umbrella, canoe, raisins.[32] When, in Samuel Richardson's *Pamela* (1740), the heroine makes her trembling way along a wainscotting when Mr B is mean to her, that is the first we know of a wainscotting. When the space is visualised in detail, it stands out for a particular emblematic purpose. Jonathan Swift's deliciously disgusting detailed descriptions of human filth in his dressing-room poems and in *Gulliver's Travels* (1726), and Delarivier Manley's or Eliza Haywood's sensuous descriptions of scenes of seduction, stand out precisely because of their atypical circumstantiality, which serve particular satirical purposes in making us see differently. Robinson Crusoe's endlessly specific and endlessly repeated details about his island habitation function as the necessary indicator of his psychological obsessions. The thickness of his description is the measure of his fear. Description enters only in times of crisis, for very specific reasons. Perhaps, indeed, Crusoe deliberately refrigerates his mind by the interruption.

I have elsewhere argued that Richardson's novels provide a telescoped history of the incorporation of careful, connected, interior visual detail in the novel, from the emblematic space of *Pamela* (1740) to the endlessly shifting implicit spaces of *Clarissa* (1747–48), to the domestication and gentrification of the guidebook tradition in *Sir Charles Grandison* (1753–54), in Harriet's descriptions of objects, colours, textures and interior spaces generally.[33] Where Richardson pioneered details of interior space, Ann Radcliffe opened up narrative landscape (as well as interiors) in similarly detailed and surface-loving ways. Sir Walter Scott credits Radcliffe with the first real demonstration of novelistic description, by arguing that she combines poetic with prose traditions: 'Indeed the praise may be claimed for Mrs Radcliffe, of having been the first to introduce into her prose fictions a tone of fanciful description and impressive narrative, which had been hitherto exclusively applied to poetry . . . Mrs Radcliffe has a title to be considered the first poetess of romantic fiction.'[34]

Radcliffe pioneered both description as setting, creating a visual space to be entered, when finished, by characters and events, and description that maps psychology directly onto landscape or interior. Both would become stock conventions of the nineteenth-century novel. In *The Mysteries of Udolpho* (1794), for example, we get a fully realised positioning of Emily St Aubert's home, La Vallée, in a context of boundedness: the boundaries of window frames, of mountain ranges, of changing climates and colours. We learn, in this context, what Emily loves best: 'It was one of Emily's earliest pleasures to ramble among the scenes of nature; nor was it in the soft and glowing landscape that she most delighted; she loved more the wild wood-walks, that skirted the mountain, and still more the mountain's stupendous recesses.'[35] This emotional and physical geography – an interior-in-exterior – is caught up again and developed further in her response to her first glimpse of the Castle Udolpho:

> Emily gazed with melancholy awe upon the castle, which she understood to be Montoni's; for, though it was now lighted up by the setting sun, the gothic greatness of its features, and its mouldering walls of dark grey stone, rendered it a gloomy and sublime object. As she gazed, the light died away on its walls, leaving a melancholy purple tint, which spread deeper and deeper, as the thin vapour crept up the mountain, while the battlements above were still tipped with splendour. From those too, the rays soon faded, and the whole edifice was invested with the solemn duskiness of evening. Silent, lonely, and sublime, it seemed to stand the sovereign of the scene, and to frown defiance on all, who dared to invade its solitary reign.[36]

The importance of description here is not just the overlap into poetic territory, but the subliminal connections. The detailed shades of light silhouette the as-yet vaguely described castle, but connect us thematically to what Emily, in fact, loves: the beautiful; her ineffectual father St Aubert; her disappointing lover Valancourt; the low hills of France. But she loves best the sublime, the mountainous, the stupendous, the phallic, the ambiguous, and, indirectly, the fierce Montoni, whose knees she has a habit of embracing. The castle gets its visual due: the melancholy of Emily and of the twilight join each other, and all Emily's 'gazing' that is here rhetorically linked to dying later translates consistently into 'awakenings'. Emblematic detail spreads out into emblematic description, from the decorative or ornamental to the explanatory and sustained.[37]

Sir Walter Scott's admiration for Radcliffe translates into his own version of detailed historical description of place. In *Ivanhoe* (1819), for example, he gives us the eighteenth-century version of descriptive placement, but then moves us vividly inside, as in Cedric's mansion, the description of its interior continuing for several detailed pages, until all its corners and all its furniture appear fully formed and minutely traced.[38] Scott, like Radcliffe, creates a space ahead of time in which to place characters and their actions. He is fully aware of the power of accumulated detail to halt the reader in her narrativised tracks. Sometimes the accumulated detail seems simply visual, an end in itself. At other moments, description serves more obviously emblematic purposes, shaping historical and social space with physical dimension:

> The other appointments of the mansion partook of the rude simplicity of the Saxon period, which Cedric piqued himself upon maintaining. The floor was composed of earth mixed with lime, trodden into such a hard substance, as is often employed in flooring our modern barns. For about one quarter of the length of the apartment, the floor was raised by a step, and this space, which was called the dais, was occupied only by the principal members of the family and visitors of distinction. For this purpose, a table richly covered with scarlet cloth was placed transversely across the platform, from the middle of which run the longer and lower board, at which the domestics and inferior persons fed, down towards the bottom of the hall. The whole resembled the form of the letter T, or some of those ancient dinner-tables, which, arranged on the same principles, may be still seen in the antique Colleges of Oxford or Cambridge.[39]

Precedence at table was as rigorously prescribed in Scott's time as it was in Cedric's, but the trappings were different, and Scott was as interested in the trappings – in the 'old-fashioned wardrobe' – as in the somewhat longer-lasting social hierarchy. Scott has Cedric himself maintaining historical and cultural boundaries through spatial maintenance, with surfaces, with interior management. The description makes the space particular so that the particulars have meaning, on their own (as in Defoe's novels) but also in relation to each other. Visual space is filled in: the house is built, the carpet laid, and the characters can now move in and begin their novelistic lives and actions.

THE TERRITORY OF THE HISTORIAN

What Radcliffe and Scott offer – and all the historical novelists for that matter, including Defoe and Fielding – is the dual perspective of the historian, who positions the present in relation to the past. 'Our modern barns' and the 'antique colleges of Oxford' mark for the contemporary reader of *Ivanhoe* a sense of progress perhaps, a sense of temporal distance certainly. But the phrases, the images, also measure spatial change. And by the end of the eighteenth century, demands were being made on the historian for some similar sort of spatial awareness and particularisation. In Hugh Blair's lecture on 'Historical Writing', for example, he warns against 'prolix detail', but repeats what he had said about poetry: 'General facts make a slight impression on the mind. It is by means of circumstances and particulars properly chosen, that a narration becomes interesting and affecting to the Reader.'[40] Although such a phrase seems simply to repeat the descriptive dicta of Rapin and the classical authorities, 'even so,' as Mark Phillips notes, 'it is striking to see the great ancient histories applauded as "picturesque" or "interesting"'.[41] More than a whiff of late eighteenth-century aesthetics mingles in the critical discourse. The *Monthly Review* noted thus of the second edition of Sir John Sinclair's *History of the Public Revenue* (1790):

> History, till of late, was chiefly employed in the recital of warlike transactions . . . The *people* were not known; the circumstances that affected *their* domestic prosperity and happiness were entirely overlooked; and the records of many ages might have been perused without obtaining the least information concerning any fact that led to a knowledge of the internal economy of the state, or the private situation of individuals.
>
> Thanks, however, to the more enlightened spirit of modern times, things are much altered in this respect.[42]

Thanks to the study of manners pioneered by Voltaire in *Siècle de Louis XIV* (1751) and *Essai sur les mœurs* (1756), we are not yet rummaging in the cupboards or being guided about the house, but the geography of interest is clearly changing from the public to the private.

David Wootton has argued that Hume, as historian, positioned himself competitively against novelists. Everett Zimmerman has countered that, in fact, Hume incorporates novelistic narrative techniques of 'rendering . . . the private world of the historical agent'.[43] Zimmerman focuses on Hume's sense of the constructedness of history writing, the 'careful placement in time that is a feature of formal realism', the connectedness of narrative through causality and contiguity, and the dual perspectives of 'both trying to understand events as they appeared to contemporary spectators and trying, as well, to grasp the less public motives of participants in historical events'.[44] Hume himself had insisted: 'An annalist or historian, who should undertake to write the history of EUROPE during any century, would be influenced by the connexion of contiguity in time or place. All events, which happen in that portion of space and period of time, are comprehended in his design, though in other respects different and unconnected.'[45] But Zimmerman, Wootton, Phillips and other analysts of Hume's historical technique tend to focus on his crafting of contiguity in time: there is virtually no mention of Hume's use of space in his *History of England* (1754–62).[46] In some ways, this is not surprising, because as Phillip Hicks points out, though some contemporaries claimed that Hume was writing history in a new manner, most 'did not object to whatever innovations Hume might have introduced into British historiography as inconsistent with neoclassical standards for history'.[47] But as Mark Phillips notes about Blair, who managed to see classical models of history through a 'picturesque' lens with no consciousness of anachronism, so the 'new manner' of writing history – the study of manners pioneered by Voltaire – perhaps created a larger space for the classical models to shift around in, a space already prepared by novelistic narrative.

As Macaulay's complaint about the proper but unfulfilled duties of the historian suggests, however, the invitation to greater spatial detail offered by the new interest in 'manners' – touring houses, sitting at tables, rummaging closets – was not taken up with any obvious lavishness. But if we rummage the wardrobes of descriptive detail, we can note significant changes. Detail itself in historical writing was getting perceptibly more vivid. Compare, for example, Arthur Murphy's 1793 translation of Tacitus's description of Capri to the version on pages 116–17:

> a small island, separated from the promontory of Surrentum by an arm of the sea, not more than three miles broad. Defended there from all intrusion, and delighted with the solitude of the place, he sequestered himself from the world, seeing, as may be imagined, many circumstances suited to his humour. Not a single port in the channel; the stations but few, and those accessible only to small vessels; no part of the island, where men could land unobserved by the sentinels; the climate inviting; in the winter, a soft and genial air, under the shelter of a mountain, that repels the inclemency of the winds; in the summer, the heat allayed by the western breeze; the sea presenting a smooth expanse, and opening a view of the bay of Naples, with a beautiful landscape on its borders: all these conspired to please the taste and genius of Tiberius. The scene, indeed, has lost much of its beauty, the fiery eruptions of Mount Vesuvius having, since that time, changed the face of the country.[48]

This description is literally longer than Gordon's, seventy years earlier. It may be, of course, that Murphy's literary talents are poised against Gordon's in translation. Yet it seems worth noting that the sea is no longer just 'open all around', but rather presents 'a smooth expanse', that mild winter is elaborated into 'a soft and genial air', that the view is now particularly of Naples, and that the eruptions have become 'fiery'. We have already seen that, in one sense, space was implicit within the economic and generalised descriptions of pre-nineteenth-century narratives, called up in the reader's mind by a tag such as 'the Silver *Thames*' (Alexander Pope's *The Rape of the Lock* (1714)), or by an act such as Pamela hopping out a window to escape Lady Davers and the naughty Jacky. But there is another sense in which description creates space. The narrative torn asunder, the act of refrigeration, the 'painting' of description, requires the act of stopping and looking – 'the *very process of spacing out*', the 'becoming space of time' as Beaujour has it.[49] The longer the description, the longer the look; the more detailed the description, the more within sight; the more within sight, the richer and multi-dimensional the sense of space.

David Hume articulated most of the classical conventions about the use of detail and description in narrative. He notes, for example, that the use of 'minute circumstances' in poetry:

> which, though to the historian they seem superfluous, serve mightily to enliven the imagery and gratify the fancy. If it be not necessary, as in the *Iliad*, to inform us each time the hero buckles his shoes and ties his garters, it will be requisite, perhaps, to enter into a greater detail than in the *Henriade*, where the events are run over with such rapidity that we scarce have leisure to become acquainted with the scene or action.[50]

Hume disliked stylistic extravagance, arguing for 'simplicity and refinement in writing'.[51] Yet he criticises Clarendon's lack of descriptive detail: 'Lord CLARENDON, when he approaches towards the catastrophe of the royal party, supposes, that his narration must then become infinitely disagreeable; and he hurries over the king's death, without giving us one circumstance of it. He considers it as too horrid a scene to be contemplated with any satisfaction, or even without the utmost pain and aversion.'[52] Such a criticism marks Hume's own opening up of interior space, in intensifying the details of a description that render the image more vivid, the space more articulated.

Mark Phillips argues that one of Hume's distinguishing innovations in history writing is his use of sentimental tableaux, moments of 'intensified sympathy', that provide a 'temporary release of feeling' in the otherwise complexly connected narrative.[53] Unlike the larger province of sentimental writing per se, in which the cumulative effect of emotional response is an end in itself, Hume's suddenly spatialised, contextualised scenes offer something of the reverse of the classical model, in which description, as one eighteenth-century writer put it, serves as 'some relaxation, some divertisement from a continued scene of horror' in 'tumultuous' works like the *Iliad*, 'whose subject is only quarrelling, fighting and death'.[54] Hume's descriptive spaces open into the scenes of horror, spacing out the linear narrative of cumulative chronology with moments for almost novelistic identification and experience. His account of Oliver Cromwell's last paranoiac days, for example, takes Clarendon as the obvious model, but rings almost novelistic changes on it. Clarendon writes:

It had been observ'd in *England*, that, though from the dissolution of the last Parliament, all things seem'd to succeed, at home and abroad, to the Protector's wish, and his power and greatness to be better establish'd than ever it had been, yet he never had the same serenity of mind he had been used to, after he had refused the Crown; but was out of countenance, and chagrin, as if he were conscious of not having been true to himself; and much more apprehensive of danger to his Person than he had used to be. Insomuch as he was not easy of access, nor so much seen abroad; and seem'd to be in some disorder, when his Eyes found any stranger in the room; upon whom they were still fixed. When He intended to go to *Hampton* Court, which was his principal delight and diversion, it was never known, till he was in the Coach, which way he would go; and he was still hem'd in by his Guards both before and behind; and the Coach in which he went, was always thronged as full as it could be, with his Servants; who were armed; and he seldom returned the same way he went; and rarely lodged two Nights together in one Chamber, but had many furnished and prepared, to which his own Key convey'd him and those he would have with him, when he had a mind to go to bed: which made his fears the more taken notice of, and publick, because he had never been accustom'd to those precautions.[55]

Hume revises this, changing the sense of distance between reader and historical figure by refining and intensifying visual details and verbal patterns:

Death, too, which, with such signal intrepidity he had braved in the field, being incessantly threatened by the poinards of fanatical or interested assassins, was ever present to his terrified apprehension, and haunted him in every scene of business or repose. Each action of his life betrayed the terrors under which he laboured. The aspect of strangers was uneasy to him: With a piercing and anxious eye he surveyed every face to which he was not daily accustomed. He never moved a step without strong guards attending him: He wore armour under his cloaths, and farther secured himself by offensive weapons, a sword, falchion, and pistols, which he always carried about him. He returned from no place by the direct road, or by the same way which he went. Every journey he performed with hurry and precipitation. Seldom he slept above three nights together in the same chamber: And he never let it be known beforehand what chamber he intended to choose, nor entrusted himself in any, which was not provided with back-doors, at which sentinels were carefully placed. Society terrified him, which he reflected on his numerous, unknown, and implacable enemies: Solitude astonished him, by withdrawing that protection which he found so necessary for his security.[56]

The various chambers are not themselves described in either account. But where Clarendon ascribes motive and feeling from a distance ('as if', 'seemed to be'), Hume penetrates the psychological interior with Richardsonian confidence and emotional particularisation: the adjectives and verbs 'terrified', 'haunted', 'piercing and anxious', 'hurry and precipitation', 'terrified', and 'astonished', vivisect the Cromwellian soul. 'Every scene of business', 'each action of his life' and 'every journey' break into smaller bits the chronology implicit in Clarendon's 'used to be', 'still', and 'always'. The term 'offensive weapons' is made particular in 'a sword, falchion, and pistols'. Where Clarendon's Cromwell is seen from without ('it had been observ'd', 'the more taken notice of, and publick'), Hume's acts from within. Hume's perspective as historian is not simply dual – past and present – but four-dimensional, unfolding space as well as time. His sense of minute circumstance creates not the visual particularity of Radcliffe or Scott, but the equally Georgian interior of the private historical agent.

CONCLUSION

Macaulay distinguished between two kinds of history: one like a map, the other like a painted landscape. The painting gives us an incomplete visualisation, without accurate dimensions, distances, or angles. The map gives exact information, but no imaginative scenes.[57] No historian, according to Macaulay, had yet successfully combined the two approaches, because history writing itself is 'under the jurisdiction of two hostile powers' – reason and imagination – 'and, like other districts similarly situated, it is ill-defined, ill cultivated, and ill regulated . . . It may be laid down as a general rule, though subject to considerable qualifications and exceptions, that history begins in Novel and ends in Essay.'[58] What Macaulay was historically marking, however, was in part the eighteenth-century remapping in narrative of the visual, the circumstantial, the surface. The geographies of description and narrative, of visualisation and factualisation, of space and time were in the process of redistribution. Although history writing would continue for the most part to ignore Macaulay's call for the spatially intimate, the novelistically constructed and the circumstantially minute, it nevertheless relocated itself from the classical world into the Georgian. The 'world of things', the interest in surfaces, meant a different perception of space as, to use Henri Lefebvre's term, something 'produced'.[59] Surfaces were recognised as both interactive with and interpretive of the social and the psychological, where description was encouraged to produce a more vivid, detailed, individualised sense of space for rather than by the reader. As Virginia Woolf said of John Evelyn (and, by extension, his world), there was one difference between his way of experiencing and ours: '*The visible world was always close to him.*'[60] Later writers needed to make the world visible. So they described it.

NOTES

1 T. B. Macaulay, *Critical and Historical Essays* (London: Longman, 1850), 50.
2 See, for example, R. Trickett, '"Curious eye": some aspects of visual description in eighteenth-century literature', in D. L. Patey and T. Keegan (eds), *Augustan*

Studies: Essays in Honor of Irvin Ehrenpreis (Newark: University of Delaware Press, 1985), 239–52.

3 P. N. Lenglet du Fresnoy, *The Geography of Children* (London: E. Littlejohn and J. Hawkins, 1737), 1.

4 See G. Genette, *Figures of Literary Discourse*, trans. A. Sheridan (New York: Columbia University Press, 1982), 134–7; P. Hamon, 'Rhetorical status of the descriptive', trans. P. Baudoin, *Yale French Studies*, 61 (1981), 1–26, quote from p. 6; M. Beaujour, 'Some paradoxes of description', *Yale French Studies*, 61 (1981), 27–59, see especially pp. 28–31, 40–2.

5 H. Peacham, *The Garden of Eloquence* (London: H. Jackson, 1577), Oiiii^v–Pi.

6 [R. Rapin], *Instructions for History: with A Character of the most Considerable Historians, Antient and Modern. Out of the French, by J. Davies of Kidwelly* (London: John Barnes, 1680), 44–5.

7 [Rapin], *Instructions for History*, 53–4.

8 *Ibid.*, 78.

9 Beaujour, 'Some paradoxes of description', 40.

10 [P. Whalley], *An Essay on the Manner of Writing History* (London: T. Waller, 1744), 17.

11 S. Johnson, *Preface to Shakespeare* (1765), in F. Brady and W. K. Wimsatt (eds), *Samuel Johnson: Selected Poetry and Prose* (Berkeley and Los Angeles: University of California, 1977), 335.

12 [Rapin], *Instructions for History*, 44.

13 *Ibid.*, 73.

14 *The Works of Tacitus*, 2 volumes, trans. T. Gordon (London: T. Woodward and J. Peele, 1723), Vol. 1, 199–200.

15 [Rapin], *Instructions for History*, 70.

16 Hamon, 'Rhetorical status of the descriptive', 4.

17 Beaujour, 'Some paradoxes of description', 29.

18 Hamon, 'Rhetorical status of the descriptive', 4.

19 S. Johnson, *Rasselas*, in Brady and Wimsatt (eds), *Samuel Johnson*, 90 and 301.

20 Quoted in A. Clutton-Brock, 'Description in poetry', in H. C. Beeching (ed.), *Essays and Studies by Members of the English Association*, 2 volumes (Oxford: Clarendon Press, 1911), Vol. 2, 94–5.

21 H. Blair, *Lectures on Rhetoric and Belles Lettres*, 2 volumes (London: W. Strahan and T. Cadell, 1783), Vol. 2, 361.

22 Quoted in Hamon, 'Rhetorical status of the descriptive', 8, citing the articles 'Descriptif' and 'Description' in the *Grand Dictionnaire Universel du XIXe Siècle*, Vol. 6.

23 [N. Boileau Despréaux], *The Art of Poetry, Written in French by the SIEUR de Boileau, Made English*, trans. Sir William Soane (London: R. Bentley and S. Magnes, 1683), Canto III, 44.

24 R. Barthes, 'Le monde-objet', in his *Essais Critiques* (Paris: Éditions du Seuil, 1964), 19–28.

25 For examples, see J. Brewer and R. Porter (eds), *Consumption and the World of Goods* (London: Routledge, 1993); J. Brewer and S. Staves (eds), *Early Modern Conceptions of Property* (London: Routledge, 1996); L. Jardine, *Worldly Goods: A New History of the Renaissance* (New York: Nan A. Talese, 1996); P. Ariés and R. Chartier (eds), *A History of Private Life*, 4 volumes (Cambridge, MA: Harvard University Press, 1989), Vol. 3.

26 E. Casey, 'Literary description and phenomenological method', *Yale French Studies*, 61 (1981), 176–201, quote on p. 199.

27 H. Fielding, *The History of Tom Jones, A Foundling* (1749), ed. F. Bowers and with an introduction by M. Battestin (Wesleyan: Wesleyan University Press, 1975), 42.

28 This phrase is frequently employed by Defoe in his *A Tour thro' the Whole Island of Great Britain* (London: G. Strahan, W. Mears, R. Francklin, S. Chapman, R. Stagg and J. Graves, 1724).

29 Fielding, *Tom Jones*, 43.

30 Trickett, '"Curious eye"', 247.

31 C. Wall, 'The rhetoric of description and the spaces of things', in D. Todd and C. Wall (eds), *Serious Reflections on Occasional Forms: Essays in Eighteenth-Century Genre and Culture in Honor of J. Paul Hunter* (Newark: University of Delaware Press, 2001), 261–79.

32 See V. Woolf, 'Robinson Crusoe', in *The Second Common Reader* (New York: Harcourt Brace, 1986), 51–8. Later critics have also argued for an essential lack of visual quality in Defoe: see, for example, M. Byrd, *London Transformed: Images of the City in the Eighteenth Century* (New Haven and London: Yale University Press, 1978), 12–13; D. Van Ghent, *The English Novel: Form and Function* (New York: Harper & Row, 1961), 34–5.

33 C. Wall, 'The spaces of *Clarissa* in text and film', in R. Mayer (ed.), *The Eighteenth-Century Novel on Film* (Cambridge: Cambridge University Press, forthcoming), and C. Wall, 'Teaching space in *Sir Charles Grandison*', in J. Harris and L. Zunshine (eds), *Approaches to Teaching Richardson* (New York: Publications of the Modern Language Society, forthcoming).

34 Sir W. Scott, *Miscellaneous Prose Works of Sir Walter Scott, Bart*, 3 volumes (Edinburgh: R. Cadall, 1847–52), Vol. 1, 324.

35 A. Radcliffe, *The Mysteries of Udolpho* (1794), ed. B. Dobrée (Oxford: Oxford University Press, 1980), 6.

36 *Ibid.*, 226–7.

37 Radcliffe also spends a good deal of time on the gynic details of Emily's room in *Udolpho* – a door that can only be locked from the outside, that leads into a dark narrow staircase up which potential rapists run.

38 Sir W. Scott, *Ivanhoe; A Romance*, in *Historical Romances of the Author of Waverley*, 8 volumes (Edinburgh: Archibald Constable, and London: Hurst, Robinson, 1822), Vol. 1, 39–40.

39 *Ibid.*, 40.

40 Blair, *Lectures on Rhetoric and Belles Lettres*, Vol. 2, 274.

41 M. S. Phillips, *Society and Sentiment: Genres of Historical Writing in Britain, 1740–1820* (Princeton: Princeton University Press, 2000), 42.

42 *Monthly Review*, 2nd. series (1790), 3, 93–4.

43 D. Wootton, 'David Hume, "the historian"', in D. Fate Norton (ed.), *The Cambridge Companion to Hume* (Cambridge: Cambridge University Press, 1993), 281–312, quote on pp. 281–2; E. Zimmerman, *The Boundaries of Fiction: History and the Eighteenth-Century British Novel* (Ithaca: Cornell University Press, 1996), 245–56.

44 *Ibid.*, 239.

45 D. Hume, *An Enquiry Concerning Human Understanding* (1748), ed. T. L. Beauchamp (Oxford: Clarendon Press, 2000), 19.

46 D. Hume, *The History of England, From the Invasion of Julius Caesar to the Revolution in 1688* 8 volumes (London: T. Cadell, 1782).

47 P. Hicks, *Neoclassical History and English Culture from Clarendon to Hume* (London: Macmillan, 1996), 199.

48 [A. Murphy], *The Works of Cornelius Tacitus: by Arthur Murphy, Esq.*, 4 volumes (London: G. G. J. and J. Robinson, 1793), Vol. 1, 305–6.

49 Beaujour, 'Some paradoxes of description', 43.

50 Hume, *Enquiry Concerning Human Understanding*, 35.
51 D. Hume, *Essays Moral, Political, and Literary*, ed. E. F. Miller (Indianapolis: Liberty Classics, 1985). See also J. J. Richetti, *Philosophical Writing: Locke, Berkeley, Hume* (Cambridge MA: Harvard University Press, 1983), 189, and less persuasively, L. Braudy, *Narrative Form in History and Fiction* (Princeton: Princeton University Press, 1970), 48–9 and 87–8.
52 Hume, 'Of tragedy', in *Essays Moral, Political, and Literary*, 223.
53 Phillips, *Society and Sentiment*, 66.
54 [J. Newbery], *The Art of Poetry on a New Plan*, 2 volumes (London: J. Newbery, 1762), Vol. 2, 230.
55 E. Hyde, Earl of Clarendon, *The History of the Rebellion and Civil Wars in England, Begun in the Year 1641*, 3 volumes (Oxford: Printed at the Theater, 1702–4), Vol. 1, 504 (Book XV, mistakenly bound in volume 1 instead of volume 3).
56 Hume, *History of England*, Vol. 7, 284–5.
57 Macaulay, *Critical and Historical Essays*, 50–2.
58 T. B. Macaulay, *Reviews, Essays, and Poems* (London: Ward, Lock, and Tyler, 1875), 323; H. Neele, *The Romance of History*, 3 volumes (London: Edward Bull, 1828).
59 H. Lefebvre, *The Production of Space*, trans. D. Nicholson-Smith (Oxford: Blackwell, 1991), 278.
60 V. Woolf, 'Rambling round Evelyn', in *The Common Reader* (New York: Harcourt Brace, 1953), 84.

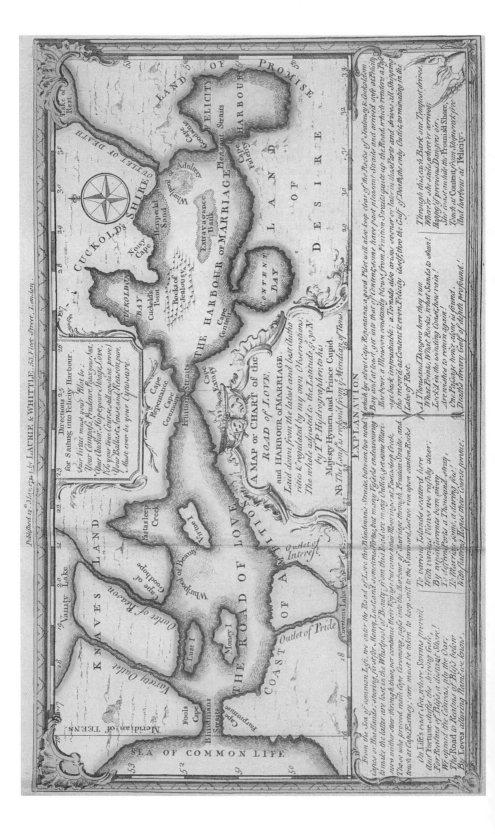

7

Spaces of erotic delight

༒

Karen Harvey

Now bound with a copy of the erotic book *A Voyage to Lethe* (1741) is the coloured engraving 'A Map or Chart of the Road of Love, and Harbour of Marriage' (Figure 7.1). The map, shaped on the Mediterranean, is designed to convey the perils and profits of courtship and marriage, and ostensibly to provide viewers with directions to reach 'Felicity Harbour'. Probably produced in the final decade of the eighteenth century, the date on the map has been erased and replaced with '1741' in hand, reinforcing the correspondence it was believed to have with this particular book. The map is a visual rendition of the journey that the fictional sea captain of this erotic text – Samuel Cock – recounts in the book, and, in particular, the engraving mirrors the cartographic approach that Sam adopts to sea and land. Nearing 'the Gulph of Venus', he enjoys a vantage point from which he 'commanded the charming Circumference of Buttock-Land'. He then travels further across 'a delightful Ivory Plain, which is terminated one way by two lovely rising Hills . . . and the other by a thick Grove of Trees, shading a Valley'. Moving along this valley, he reached the place called 'Beth-Eden' at its furthest end, before finally entering the gulf.[1] In this erotic text, of course, Lethe was not simply a place, but also a female body. The movement from left to right across 'A Map or Chart of the Road of Love' – from the 'Sea of Common Life' through 'Fruition Straights' to 'Felicity Harbour' – mirrored Sam's description of his journey across, through and into Lethe.

Why were the map and the travel book suitable models for erotic depictions of sex? Erotica shrouded bodies in metaphor and depicted sexual

facing] 7.1 'A map or chart of the road of love, and harbour of marriage' (*c.* 1781), insert in *A Voyage to Lethe* (1741). (By Permission of the British Library: Cup.1001.c.4)

activity with deferral and silence, and in part the map and the travel book provided effective means of disguise for erotic authors. But these writers were also firmly embedded in eighteenth-century print culture, and the combination of the book and the engraved print in *A Voyage to Lethe* serve as clues to how depictions of sex and sexual relations were shaped by geographical knowledge and its modes of expression. The image clearly adopted a common form of geographical expression in the map and the text aped popular accounts of voyages. These geographical modes permeated widely. Eighteenth-century fiction and travel literature were closely related. Fiction used the itinerary as a narrative form, and in much writing narrative was conceived 'as spatial design'.[2] Novelists also responded to famous voyages by writing their own travels.[3] But the depiction of the experiences of sex and female bodies as spatial experiences was also part of a broader spatial approach to women. Indeed, the category of gender is indispensable to understanding spatial knowledge: sexual difference, gender and sexuality were cast into spatial forms and relations in space. Geographical knowledge and its modes of expression were linked to other practices of viewing. It has been noted that 'geographical knowledge was an active part of Enlightenment knowledge', and erotic authors were skilled at drawing on new knowledge and its practices.[4] The combination of 'A Map or Chart of the Road of Love' with a description of a landscape to represent the female body alluded to other forms of mapping bodies, notably in science and medicine. Michel de Certeau has argued that the mapping mode was central to modern scientific knowledge, and to the power that such knowledge could wield. This stood in contrast to the itinerary or story mode, which was dominant in imaginative literature.[5] In the eighteenth century, however, the map/itinerary dichotomy does not correspond to science/literature. As Matthew Edney has argued, the 'linear route of the geographical traveller' emphasised by reconnaissance, and 'the systematic conceptualization and description of discrete areas across the earth's surface' entailed in mapping, are distinguishable but interdependent aspects of Enlightenment geographical knowledge.[6] In erotica, narrative leads smoothly to mapping with hardly a shift in register.

Power is an important theme of recent discussions of geographical knowledge and its practices, particularly of cartography.[7] In erotica, related modes of expression also conveyed gendered associations of power. In metaphorical descriptions of sex, the movement of the male narrator/viewer progressed from a position above the stationary female body, across and then into the body. The implied movement of men in these descriptions thus transformed from a cartographic viewpoint into a position akin to a medical examination or geographical exploration. These patterns of movement shaped sexual encounters. The chapter argues that forms of geographical or spatial knowledge facilitated certain forms of gendered, inequitable relations. Certain patterns of male movement were associated with the quest for knowledge and the assertion of force. Notions of male movement and female immobility permeated erotic material, and these gendered patterns of movement mutated into male force and female submission. Moreover, these gendered rules shaped both imagined and actual encounters. Erotic authors drew on contemporary geographical knowledge and approaches to space in their discussions of sex, sexuality and gender, conveying gendered power relations.

WRITING EROTICA

Female bodies in erotica – the type of body that featured most often – were frequently described in such a way that laid them out for the reader. When described as bodies rather than as landscapes, for example, this was achieved by listing distinct body parts in quick succession. In one poem,

> the girl was wond'rous fair,
> Black were her eyes, and brown her hair;
> Upon her cheeks sat blooming youth,
> And charming was her little mouth:
> Uncover'd was her lovely breast,
> That swell'd, as wanted to be prest.[8]

While each description stressed different aspects of bodies, the manner in which they were listed was extremely common. Another woman was a collage of delightful parts:

> Her hair, that was as raven black,
> Hung o'er her shoulders and her back;
> Her breasts were like the driven snow,
> On which her nipples warmly glow;
> Her arm, her waist, her legs, her thighs,
> The Squire beheld with wond'ring eyes.[9]

The quick-fire naming of body parts forged the semblance of complete female bodies. Descriptions of men lacked the sheer range of body parts, the lucid details of brilliant colours, gentle contours, graceful shapes and sensuous textures. These depictions rarely displayed the vividness of descriptions of female bodies, and underlined size and strength alone. Most importantly, descriptions of male bodies spotlighted very small areas of the body.[10]

In contrast, descriptions of female bodies gave some semblance of a whole woman, whose individual parts blended into one harmonious whole. The narrator of A Description of the Temple of Venus (1726) imagined a woman who visited him in a dream, explaining that although 'each distinct feature was not exactly regular . . . the whole was surprisingly beautiful'.[11] A second man described his lover in a similar way: 'She has a lovely Shape, a majestick, but modest Air; a piercing Eye, that will soon look yielding: Features exactly suited to each other.'[12] The concern was for the whole body, rather than distinct parts. One fictional female's description of herself at the age of fifteen seems to have been founded on similar exacting requirements:

> I was already above the middle stature, with a fair skin, clear sparkling black eyes, a well-shaped nose, pouting ruby lips, regular white teeth, and an agreeable dimple in my cheek; my hair was of a dark brown, which flowed in ringlets down a neck that was taper and well-shaped; an easy fall of the shoulders took off, in some degree, from that plumpness before, which is uncommon at my age; my shape was not remarkably slender, but proportioned to my body, and my legs and feet, which were particularly genteel, received grace from an easy unaffected air I was naturally possessed of; my hand and arm, already formed, were of the number of those which painters so attentively imitate.[13]

Moving from head to toe, women's bodies were transformed into agreeable and proportionate collections of separate parts. Such descriptions furnished the male narrators and readers with a view which enabled them to 'take in' the whole female body. Like maps, these descriptions allowed readers to glide across the landscape of female bodies.

Importantly, descriptions of female bodies often transported the reader from the top of the body to the bottom, ending with a descent into the body. At this point, architectural metaphors which envisaged bodies as collections of parts coalesced with topographical metaphors, which portrayed bodies being viewed, traversed and entered. The swift movement across the surface of a body was most pronounced in those texts which employed an extended metaphor of land for the body. Male bodies were occasionally portrayed in terms of land, but these descriptions did not conclude with a descent into the body.[14] In contrast, in the poem *Consummation* (1741), Venus tempted Adonis by asking him to 'o'er all these various Charms unbounded rove' before inviting him across and into her body:

> In these fair Locks, that o'er my Neck incline,
> Behold the Tendrils of the wanton Vine;
> In those soft Breasts you press, the Hills are seen,
> And the low Valley in the Space between;
> Thence see the Plain, the level Lawn extend,
> In sweet Declension see the Margin bend;
> There Ever-fruitful, pregnant with Delight,
> The Moss-grown Fountain courts the roving Sight.[15]

At the close of the century, this 'roving sight' was still being satisfied, and readers could be whisked across a woman's neck, breasts, waist, legs and arms, before resting in the darkened area of her genitalia.[16]

The implied movement of the narrator and the reader in these descriptions was reminiscent of the position of the artist in much contemporary writing on landscape and gardens. The picturesque mode transformed the way the landscape was described, changing the imaginative position of the author, artist, observer or reader. In some picturesque visual and written culture, a high position was replaced by a low position, in which the spectator had the feeling of 'moving through rather than surveying' the landscape, and even of being submerged or 'enveloped'.[17] In erotic descriptions, the spotlight moved across the surface of bodies in a fashion parallel to the way in which these contemporary writers on land moved across their landscapes. Readers were given a reconnoitre of the body from above, as they were invited to 'o'er her neck take nimble flight', or 'to range'.[18] But this position was quickly transformed as the description would skate over the body, traversing it through a horizontal movement over the surface. Ultimately, an entry into the body was made as the description shifted and gave the sense of moving down vertically.

The descriptions of female bodies in *The Fruit-Shop* (1765) switched between envisaging them as large areas of land to be viewed aerially or cartographically, and as smaller patches to travel through and into. In 'A description of the garden wherein the first fruit tree stood', the author proposed to proceed in the manner of 'strenuous naturalists' by giving 'a geographical delineation of that chosen and happy spot'.[19] Though choosing not to employ such a method, he carved up the world into continents, assessing which area had experienced the fruit-shop (the male genitalia) first. Describing female bodies as Asia, 'Africk', Europe and America, the author conjured images of maps.[20] Soon, however, the female body was transformed into a garden that seduced and teased the viewer with surprises: 'the raptured mind was in a manner lost, while it enjoyed the sweet variety, and strayed through such windings of successive wonders'.[21] This description was akin to the erotic manipulation of sight in eighteenth-century gardens. A series of concealments and revelations teased the viewer, such that these gardens have been likened to a striptease.[22] The movement of the narrator or reader in eighteenth-century erotica echoed this sense of moving through, of being enveloped and teased by, the landscape.

The places in which erotic explorers ended their wanderings through and into the landscape often took the form of grottoes and groves.[23] In contrast to seventeenth-century grottoes that were often built inside houses, eighteenth-century grottoes were commonly situated in gardens.[24] They were envisaged as a crucial component of a new style of garden experience, one less regimented than in previous centuries and in which 'many layers only gradually unfold'.[25] Grottoes were also thought to express the enduring relationship between culture and nature: 'Art imitating and surpassing nature' was a theme which endured in the history of the grotto.[26] By the eighteenth century, however, the relationship had shifted: 'now the wonders of nature were to supercede those of art, at least in theory'.[27] In accordance with such changes in garden design, the grottoes in eighteenth-century erotica were apparently naturally occurring. Women's genitalia were inviting, shaded recesses and snug, moist caves: 'a dark, tho' pleasant, Way', the 'mossy spot', and 'Love's Grotto'.[28]

In frequently presenting women's bodies as grottoes, eighteenth-century authors compounded women with nature. And in depicting men exploring these places of nature, these authors can be situated in the tradition described by Genevieve Lloyd: '[r]ational knowledge has been construed as a transcending, transformation or control of natural forces, and the feminine has been associated with what rational knowledge transcends, dominates or simply leaves behind'.[29] Mark Wigley has proffered a similar gendered interpretation of classical architecture, in which 'the actual body that is being composed, the material being shaped, is a woman ... Man is a cultural construction which emerges from the control of the feminine'.[30] As Carole Fabricant has observed, gardens were personified as women, and were to be 'controlled and possessed' by male gardeners, designers and writers.[31] The depictions of women in erotica as constructions of parts and as landscapes to be viewed, traversed and entered should be understood in these contexts: the feminine was matter to be explored.[32]

Descriptions of women's bodies as land did not always incorporate a mapping and controlling male gaze, and, as I have argued elsewhere, 'feminine spaces were to be neither undermined nor conquered'.[33] These descriptions were, however, power-laden. This can be demonstrated by placing them in the context of other descriptions of women's bodies and considering the various approaches to space incorporated in explorations of female land and bodies. *A New Description of Merryland* (1741), by Charles Stretser, was ostensibly written as a corrective to the work of 'modern Geographers', and to atlases, globes and modern histories, which neglected to describe this country.[34] The book begins with an overview of the female body of 'Merryland'. The first chapter gives an account 'OF THE NAME OF MERRYLAND AND WHENCE IT IS SO CALLED', while the second chapter adopts an aerial approach, concerning 'OF THE SITUATION OF MERRYLAND'.[35] Here, Merryland was placed within a 'continent', and the type of territory flanking it, and its longitude and latitude were all reported.[36] The focus later transforms in the chapter 'OF THE AIR, SOIL, RIVERS, CANALS, &C', in which the reader learned of the lake 'VSCA' (vesica, or bladder) and the deep 'canal' (vagina) that ran through the middle of the land.[37] It was in this chapter that the author described the journey along the canal 'up to the Country', passing through the labia, the nymphae and hymen.[38] The remaining chapters relayed details of the inhabitants, the products and commodities, the rarities, the government, and the religion of the land, before concluding with a lengthy description of penetrative sex conveyed in the tale of the author's attempt to bring his boat to anchor in the harbour of Merryland.

The author confirmed the geographical approach when he apologised for not providing a map, claiming it would have been too expensive. He did, however, refer readers to a 'map' in a book by 'Mr. Moriceau', though quickly confessed that the model invented by 'Sir. R. M.' gave 'a better Idea of MERRYLAND than can possibly be done by the best Maps, or any written Description'.[39] The model referred to was a wax model of the female body by physician Richard Manningham, who gave lectures on midwifery and founded the first of London's lying-in hospitals in 1739.[40] The map, from Francis Mauriceau's treatise on female health and childbirth, was almost certainly one of the engravings which depicted female torsos splayed open (Figure 7.2).

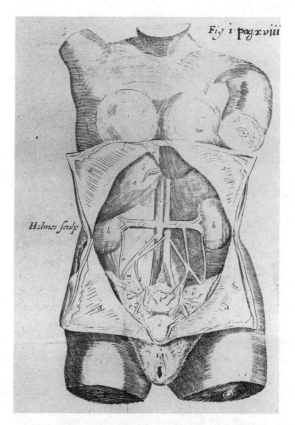

7.2 'A female torso and reproductive organs', from Francis Mauriceau, *The Diseases of Women with Child* (1736). (By Permission of the British Library: 1484.cc.20)

Geographical and anatomical approaches collapsed together here. In a later satirical critique of his own book, the author of *A New Description of Merryland* criticised Mauriceau for demonstrating 'but very little Skill in Anatomy in his description of these several Parts'. He denounced the medical 'Map of Merryland' as a 'baudy-Print' designed to entertain his readers, 'rather than to give them any useful Instruction'.[41] But such medical maps were well suited to an erotic book such as *A New Description of Merryland*. Allowing the viewer to peer past the flesh and into the body, they gave the impression of descending into the corpse. Just as the author of *A New Description of Merryland* described the female body as land, so Mauriceau had wielded this metaphor in denouncing other writers on female health as comparable to 'those Geographers who give us the Description of Countries they never saw, and (as they imagine) a perfect Account of them'.[42] Languages of geography and anatomy in descriptions of female bodies were used by erotic and medical writers alike.

A 'new preoccupation with depth' infused the texts and practices of eighteenth-century science and medicine. Information was imagined to be 'based on looking deeply into and thereby intellectually mastering nature'.[43] By constructing 'the route to knowledge as a form of looking deep into the body', this model derived a significant erotic dimension.[44] Scenes of inspection of female bodies in erotic material – which allied a descent into female bodies with the attainment of knowledge – were clearly sexualised encounters. A series of passages in *A Description of the Temple of Venus* (1726), for example, recounted the display and unveiling of groups of women of various nationalities in turn in front of the male narrator, and his assessments of each group.[45] This theme could also take the form of the classical story of the Judgement of Paris, in which Paris chose the most beautiful of three goddesses. In 'The Rival Beauties' (1770), for example, a man likened himself to Paris, describing the way in which three women 'Display'd their charms before my critic eyes'.[46] At other times such events were conveyed through scientific metaphors. In *The Fruit-Shop* (1765), for example, women were likened to comets which endured 'the prying power of our auxiliary glass tubes, telescopes, &c'.[47] Indeed, in *Did you ever see Such Damned Stuff?* (1760), the King restrained his wife forcibly and inspected her naked body with a magnifying glass.[48] As with anatomical practices, botanical and geographical investigation promised to yield knowledge. Several botanists, the author of a book on the female 'plant' wrote, had long tried 'to dive deep into the secret qualities of this unfathomable Shrub'.[49] Similarly, as the 'curious Enquirer' into the land of Lethe stated, being 'ambitious of transmitting Materials to Posterity for the Benefit of future Historians and Geographers', he resolved 'to make it my Business this Voyage to dive into everything worth knowing'.[50] A range of intellectual endeavours – writing about the landscape and garden design, geography, botany, science and medicine – associated an exploration of depth with the production of specialised knowledge and the expression of power. Curiosity and 'prying power' were gendered and sexualised preoccupations.

Descriptions of female bodies allowed narrators and readers to explore and enter these bodies, whether as land, plant, sea, grotto or corpse. These descriptions also rendered female bodies stationary objects of exploration and this asymmetrical capacity for movement emerged again in depictions of liaisons between male and female characters. Of course, both female and male characters moved in erotica. But women were typically associated with stasis, waiting for men in an exposed and vulnerable state. Princess Tricolora prepared for sex with her lover Prince Discreet by placing herself 'on one of those long low chairs so pure and convenient for Pleasure to give Virtue a fall, and lay sprawling on her back'.[51] In *A Chinese Tale* (*c*. 1740), Cham-Yam reclined on a sofa to engage in the masturbation which prompted the climax to the poem, while one woman in *The Prostitutes of Quality* (1757) was found by her lover in a 'languishing Posture, lying on a Couch, all undressed'.[52] The collection *Forty Select Poems* (1753) contained a series of encounters in which a man approached an immobile woman. One woman was discovered by a 'youthful swain' lying on the grass with her petticoat and gown over her head, before they had sex; another man found a woman apparently asleep, clambered on to her bed, and 'began to downright sinning'; while a nun's pregnancy came about because 'father Stiffrump' entered her room as she lay naked on the bed.[53] Poems in the later collection *The Festival of Love* (1770) depicted Palemon discovering Phyllira reclining on a couch, and Lubin approaching Lydia as she 'on a bank reclining lay'.[54]

It is striking that many visual images in these books employed similar gendered codes of movement. In the frontispiece to *The Surprize* (1739) (Figure 7.3), Timante had bounded up the stairs and entered Araminta's room where she lay prostrate on the bed.[55] Several of the images inserted in *A Voyage to Lethe* were remarkably similar. In 'A Fine Subject on the Carpet', for example, the woman lay prostrate on the floor, and her outstretched arm could have indicated a request for help, or an invitation to the standing man to join her.[56] Such depictions of women reclining and awaiting men contextualise Stretser's reference to Richard Manningham's wax model in *A New Description of Merryland*. Late eighteenth-century wax anatomical models of female figures invariably reclined on lush cushions in 'passive, yet sexually inviting poses', in stark contrast to wax models of male bodies, which were 'upright muscle men'.[57]

The women portrayed waiting for men resembled not just wax models, but statuesque figures. In one episode in *The Fruit-Shop*, a woman retired to her house 'to be there in readiness for his reception', and was positioned

7.3 'Timante enters Araminta's room': frontispiece to
The Surprize (1739). (By Permission of the British Library:
PC.19.a.14)

so that she became the statuesque centrepiece to the marble artwork of
the bed:

> She was placed on a bed of the most elegant, as well as costly workmanship;
> all around it were fixed Cupids of Parian marble, each connected to the other
> by flowery wreaths. On Alexander's entering the apartment, she by a bound of
> affected emotion, so contrived matters that part of the bed-covering was thrown
> off, and he had so full a view of her well-formed limbs, &c. that he could no
> longer refrain.[58]

An almost indistinguishable scenario greeted Anthony as he entered Cleopatra's room for the first time. Again surrounded by marble Cupids, this bed was also covered with a painted canopy depicting Mars and Venus. All was arranged so that as Cleopatra undressed, the marble Cupids became animated, and the face of the painted Venus 'was suddenly vermillioned over with a blush of rivalship'.[59] In this coordinated performance, distinctions between the painted, sculpted and human figures were elided. It was appropriate that female characters should be presented as statues. In the realm of art and the garden such carved female figures were gazed upon by connoisseurs – men whose artistic explorations and investigations gleaned them elite knowledge of considerable status.[60] Such men were likely to have been a large constituency of the readership of erotica, a readership that required (so the texts implied) some knowledge of novels and poetry, classical mythology, biblical tales, theology, ancient and modern world history, European conflicts, ancient medicine, recent science and contemporary quackery, botany, natural history and reports of voyages and expeditions.

Women did not always remain still in erotic encounters. The men who discovered them often proceeded to move the bodies of their female lovers around. Most encounters closely resembled the experience wished for by one man:

> My arms! that shall, with eager haste,
> Encircle now your slender waist;
> Now round your neck be careless hung,
> And now o'er all your frame be slung:
> About your limbs my limbs will twine,
> And lay your glowing cheek to mine;
> Close to my broader, manlier chest,
> I'll press thy firm, proud-swelling breast;
> My murm'ring tongue shall speak my bliss,
> Shall court your yielding lips to kiss;
> Each kiss with thousands I'll repay,
> And almost suck your breath away;
> A thousand more you then shall give,
> And then a thousand more receive;
> In transport half dissolv'd we'll lie,
> Venting our wishes in a sigh![61]

The contrast between the perpetual movement of the man and the stationary figure of the woman who he moved around and over was striking. This woman is absolutely still apart from returning kisses and being pressed by her male lover.

The actions of men who manoeuvred their lovers before having sex could lack violence: one man who came across a female friend in the woods 'gently laid' her on the grass and had sex.[62] In other descriptions, a man stole into

Sally's room and 'lay her on the bed', while another man spied a woman and 'laid her down, amongst the dew'.[63] On most occasions, however, this act of manoeuvring women's bodies just prior to sex was described in terms which suggested a degree of force. Maria Brown's first lover followed her to her bed-chamber and, as Maria described it, 'threw me upon the bed', while another virgin told how a man 'flew into the room' and 'threw me down on the bed'.[64] In the poem 'Caelia Enjoy'd in Her Sleep', many of these themes converged. The male narrator, whose previous attempts to have sex with Caelia had been scuppered by her 'stubborn will', whispered to the sleeping woman and interpreted her rising breast and the lack of 'rude Alarms' as the permission he had sought. He eagerly won the 'Fort', noting her consent even though she was also described as 'insensible and dead'.[65] The codes of female immobility and male mobility transformed seamlessly into female vulnerability and male aggression.

READING EROTICA

These gendered codes of movement governed both imagined and actual encounters. The ways in which literary, geographical, scientific and medical modes of approaching the spaces of women's bodies shaped actual encounters between men and women can be observed through a brief consideration of the reading of erotica.[66]

Within erotic texts, readers of erotica were imagined to be female readers situated alone in private spaces. Such was the association of women and suggestive material, that a pornographic library was described as 'the Female-Classics'.[67] In numerous erotic stories, women who masturbated or who became sexually responsive were depicted as having read suggestive material.[68] Visual depictions of female readers confirmed the image of the sole female reader absorbed in the erotic text. The engraving 'The Female Lover' in *The Cupid* (1736) (Figure 7.4) displayed such a female reader in this way accompanied by the rhyming couplet: 'Plays, Poems & Romances melt ye Heart/ And Love finds easy entrance for his Dart'.[69]

Just as women were stationary and reclining figures waiting for men in erotic narratives, so women readers were often reclined and susceptible to the temptations and persuasions of print. These associations corresponded to widely-held anxieties about reading. The image of the reading woman operated as 'a key icon' through which the dangers of new kinds of private and intimate reading were expressed.[70] Reading was considered a potential threat to both body and mind in the eighteenth century. In situating the reading of erotica in private, female-only environments, authors of erotica seemed to insist that it was women that were susceptible to erotic literature and the particular perils of solitary reading.

The Female Lover.

Plays Poems & Romances melt y Heart.
And Love finds easy entrance for his Dart.

7.4 'The female lover', from *The Cupid* (1736). (By Permission of the British Library: 991.c.35)

This image of the vulnerable, solitary female reader within erotic texts contrasts with the reader at the centre of the model of reading manufactured by erotic authors and readers: a free-thinking, witty man situated in a homosocial environment. In some cases, this model also rendered this man a scientific, medical observer. The 'Beggar's Benison and Merryland' of Anstruther, Scotland, was an extreme form of male club, a notorious group which ran from 1732 well into the nineteenth century.[71] This libertine Scottish group was male, apart from female prostitutes who sometimes attended.[72] Erotic material formed an important component of this group's meetings, but the manner of reading was quite different to the solitary perusals of imaginary women. Members were required to read 'amorous' passages aloud during the initiation ceremony, and later in the meetings the men sang songs, recited toasts and bon mots, and read classic erotic texts. Poking fun at both the religious and medical men, they also read what they described as '[a]natomy and anatomical Bible texts': extracts from the Bible which referred to either sex or birth, or both.[73]

These men christened themselves devotees of 'our Celebrated Territories of MERRYLAND'.[74] In doing so they knowingly allied themselves to the textual conventions of treating and exploring women's bodies as land. The practices of these men were rendered more legitimate – and witty – by the way they echoed contemporary geographical books. As Percy Adams has explained, 'It was the age of gold for travellers, both real and imaginary. And, as a result, it was the age of opportunity for travel lies.'[75] Erotic authors mimicked such travel lies in many ways, for example, using prefaces which emphasised the truth and objectivity of the account.[76] Stretser's *A New Description of Merryland* defiantly told readers that he was only going to share with them information on the parts of the country that he had experienced, rather than 'amuse Mankind with the uncertain Guesses and fabulous Relations of idle Travellers'. His aim was to 'distinguish Truth from Fiction', because 'the World is no longer to be amused with the fabulous Relations of Travellers and Historians, any more than with the Dreams of Superstition and Enthusiasm'. '[R]elations monstrous and unnatural may please the Weak and Indolent,' he announced, 'but Truth and Nature only can satisfy the Wise.' As already mentioned, Stretser later satirised *A New Description of Merryland*, and one of his first accusations was that the book was a travel lie:

> The first Conception was owing to our Author's accidentally reading in Gordon's Geographical Grammer these Words, which Mr. Gordon uses in speaking of Holland, viz. 'the Country lying very low, it's Soil is naturally wet and fenny'. Ha! said he, the same may be said of a * * * * as well as of Holland; this Whim having once entered his Noddle, he resolved to pursue the Hint, and try how far he could run the Parallel; his wise Head fancied here was a fine Scope to ridicule the Geographers, so he sets to scribbling.[77]

In satirising such works, erotic readers demonstrated their wit and their knowledge. Erotica was multi-dimensional, and in this respect it had a double function. While reproducing ways of thinking and representing space that embodied gendered inequalities of power, these men may have reproduced the power relations expressed in and constituted by those practices. To some extent, however, the satirical and playful nature of the erotica and its contexts might work simultaneously to undermine those practices. Men involved in erotic culture certainly played with notions of myth and of truth and knowledge, blurring the distinction between empirical knowledge and imaginary knowledge so important to geographical exploration.[78] This was also, of course, the age of the Grand Tour, and these men manufactured a particular version of the idea that topography should yield both pleasure and improvement.[79]

The pretensions of these men to improvement was clearest in their adoption of practices of viewing women's bodies as medical objects of inspection. As noted, these men claimed to have read '[a]natomy and anatomical Bible texts', but reading aloud was one ritual among many for the Beggar's Benison. They sometimes had sex with prostitutes, and on one occasion in 1734 there were '24 present and 4 Novices tested and frigged'.[80] At other times, men inspected the bodies of women paid to display themselves. The records of the society report: 'One Feminine Gender, 17, was hired for One Sovereign, fat and well-developed. She stripped in the Closet, nude; and was allowed to come in with face half-covered. None was permitted to speak or touch her. She spread wide upon a seat, first before and then behind.' The full description of this latter event – in which 'every Knight passed in turn and surveyed the Secrets of Nature' – was suggestive of attempts to intellectualise this voyeuristic and supposedly deeply physical enjoyment.[81] These men were rendering their appreciation of women's bodies into a pseudo-scientific exercise. Actual women were being inspected – or reported as having been inspected – in the same way as imaginary women were in the texts.

Just as some actual women were treated as imaginary women – albeit in exceptional circumstances – so other men explored actual space in the same sexualised way as texts explored feminine landscapes. Sir Francis Dashwood presided over the meetings of the notorious Hell Fire Club. His West Wycombe garden, in a Buckinghamshire valley, was designed to represent a female body. It was replete with 'two little mounds, each surmounted by a bed of bright flowers' which shot streams of milky water into the air, and 'a triangle of dense shrubbery' from which gushed a stream of water. A Temple of Venus, built in 1748, stood atop a mound at the centre of the garden.[82] Of course, Dashwood's garden was unusual if not unique, and may well have been shocking to many contemporaries. Similarly, although Tim Hitchcock has suggested that the practice of a woman stripping to reveal her genitalia was common at male clubs, many of the activities at the Beggar's Benison would have been anathema to powerful ideals of masculine politeness and gentility.[83] Indeed, it could be that an attempt to translate representational strategies towards female bodies into actual practices in meetings was a response to the restrictions of dominant modes of polite masculinity. Nevertheless, excess was limited not only by picturing men in the sociable and public (if exclusive) spaces of erotic reading, but by couching their practices in modes of geographical and scientific enquiry.

These modes gendered forms of erotic pleasure, but the patterns of movement expressed in geographical, medical and scientific modes of exploration were potent expressions of gendered power relations. In erotic narratives, male bodies were portrayed moving and acting in space and certain patterns of male movement were associated with the quest for knowledge and the assertion of force. In metaphorical descriptions of sex, the movement of the male narrator/viewer progressed from a position above the stationary female body, across and then into the body. The implied movement of men in these descriptions thus transformed a cartographic viewpoint into a position akin to a medical examination or geographical exploration. Notions of male movement and female immobility were again revealed in descriptions of men and women encountering one another prior to sex, in which women were depicted waiting for men. From explorations of stationary female bodies to encounters of some violence, the gendered patterns of movement which endorsed male movement and female immobility mutated into male force and female submission. Both in cases of implied movement in metaphorical descriptions and in depictions of male and female characters, male motion implied knowledge, power, independence and self-control. The ability to move both oneself, and a female lover, was constitutive of a man's masculinity: during one encounter, a man's motion was initiated precisely 'to shew he was a man'.[84] The movement of men in erotic texts contrasted sharply with the statuesque immobility of women. Gender and sexual difference was being shaped in large part by the associations and the navigations of space: the involvement of men in eighteenth-century erotic culture was grounded in their navigation, exploration and inspection of imaginary, metaphorical and material Maps of Love.

NOTES

My thanks to the audience at the Georgian Geographies conference, to Charlotte Grant, Mark Jenner, Roy Porter and, particularly, to Penelope J. Corfield, Miles Ogborn and Amanda Vickery.

1 Captain Samuel Cock [pseud.], *A Voyage to Lethe; By Capt. Samuel Cock; Sometime Commander of the Good Ship the Charming Sally. Dedicated to the Right Worshipful*

Adam Cock, Esq.; of Black-Mary's-Hole, Coney-Skin Merchant (London: J. Conybeare, 1741), 27–30.

2 R. Varey, *Space and the Eighteenth-Century English Novel* (Cambridge: Cambridge University Press, 1990), 4.

3 P. G. Adams, *Travellers and Travel Liars, 1660–1800* (New York: Dover Books, 1980), 224.

4 C. W. J. Withers and D. N. Livingstone, 'Introduction: on geography and Enlightenment', in D. N. Livingstone and C. W. J. Withers (eds), *Geography and Enlightenment* (Chicago: University of Chicago Press, 1999), 1–32, quote on p. 13.

5 M. de Certeau, *The Practice of Everyday Life*, trans. S. Rendall (Berkeley: University of California Press, 1984), 199–21.

6 M. H. Edney, 'Reconsidering Enlightenment geography and map making: reconnaissance, mapping, archive', in Withers and Livingstone (eds), *Geography and Enlightenment*, 165–98, quote on p. 175.

7 *Ibid.*; see also J. Black, *Maps and Politics* (London: Reaktion, 1997), 11–28.

8 'The Chrystal Bottle', *Forty Select Poems, on Several Occasions, by the Right Honourable The Earl of —— (London: no publication details, c. 1753)*, 10.

9 'The Squire', *The Festival of Love; Or, a collection of Cytherean Poems*, sixth edition (London: M. Smith, c. 1770), 231.

10 See, for example, 'The Ink Bottle', *Forty Select Poems*, 47; 'The Filthy Beast', *Forty Select Poems*, 124.

11 [Anonymous], *A Description of the Temple of Venus, at Cnidus* (London: Tho. Edlin, 1726), 36.

12 *Ibid.*, 39.

13 [Anonymous], *Genuine Memoirs of the Celebrated Miss Maria Brown. Exhibiting the Life of a Courtezan in the Most Fashionable Scenes of Dissipation*, 2 volumes (London: I. Allcock, 1766), Vol. 1, 63–4.

14 See, for example, *Voyage to Lethe*, 8.

15 [Anonymous], *Consummation: Or, the Rape of Adonis* (London: E. Curll, 1741), 8–9.

16 'The Bridal Night', *The Pleasures that Please on Reflection. Selected from the Album of Venus* (London: W. Holland, 1789), 47.

17 M. Andrews, *The Search for the Picturesque: Landscape Aesthetics and Tourism in Britain, 1760–1800* (Aldershot: Scolar Press, 1989), 61; J. D. Hunt, *The Figure in the Landscape: Poetry, Painting, and Gardening during the Eighteenth Century* (Baltimore, MD: Johns Hopkins University Press, 1976), 228, 247.

18 'The Bridal Night', 47; 'Venus and Love', *The Bacchanalian Magazine and Cyprian Enchantress. Composed Principally of New and Convivial and Amorous Songs* (London: H. Lemoine, 1793), 15.

19 [Anonymous], *The Fruit-Shop. A Tale*, 2 volumes (London: C. Moran, 1765), Vol. 1, 19.

20 *Ibid.*, Vol. 1, 22.

21 *Ibid.*, Vol. 1, 42.

22 S. Pugh, *Garden–Nature–Language* (Manchester: Manchester University Press, 1988), 109. Pugh is inspired by Barthes's notion of the erotic: see R. Barthes, *The Pleasure of the Text* (Oxford: Blackwell, 1990).

23 These places of female bodies were compounded with the places in which sex took place: women's bodies were indistinguishable from sexualised locations. See K. Harvey, 'Gender, space and modernity in eighteenth-century England: a place called sex', *History Workshop Journal*, 51 (2001), 158–79.

24 B. Jones, *Follies and Grottoes* (London: Constable, 1974), 145.

25 N. Miller, *Heavenly Caves: Reflections on the Garden Grotto* (London: Allen & Unwin, 1983), 78.

26 *Ibid.*, 10.

27 *Ibid.*, 77.

28 [Anonymous], *Little Merlin's Cave*, fourth edition (London: T. Read, 1737), 6; 'The Girdle of Venus Unbuckled', *Festival of Love*, 40; *Pleasures That Please*, 8; Harvey, 'Gender, space and modernity', 165–6.

29 G. Lloyd, *The Man of Reason: 'Male' and 'Female' in Western Philosophy* (London: Methuen, 1984), 2.

30 M. Wigley, 'Untitled: the housing of gender', in B. Colomina (ed.), *Sexuality and Space* (New York: Princeton Architectural Press, 1992), 327–89, quote on p. 357.

31 C. Fabricant, 'Binding and dressing nature's loose tresses: the ideology of Augustan landscape design', *Studies in Eighteenth-Century Culture*, 8 (1979), 109–35, quote on p. 131.

32 By the end of the eighteenth century, however, the situation was more complicated. Two views of men's involvement in landscape taste had emerged in Gothic writing, 'aristocratic, homosocial, and libertine on the one hand, professional, heterosocial, and polite on the other': see S. J. Daniels, 'Gothic gallantry: Humphry Repton, Lord Byron, and the sexual politics of landscape gardening', in M. Conan (ed.), *Bourgeois and Aristocratic Cultural Encounters in Garden Art, 1550–1850* (Washington DC: Dumbarton Oaks Research Library and Collection, 2001), 311–36, quote on p. 312.

33 Harvey, 'Gender, space and modernity', 174.

34 Roger Pheuquewell [pseud., alias Thomas Stretser], *A New Description of Merryland. Containing a Topographical, Geographical, and Natural History of that Country*, seventh edition (London and Bath: J. Leake, and E. Curll, 1741), xi–xii.

35 *Ibid.*, 1, 3.

36 *Ibid.*, 3.

37 *Ibid.*, 11.

38 *Ibid.*, 15–17.

39 *Ibid.*, 18. The model was described as 'the curious Model or Machine' or 'Artificial Matrix'. See [Thomas Stretser], *Merryland Displayed: Or, Plagiarism, Ignorance, and Impudence Detected. Being Observations upon a Pamphlet Intituled A New Description of Merryland* (Bath: J. Leake, 1741), 36.

40 A. Wilson, *The Making of Man-Midwifery: Childbirth in England, 1660–1770* (London: University College London Press, 1995), 85, 114–16.

41 [Stretser], *Merryland Displayed*, 35–6.

42 F. Mauriceau, *The Diseases of Women with Child: As also the Best Means of Helping them in Natural and Unnatural Labours*, seventh edition (London: T. Cox and J. Clarke, 1736), viii.

43 L. Jordanova, *Sexual Visions: Images of Gender in Science and Medicine Between the Eighteenth and Nineteenth Centuries* (London and New York: Harvester Wheatsheaf, 1989), 57–8.

44 *Ibid.*, 50. The erotic element of this model of knowledge is discussed by Jordanova between pp. 87–110.

45 [Anonymous] *Description of the Temple of Venus*, 17–26.

46 *Festival of Love*, 29; see also *Arbor Vitae: Or, the Natural History of the Tree of Life* (London: E. Hill, 1741), 20 and *Forty Select Poems*, 31.

47 *Fruit-Shop*, Vol. 1, 68.

48 [Anonymous], *Did you ever see Such Damned Stuff? Or, So-Much-the-Better. A Story without Head or Tail, Wit or Humor* (London: C. G. Seyffert, 1760), 139–44.

49 [Anonymous], *Natural History of the Frutex Vulvaria* (London: E. Hill, 1741), 11.

50 *Voyage to Lethe*, 74.

51 *Did you ever see Such Damned Stuff?*, 102.

52 W. Hatchett, *A Chinese Tale. Written originally by that prior of China the facetious Sou ma Quang* (London: J. Cooper, *c.* 1740), 19, 25; [Anonymous], *The Prostitutes of Quality; Or, Adultery a-la-mode. Being Authentic and Genuine Memoirs of Several Persons of the Highest Quality* (London: J. Cooke and J. Coote, 1757), 170.

53 'The Raven', 185; 'The Chaplain', 45; 'The Nun', 133, all in *Forty Select Poems*.

54 'The Girdle of Venus', 31–5; 'Epigram', 5, both in *Festival of Love*.

55 See [Anonymous], *The Surprize: Or, the Gentleman turn'd Apothecary. A Tale written originally in French Prose; afterwards translated into Latin; and from thence now versified in Hudibrastics* (London: Printed and sold by the booksellers of London and Westminster, 1739), the description is on p. 7.

56 For a discussion of this and other images, see K. Harvey, *Bodies and Gender in Eighteenth-Century English Erotic Culture* (Cambridge: Cambridge University Press, forthcoming).

57 Jordanova, *Sexual Visions*, 44–5.

58 *Fruit-Shop*, Vol. 1, 55–6.

59 *Ibid.*, Vol. 1, 68–9.

60 J. Barrell, 'The dangerous goddess: masculinity, prestige and the aesthetic in early eighteenth-century Britain', in J. Barrell, *The Birth of Pandora and the Division of Knowledge* (Basingstoke: Macmillan, 1992), 63–87; J. Brewer, *The Pleasures of the Imagination: English Culture in the Eighteenth Century* (London: HarperCollins, 1997), 252–87; A. Bermingham, 'The aesthetics of ignorance: the accomplished woman in the culture of connoisseurship', *The Oxford Art Journal*, 16 (1993), 3–20, on the male viewing of women in the home.

61 'To Cynthia', *Festival of Love*, 18.

62 'The Apocrypha', *Forty Select Poems*, 130.

63 'The Black Ey'd Maid', *Bacchanalian Magazine*, 100; 'The Chrystal Bottle', *Forty Select Poems*, 12.

64 *Genuine Memoirs of . . . Miss Maria Brown*, Vol. 1, 117; 'The Maidenhead', *Bacchanalian Magazine*, 45–6.

65 'Caelia enjoy'd in her sleep', in Tim Merriman [pseud.], *The St James's Miscellany, Or the Citizen's Amusement* (London: T. Payne, T. Ashley, A. Dodd, and E. Nutt, *c.* 1730), 14–15.

66 For more on this model, see Harvey, *Bodies and Gender*, chapter 2.

67 [Charles Cotton], 'Erotopolis; Or, of the Situation of Bettyland', in Philo-Brittanniae [pseud.], *The Potent Ally: Or, Succours from Merryland*, second edition (Paris: printed by direction of the author, 1741), 30–1.

68 [William Hatchett], *A Chinese Tale* (London: J. Cooper, *c.* 1740), 15–6; *Did You ever see Such Damned Stuff?*, 20.

69 [Anonymous], *The Cupid. A collection of Love Songs, in Twelve Parts. Suited to Twelve different Sorts of LOVERS, VIZ.* (London: J. Chrichley, for R. Dodsley, 1736), facing p. 1.

70 J. Pearson, *Women's Reading in Britain, 1750–1835: A Dangerous Recreation* (Cambridge: Cambridge University Press, 1999), 219; P. de Bolla, *The Discourse of the Sublime* (Oxford: Basil Blackwell, 1989), 249–50.

71 P. Wagner, *Eros Revived: Erotica of the Enlightenment in England and France* (London: Secker & Warburg, 1988), 58.

72 [Anonymous], *Records of the Most Ancient and Puissant Order of the Beggar's Benison and Merryland, Anstruther* (Anstruther: For private distribution, 1892), 5–6, 21–6. For a discussion of this club and its activities, see D. Stevenson, *The Beggar's Benison: Sex Clubs of Enlightenment Scotland* (East Linton: Tuckwell Press, 2001).

73 *Records of the Most Ancient and Puissant Order of the Beggar's Benison*, 9–10.
74 *Ibid.*, 6.
75 Adams, *Travellers and Travel Liars*, 9; Edney, 'Reconsidering Enlightenment geography', 177–85.
76 On this practice in the travel lie genre, see Adams, *Travellers and Travel Liars*, 228–9.
77 [Stretser], *Merryland Displayed*, x.
78 J. L. Allen, 'Lands of myth, waters of wonder: the place of the imagination in the history of geographical exploration', in D. Lowenthal and M. J. Bowden (eds), *Geographies of the Mind: Essays in Historical Geosophy* (Oxford and New York: Oxford University Press, 1976), 42–53.
79 C. Chard, *Pleasure and Guilt on the Grand Tour: Travel Writing and Imaginative Geography, 1600–1830* (Manchester: Manchester University Press, 1999), 22–6.
80 *Records of the Most Ancient and Puissant Order of the Beggar's Benison*, 14.
81 *Ibid.*, 13.
82 D. P. Mannix, *The Hell Fire Club* (London: Four Square Books, 1961), 5; L. C. Jones, *The Clubs of the Georgian Rakes* (New York: Columbia University Press, 1942), 99–100; D. McCormick, *The Hell-Fire Club: The Story of the Amorous Knights of Wycombe* (London: Jarrolds, 1958), 120; B. Partridge, *A History of Orgies*, (London: Spring Books, 1966), 133–48; Miller, *Heavenly Caves*, 79. I am grateful to Anna Clark for bringing this point to my attention.
83 T. Hitchcock, *English Sexualities, 1700–1800* (Basingstoke: Macmillan, 1997), 22.
84 'The Filthy Beast', *Forty Select Poems*, 126.

8

Joseph Banks, mapping and the geographies of natural knowledge

ℰ

John Gascoigne

'WHAT IS ENLIGHTENMENT?'. The question that Kant set out to answer in the late eighteenth century continues to echo down the centuries as both modernists and postmodernists define themselves as either with or against the 'Enlightenment project' – a project that attempts to organise our knowledge of the world around universal canons of rationality and predictability. Yet, in the eighteenth century itself – in the very age of the Enlightenment – the establishment of such universal canons was a gradual and often contested process as local and traditional ways of understanding the world were challenged by more all-encompassing modes of thought.[1] The spread of Enlightenment values often depended more on a series of beachheads than on the advance of a continuous front. National institutions were sometimes impervious to Enlightenment values while local institutions and practices were reshaped to provide a terrain in which Enlightenment values could take root.[2]

It is this transformation of geographies of knowledge that is the theme of this chapter. What follows focuses on the case of Joseph Banks – a figure whose life and works were largely devoted to the task of promoting greater order and system, either in the natural sciences, in cartography, or in the workings of the British state. And yet, as a landed gentleman, he was rooted in a culture that gave particular status to local knowledge and to the country connections with which it was bound up. Banks's significance is linked, then, with the ways in which his promotion of the mapping of knowledge could operate on different scales and different projections: from the local to the national and thence to the imperial. As one who was very conscious of his dignity as a member of the landed elite, Banks represents, too, an ideal of genteel learning that was sympathetic to forms of knowledge that could be readily assimilated into that world of clubs and learned societies to which he naturally belonged. The corollary to this, however, was his opposition to the growth of more differentiated forms of knowledge based on disciplinary expertise. For Banks, the map of knowledge should be a general one without those specialised markers which would set apart regions of the world of learning as the domain of a select few.

BANKS AND ENCYCLOPAEDIC KNOWLEDGE

Banks's views on the need for knowledge to form part of the general culture of the governing classes were widely shared. Just as the eighteenth-century state with the active support of its Enlightenment-trained bureaucrats sought to reduce the role of rival jurisdictions – whether of the Church, the aristocracy, the guilds or the universities – so, too, the theorists of the Enlightenment aimed to bring all knowledge under a common banner. Claims to a separate space for knowledge derived from divine knowledge or even from traditional lore were eroded by an insistence on the interrelated character of all knowledge and its need to be exposed to public scrutiny.

One of the most characteristic features of the Enlightenment mentality was the encyclopaedia with its assumption that all forms of knowledge could be brought into a methodically organised synthesis. As Yeo has argued, the tensions between the convenience of an alphabetical organisation and the need to classify knowledge in terms of fundamental organisation were generally solved by establishing a prefatory map of knowledge.[3] This metaphor of a map of knowledge was an eighteenth-century commonplace. Francis Bacon, the great mentor of the encyclopaedists, had underlined the parallel between the conquest of geographical space and the conquest of knowledge with the frontispiece to his influential *Novum Organum* (1620) depicting the ship of learning sailing beyond the Pillars of Hercules, the traditional edge of the classical world. Maps were an embodiment of many of the central features of the Enlightenment: they were empirically based, scientifically organised, synthetic in the extent to which they drew together a diverse body of knowledge and they shed light on the dark corners of the globe: all goals shared by the encyclopaedists.

The encyclopaedists, however, keen to avoid the dogmatism of their seventeenth-century rationalising predecessors and still more that of the scholastics, were prepared to acknowledge that the form that the mapping of knowledge took could be, like the mapping of the world, a matter of convenience. What mattered was that there was some system or order, not that there was some absolute unassailable Truth. As D'Alembert wrote in the *Discours*

Preliminaire to the *Encyclopédie*, 'We may therefore figure to ourselves as many different Systems of Knowledge, as there are general Maps of different Projections: and each System may have some Advantage over the rest.'[4] What mattered for the encyclopaedists was that knowledge should be made available, not sheltered in the private domains of privileged corporations. Above all, knowledge should be tested by the extent to which it yielded fruit: there was no point debating its precise boundaries so long as knowledge could be put to practical effect by being rendered accessible through clear organisation.

This was a point developed by Ephraim Chambers in the encyclopaedia which D'Alembert and Diderot took as their starting point. In a telling metaphor, knowledge for Chambers was like a part of the countryside that had become fruitful and well ordered thanks to enclosure with its challenge to traditional open-field systems of agriculture: 'In the wide field of intelligibles, appear some points which have been more cultivated than the rest . . . These spots, regularly laid out, and conveniently circumscribed, and fenced round, make what we call the *Arts and Sciences*.' But, like D'Alembert, he acknowledged that the actual layout of such fruitful fields was, in some ways, a matter of convenience: 'And yet this distribution of the land of Science, like that of the face of the earth and heavens, is wholly arbitrary; and might be altered, perhaps, not without advantage.'[5]

For Chambers and for Diderot and D'Alembert, the test of a map was its utility, in particular its utility in transforming what was traditional and unsystematic into the fruitful and the orderly. The encyclopaedists' maps of knowledge were emblematic of the fundamental Enlightenment quest to make the world more comprehensible through system and classification with the ultimate goal of utilising knowledge for the Baconian ambition of ministering to 'the relief of man's estate'. But to arrive at such geographies of knowledge meant erasing traditional types of maps or, at least, incorporating them into more wide-ranging forms of projection which merged the local with the more universal (see also Clayton's discussion of mapping, Chapter 2, pp. 39– 43). The ultimate example of the clash of such knowledge systems was the dismissal of indigenous maps since they had no meaning to the scientific cartographer – a clash recounted in Turnbull's account of Cook's inability to make sense of the map of the Society Islands drawn by the Tahitian, Tupaia.[6] The compilers of the great map of Egypt commissioned by Napoleon were equally dismissive of indigenous knowledge systems.[7] The ways in which Tupaia's map was superseded by that of Cook or the manner in which the French took cartographic control of Egypt are potent illustrations of Francis Bacon's adage that knowledge is power. Representation of the world in schematic form brings with it the possibility of control and effective possession.[8] In many senses, a map captures a portion of the globe making it accessible and linking it with larger pictures and understandings of the world. As William

Blaeu put it in the letter to Louis XIV which prefaced his twelve-volume *Grand Atlas* (1663), 'maps enable us to contemplate at home and right before our eyes things that are farthest away'.[9]

Bruno Latour has underlined these points with his concept of 'centres of calculation' which pull together the fruits of a 'cycle of accumulation'.[10] In such a conception, the world is reconstructed in the rational form of a map, or some other ordered schema, through scientific institutions usually located at the centre of an imperial power. Along with all the other cargo that is the natural outcome of imperial exploration, knowledge – in the form of detailed charts and precise geographical data – is brought back to the centre to be transformed into maps which make possible yet further exploration and the discovery of still more detailed information. Yet maps are but one form of such a rational reconstruction of the world. Other types of data about the natural world and its human population are also transformed into orderly models which make possible understanding and exploitation of a world increasingly denuded of its dark and inaccessible corners. Once such models are constructed in the 'centres of calculation' they make possible the establishment of networks which can seek to reconstruct the world along the lines of the models themselves. One instance of such a reordering of the world was Banks's work in moving around species of plants and animals the better to serve the economic interests of the British empire – a process made possible by the network of botanical gardens that radiated around the world from Kew.

BANKS AND CARTOGRAPHIC KNOWLEDGE

European explorers like Banks brought back to such centres of calculation intellectual capital of all kinds: outlines of coasts, variations of the compass that enabled one to distinguish between the true and the magnetic North, information about tides, winds and currents and cases and cases of natural history specimens. Such information was then incorporated into a multiplicity of maps: charts for navigation, hydrographic maps describing the sea and its currents, diagrams of magnetic variations and, of course, vast volumes describing and classifying the natural world including its human population. Such maps, through their ability to abstract features of key interest, enabled the imperial powers to draw new sectors of the world into their networks either through trade or outright annexation. Whether at home or abroad, maps provided the readiest means of drawing knowledge together into an easily comprehensible form, a particularly important *desideratum* for the encyclopaedia-minded eighteenth century.[11] In the Georgian world, few individuals knew better than Joseph Banks the political uses of knowledge and, in particular, knowledge of the natural world. If, as William Harvey claimed, Francis Bacon wrote philosophy like a Lord Chancellor, Banks conducted science as a Privy Councillor alert to the ways in which the pursuit of knowledge could serve the state. And, if natural knowledge was to be usable, he well appreciated that it must be put in orderly forms of which the map was one obvious expression.

Banks in a certain sense served his scientific apprenticeship as part of cartographic enterprises. His first voyage abroad, to Newfoundland and Labrador in 1766, was part of an expedition which included among its aims the mapping of some of the territories over which Britain was exercising more effective control, thanks to its victories in the Seven Years War. The *Endeavour* expedition (1768–71) was under the command of James Cook, the map maker who had helped to make that victory possible through his charts of the St Lawrence and whose Pacific voyages were dominated by the quest for accurate maps. Indeed, this enterprise determined the very choice of vessel, the shallow-drafted Whitby colliers, which made it possible to come close to shore to conduct the precise observations on which accurate maps depended.

On both expeditions, the presence of Banks enabled the mapping to extend to a survey of the natural history of the areas encountered, including accounts of the human population. Such maps helped to make eventual imperial control of these areas of the globe more possible, particularly as Banks brought back not only maps of their natural history in the form of classification and taxonomic description, but also physical samples. These extended beyond pressed plants and stuffed animals to 'natural curiosities' and ethnological material. Banks even sought to bring back live human beings and, although the Tahitian Tupaia died en route, Banks was closely involved with the eventual visit of the Tahitian Omai. In all these ways, Banks added to the 'cycle of accumulation' which made it possible for his house in Soho Square – the eventual nucleus of the British Museum (Natural History) – to become a 'centre of calculation' by providing in accessible form systematic knowledge of the Pacific world.

Banks continued to use his influence to promote the more accurate charting of the globe, the most significant instance being his sponsorship of Matthew Flinders's circumnavigation of what was then New Holland with the *Investigator* expedition of 1801–3. The outcome was a map of the entire Australasian continent which made its European inhabitants more conscious of the land that they had come to inhabit and more inclined to adopt the new name, 'Australia', given to it by Flinders (see Figure 8.1). It served as an instance of a more general phenomenon: the way in which, by literally giving shape to a nation, map makers could be agents in shaping a sense of national identity.[12] More effective possession of the world through mapping was an activity that was as important at home as it was abroad. As the eighteenth century saw the consolidation of the state largely under the impulse of war, it

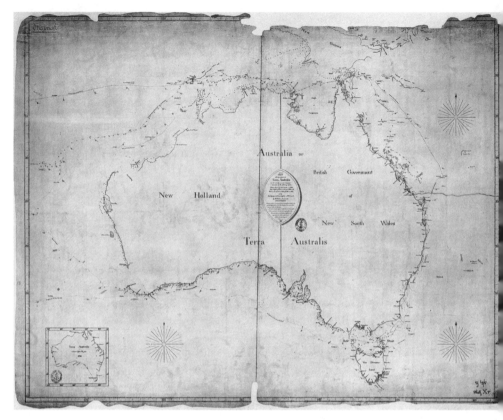

8.1 Matthew Flinders's Chart of Terra Australis (1804). (© British Crown Copyright 1998. Reproduced by permission of the Controller of Her Majesty's Stationery Office and the UK Hydrographic Office)

became ever more important to take effective stock of the resources that the state commanded. Following the lead of France, the state which first attempted to integrate science in the conduct of government policy, the British government began to institute a programme of mapping its own territory.[13] The connections between mapping and war were evident in the very origins of this enterprise.

MAPPING BRITAIN

The British Ordnance Survey effectively began following the suppression of the Jacobite uprising of 1745–46 when it was realised that knowledge of the Highlands by the Duke of Cumberland's forces was hampered by the lack of maps of the north and west of Scotland. This prompted the Military Survey of Scotland conducted from 1747 to 1754 under the initial leadership of Colonel David Watson and completed by William Roy.[14] As a consequence of these endeavours, William Roy, who was to be one of Banks's closest allies within the Royal Society, was appointed in 1765 to the newly-created position of Surveyor General of Coasts and Engineer of Directing Military Surveys in Great Britain under the Board of Ordnance, the wing of government whose function at its foundation was to supply military equipment. The position brought with it the responsibility 'to inspect, survey and make reports from time to time of the state of the Coasts, and Districts of the Country adjacent to the Coasts of the Kingdom, and the Islands thereunto belonging', a role that makes evident the association between mapping and defence of the kingdom.[15] It was also a post that made possible the development of mapping on a more rigorously scientific basis than had been employed in the survey of Scotland which was not based on triangulation but rather sought to put in schematic form a military reconnaissance of the area.[16] The alliance between Banks and Roy, together with others linked with the early work of the Ordnance Survey such as Charles Blagden and John Lloyd, was strengthened by their close association as founding members of the Royal Society Club (which lasted from 1775 until 1784).[17] From the project's beginnings in 1783, Banks was closely involved in Roy's great enterprise of providing a sound scientific basis for the accurate mapping of Britain through the construction of a baseline which would make possible precise trigonometrical calculations (see Figure 8.2).[18]

This baseline, which eventually ran for five miles across Hounslow Heath, served as the foundation for a series of triangles that extended to Dover. At Dover, it linked with the work of the French who, under the leadership of the Cassini scientific dynasty, had pioneered the techniques of accurate measurement of the earth's surface on which the British Ordnance Survey built.[19] Not the least of Banks's services was liaising with the brilliant but difficult instrument maker, Jesse Ramsden, who developed a form of theodolite which made Roy's work possible. The project was considered sufficiently important to the state to attract a royal grant of £3000 which was administered by Banks as President of the Royal Society.[20] Banks's deputy in Royal Society matters, Charles Blagden, was dispatched to France in 1787 following Roy's request to the Royal Society that 'a Commissioner might be appointed . . . to join the French Commissioners in their co-operation for carrying the trigonometrical measurements across the straits of Dover'.[21]

The motives for undertaking this project were made clear by Roy in the *Philosophical Transactions of the Royal Society of London* in 1785. He noted that: 'Accurate surveys of a country are works of great public utility, as affording the surest foundation for almost every kind of internal improvement in time of peace and the best means of forming judicious plans of defence against the invasions of an enemy in time of war.' Surveying was a route to

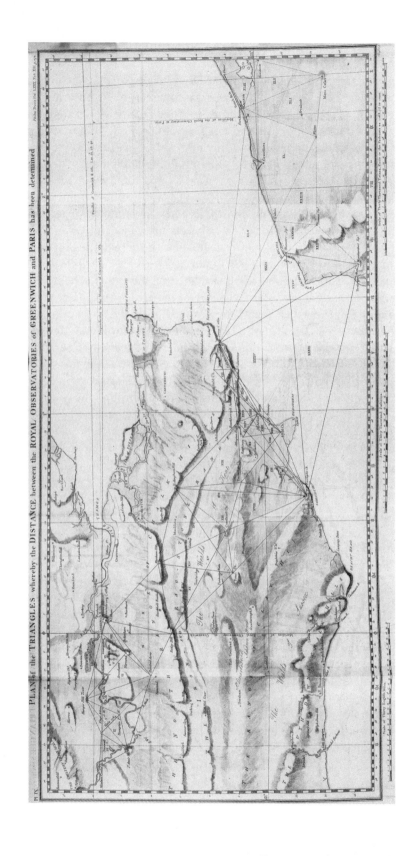

PLAN of the TRIANGLES whereby the DISTANCE between the ROYAL OBSERVATORIES of GREENWICH and PARIS has been determined

economic progress and military power. It was a means of turning knowledge into power through the full exploitation of a country's resources and of ensuring that rival powers were denied access. As Roy himself acknowledged, the initial stimulus for the project had been the 1745 Jacobite Rebellion, a fact which had prompted him to suggest that the needs of war were the most potent impulse for mapping: 'a state of warfare generally produces the first improvements in its [a country's] geography'.[22]

Such mapping had an international as well as a national character. Roy's triangulation project was one that had obvious national benefits but it had, from Banks's point of view, the further merit of fostering a scientific partnership with France since the British and French networks were connected across the Channel in 1787. Roy himself spoke of the way in which through these 'combined operations', as he termed it, 'the two most famous observatories in Europe, Greenwich and Paris, would be more accurately ascertained than they are at present'.[23] Although national considerations always came first for Banks, science retained for him a cosmopolitan character that was reinforced by the network of scientific academies of which the Royal Society formed a part.[24]

Characteristically, it was a project that was initiated by the French who had gone further than the British in linking science with the workings of government. Particularly important to the French state was the accurate mapping of its territories – an endeavour in which astronomy with its traditions of precise measurement joined with geography.[25] French geographers served the needs of a centralising French state for which accurate maps provided more effective control over its own population and the means better to defeat its enemies.[26] By linking with the British triangulation project in measuring precisely the distance between the French and the English Royal Observatories, the French scientific establishment helped both to extend the range of its own measurements and to widen the channels of scientific communication which the cosmopolitan world of the scientific academies served to foster.

MAPPING EMPIRES

With the metropolitan model of mapping and surveying established, such techniques were then gradually applied to the empire. An early transference was the work of James Rennell whose interest in applying European surveying techniques to India led to his appointment as Surveyor General of Bengal

facing] 8.2 'Plan of the triangles whereby the distance between the Royal Observatories of Greenwich and Paris has been determined' (based on the Hounslow baseline). From *Philosophical Transactions of the Royal Society*, 80 (1790), 272. (Courtesy of the John Rylands Library, University of Manchester)

in 1764. The fruits of his labour were embodied in his *Bengal Atlas* (1779) and a map of India that appeared in 1783. These works led to Rennell being awarded the Royal Society's Copley Medal in 1791 and elicited enthusiastic praise from Banks[27] who contrasted the accuracy of Rennell's mapping of Bengal with the relatively incomplete state of the mapping of Britain.[28] For Banks, Rennell's work was a potent illustration of the benefits that could accrue to the British empire and, more remotely, to humankind as a whole, from a scientifically-based scrutiny of the resources under the sway of British rule. Mapping required an orderly classification of the chief features of the land thus enabling its improvement and exploitation.

As Edney stresses, Rennell's map of India in many ways created the image of the subcontinent in the mind of the British imperial classes.[29] Like Flinders's map of Australia (See Figure 8.1, p. 156), Rennell's map of India gave reality to a national abstraction – the difference, of course, being that Australia largely became ethnically and demographically an extension of the British Isles. Rennell's India, on the other hand, served to foster a sense of trustee-ship over an alien people lacking the scientific and organisational skills which maps such as Rennell's illustrated. Indeed, argues Edney in the manner of Latour, Rennell's work and the subsequent more accurate maps based on triangulation made it possible for the British to reassemble, as it were, a form of India in Britain. Precise cartography made it possible to construct a 'centre of calculation' in the imperial metropolis so that India could be largely ruled from afar. As Edney puts it: 'the archive could be shipped back to Britain as a symbolic appropriation of the territories and peoples in India'.[30] Godlewska makes a similar claim for the Napoleonic survey of Egypt which, as she writes, 'creates the Egypt that could be claimed and taken home and mathematically and rigorously interpreted in the silence of French libraries, laboratories and museums without the difficult complications associated with colonialism, subject peoples and the bizarreries of other cultures'.[31]

India offered the possibility of greater British self-sufficiency in key prod-ucts and Rennell's maps helped to establish the route to such goals. Banks turned to Rennell, for example, for expert advice on how to reshape the ecology and economy of parts of India in order to provide Britain with the tea that it was consuming in greater and greater quantities. It was Banks's hope that this would spare the British economy the transfer of vast sums of money to purchase Chinese tea. Rennell responded enthusiastically to Banks's suggestion writing in 1788 that 'the culture of ye Tea ... would suit the Hindoos most perfectly; their patient industry, & pliable fingers would man-age the whole business to great advantage'. Furthermore, continued Rennell, it might be possible not only to bypass China with regard to tea but also to transplant to British India another major product, namely silk. For Rennell, 'The culture of the Mulberry for Silk worms strikes me as being something like that of the Tea Shrub, by the historical drawings that I have seen brought from China.'[32]

Rennell's early cartographic work led in turn to the application of triangulation methods in Madras in 1802, and eventually to the Great Trigonometrical Survey of India begun in 1818. One point of continuity between the metropolitan and imperial projects was the sending to India of a Ramsden theodolite.[33] Rennell also urged the expansion of imperial cartography in another direction through his involvement with the African Association, a body founded in 1788 to promote the exploration of Africa and which largely owed its origin to Banks. The data brought back by those explorers sponsored by the Association provided the basis for maps that would make possible greater European knowledge and eventual control of the African interior. Rennell, for example, drew on the accounts of Mungo Park and others to construct in 1798 'A Map showing the progress of discovery and improvement, in the geography of North Africa' – a map that, in retrospect, reveals the still sketchy European knowledge of that continent. In the following year he contributed eleven maps to the account of Park's travels.[34] When Banks and Park collaborated on plans for a further voyage to trace where the Niger entered the sea, Rennell attempted to dissuade both from a voyage that, all too accurately, he predicted was dangerous. But Banks was not to be lightly deflected from promoting the advance of cartographic knowledge writing that 'it is by similar hazards of human life alone that we can hope to penetrate the obscurity of the internal face of Africa'.[35] Park set off on his second and last expedition to the Niger in 1805 and perished in the cause of geographical knowledge and British commercial interests.

Undeterred by such sacrifices, African exploration remained an abiding interest for Rennell. In 1813, for example, he wrote to Banks in praise of the contribution made by Johann Burkhardt on an expedition sponsored by the African Association, particularly since, as Rennell put it, 'he has given us Notices, respecting a Country that we know as little of, as of Sudan'.[36] Rennell and Banks worked together in promoting the scientific exploration of much of the globe. Along with their common interest in India and Africa, Banks consulted Rennell in 1791 over plans for the Vancouver voyage to Northwest America. In 1810 when Banks focused on the promotion of Arctic exploration, he again turned to Rennell to provide detailed advice on such matters as winds and sea currents. When Matthew Flinders was working on his account of the circumnavigation of Australia in 1811, Rennell was among the visitors when Flinders called on Banks at Soho Square.[37] The Banks–Rennell partnership was, then, a potent illustration of the extent to which the Banksian ideals of improvement at home and abroad were closely allied to the promotion of mapping as a practice of geographical enquiry that aimed to benefit Britain at home and overseas.

MAPPING LOCAL RESOURCES

Mapping had its local as well as its national and imperial dimensions and Banks shared the English land-owning class's ability to be evident and involved in both the affairs of the city and the country. For three or four months each summer the President of the Royal Society and adviser to government became the Lincolnshire squire with his seat at Revesby Abbey and his well-honed political connections throughout the county. Whether in the city or the country, Banks kept in touch with both worlds through diligent lieutenants whose copious correspondence he kept classified to a degree that paralleled the orderly classification of the natural world made possible by the system of Linnaeus and his successors. At Banks's family seat at Revesby, a contemporary recorded that

> Nests of drawers numbered consecutively lined the walls; and it was Sir Joseph's custom to have two catalogues, descriptive of their contents; one of which always accompanied him, the other remained at Revesby. Thus, if when in London, he required any paper contained in the drawers, he had merely to refer to his catalogue, and sending the number to his steward at Revesby, the latter was enabled, by means of the Catalogue in the office, to put his hand in a moment upon the desired document, and forward it to his master.[38]

As an improving landowner much involved in the draining of the fens, Banks was well aware of the uses to which maps could be put in consolidating estates and of effecting that move to clearer and more exclusive forms of private ownership of the land which were closely linked to the agricultural revolution.[39] One graphic illustration of the importance to Banks of such cadastral or estate maps and their iconographic role as an agent of improvement is that he is depicted as holding one such, linked to the draining of the fens, when his portrait was painted in the uniform of the Lincolnshire Volunteers (Figure 8.3). Accurate mapping enabled an improving landlord such as Banks to exploit more effectively the resources of his estate both above and below ground. Estate maps facilitated enclosure and the draining of the fens. Effective mapping brought with it the system and order embodied, for example, in the plans and surveys of his Revesby estate carried out for Banks by Thomas Stone in 1794 with their lists of tenants, field names, acreages of pasture, arable and so forth.[40] That apostle of agricultural improvement, Thomas Young, was so impressed by Banks's maps of the Revesby Estate that he incorporated them in his *General View of the Agriculture of the County of Lincolnshire* (1799, 1813). It was a work that further strengthened Banks's resolve to drain what Young called those 'horrid fens',[41] a project that was preceded by further mapping in the form of a survey by the Scottish engineer, John Rennie, with a view to establishing the best means of drainage.

8.3 Joseph Banks, by Thomas Phillips (1814). (By kind permission of Boston Borough Council)

Sub-surface geological mapping enabled Banks to take advantage of what mineral wealth was available, in particular, the deposits of lead and coal on his Overton estate in Derbyshire. Soon after he inherited this estate from his uncle, Robert Banks-Hodgkinson, Banks proceeded to have a local surveyor, George Nuttall, map the area paying particular attention to possible coal deposits. Nuttall's map was to serve as a model which helped stimulate the later surveys of John Farey which formed part of the pre-history of the Geological Survey of Britain.[42] Farey's position from 1792 as agent to the Duke of Bedford is further indication of the close links between agricultural improvement and mapping. Significantly, too, Farey's major work, the two-volume *Survey of the County of Derby including a General View of its Agriculture & Minerals* (1811–13), was published under the aegis of the Board of Agriculture, the chief body dedicated to the promotion of agricultural improvement (with the enthusiastic support of Joseph Banks). This *magnum opus*, which was commissioned by Banks, grew out of Farey's geological transect of the Lincolnshire coast and the area around the Overton estate. Farey's geological mapping was combined with Nuttall's land survey in a hand-coloured map which was exhibited in 1808–9 'as a matter of Science' at Banks's house in Soho Square.[43]

Farey's work was given scientific shape and direction by the principles of William Smith who helped to establish the ordering of English geological strata. By so doing, Smith helped promote the transformation of sub-surface geological mapping into a theoretically-based cartography of the successive ages of the earth. It brought to bear on the routine concerns of mine owners and estate owners the findings derived from the wider scientific context concerning the ways in which the landscape had changed over time. Mapping here drew attention to the role of time as well as space by establishing in pictorial form the inferences made possible by the study of outcrops. Smith's ordering of strata provided the nucleus which Farey expanded to develop a more comprehensive mapping of the world beneath the feet of improving landlords such as Banks who were his patrons.[44]

Banks's patronage of Farey was consistent with his attempts to encourage other improving landlords to use the techniques of geological surveying to promote the better exploitation of mineral resources. In 1784, for example, he had advised Lord Palmerston on the best method of undertaking 'the tryal intended to be made for Coal in your Lordships neighbourhood'. In return he requested 'an exact account of the Strata passed through with the depth of Each'.[45] Coal, that most basic of all commodities in fuelling the industrial revolution, remained an abiding preoccupation of Banks. This is apparent from his 1797 'Essay regarding the coal trade, the number of persons it employs, revenue gained from it & the importance of the coal trade to the naval strength of Great Britain'.[46] As Banks was well aware, the location of Britain's coal reserves required detailed mapping. This fact explains why, in 1794, Banks acquired a chart giving depths of a mine at Newcastle.[47] It accounts also for his enthusiastic support for William Smith's *A Delineation of the Strata of England and Wales, with Part of Scotland, exhibiting the Collieries and Mines*, which was published in 1815 and dedicated to Banks.[48]

MAPPING STATE POWER

Mapping – whether above or below ground – was one of the most potent ways in which the modernising state could take command of its resources.

The late eighteenth-century state provided itself in other ways with charts of its population and its economic activities.[49] As John Brewer has stressed, the increasing cost of war made a more accurate knowledge of a nation's resources – and, ultimately, its tax-paying capacity – more and more vital. 'To be more effective government required greater knowledge', writes Brewer, 'skilled government needed more detailed and precise information'.[50]

The close conjunction between the beginnings of the Ordnance Survey in 1791 and the first British census in 1801 reflects the fact that both sprang from the same impulse: to provide a more secure framework of knowledge on which to construct state policy. Both maps and a census represent the world (natural and human) in abstracted terms which remove the data away from their local setting. Both are ways in which the state can better define itself by establishing its boundaries and the extent of population within those boundaries. Such a connection between mapping and the beginnings of national censuses is apparent in the correspondence between Banks and John Rickman, the man who conducted the first British census in 1801. As part of his more general investigations of the impact of population on agriculture, Rickman wrote to Banks on several occasions seeking, for example, to borrow General Roy's map of Scotland.[51] The common thread that drew Banks and Rickman together was that of agricultural improvement. Banks was prepared to acknowledge that agricultural change could disrupt traditional ways of life but argued that its benefits would ultimately extend to all. Banks discussed with Rickman the impact of the increase in the number of sheep in Scotland on the human population taking the sanguine view that, in the long run, the evicted population might be better off since the ultimate outcome of such Highland clearances might well be that those so displaced 'may reappear with their mouths full of mutton in our manufactories'.[52] Rickman was of like mind: 'I quite agree with you in the fitness of dislodging Highlanders for Sheep farming.'[53] Such clearances were a potent example of the way in which agricultural improvement and the techniques of surveying were closely allied as the land was put to more efficient use by its landowners. They also served as an exemplar of the way in which modernising scientific knowledge could be corrosive of traditional ways of life whether in Britain itself or in the empire more generally.[54]

Rickman's work extended to considering the effects of such a transformation on the area's human population – in effect the mapping of demographic change and resources. More accurate data on the distribution of population, like improvements in surveying, were intended to promote better planning to assist economic growth and political order. Rickman's work formed part of that same drive for order and system that informed the quest for systems of classification in the natural world. As Rickman told Banks in 1805, 'The favourite object of my life, is to distribute England into such orderly Divisions or Districts, that information may be obtained and good government enforced in the most effectual manner.'[55]

The systematisation of weights and measures in Great Britain from 1826 also forms part of the same consolidation of the state and its central authority as the definition of territory through mapping and the establishment of the extent and character of its population through the census. One instance of this connection is illustrated by the French metrical system which grew out of work to establish the exact shape of the earth. The metre was one ten-millionth of the quadrant of the terrestrial meridian which ran through France.[56] In England, William Roy's work on establishing the scientific basis on which the mapping of the Ordnance Survey was based was also linked with the legal definition of the standard yard.[57] Banks's close associate within the Royal Society, Henry Kater, was working in the same tradition when he combined measurement of longitude with advice to the Russian government on weights and measures.[58] Kater's main contribution to the reform of British practice was, however, to provide accurate data so that weights and measures could be based on the amplitude of a swinging pendulum.[59]

By the early nineteenth century, however, the need for some scientifically-based system had become urgent, particularly given the example of the recently-introduced French metric system. In 1802, Banks assured a French scientific correspondent of the Royal Society's willingness to adopt any system 'whether it is discovered in France in England or elsewhere on Condition however that the Principles on which it is Founded are simple & sufficiently correct to allow it in case of need to be reconstructed with rigorous exactitude in every part of the Globe'.[60] Hostility to things French and anti-revolutionary sentiment, however, stood in the way of the introduction of this system. From the deliberations of a parliamentary committee chaired by Banks between 1817 and 1819, the imperial system of weights and measures based on the pendulum rather than the quadrant finally emerged in 1826. Banks sought to justify this as a matter of contemporary expediency: 'lest it [the quadrant] should in Future be remeasured & proved different from what is now believd to be the amount'.[61]

Banks's exertions in improving the mint also assisted the more effective standardisation of one of the most potent symbols of state power: the issuing of coin of the realm.[62] In the tradition of Sir Isaac Newton, who had served both as Master of the Mint and as President of the Royal Society, Banks was called upon to provide scientific advice to government in relation to the national coinage. He served on the Privy Council Committee on Coinage from 1787 and took an active part in the recoinage of copper money in 1797. This recoinage was facilitated by Banks's friendship with Matthew Boulton whose steam engines provided the technological power to reform the Mint's antiquated practices. When the problem of wear of metal in coins was referred to Banks, he arranged for a series of experiments to be conducted by the Royal Society under Henry Cavendish and Charles Hatchett, the results of which, despite fears about confidentiality, were published in 1803.[63] In 1819, a year before his death, Banks was called upon to chair a committee to enquire into methods of preventing the forgery of banknotes. Such endeavours were a yet further reflection of that same mentality that prompted late eighteenth-century states to establish more clearly the boundaries of their powers.

BANKS AND THE CLASSIFICATION OF KNOWLEDGE

This quest for the better ordering of the world through maps, censuses and uniform systems of weights and measures was linked with the eighteenth-century preoccupation with classification. This had its most conspicuous scientific manifestation in the Linnean system for bringing order to the natural world. To Linnaeus, his taxonomic order was a 'map of nature'.[64] For botanists like Banks engaged in coming to terms with what, for Europe, was the new world of the Pacific, the Linnean system gave a sense of purpose and direction as thousands of natural specimens were fitted onto a map of the natural world which could become comprehensive without being over-whelmed by the information it contained. Banks's herbarium at Soho Square, for example, contained some thirty thousand specimens arranged according to Linnean principles.[65] Banks's vast collection, together with those amassed at Kew, formed a centre of calculation which made possible the reordering of the world as plants were moved around the world to promote economic growth.[66]

There were, it is true, debates about whether the Linnean system of classification, based as it was on artificial principles, was the best method of reflecting the actual realities of the natural world. In 1817, three years before his death, Banks commented to Sir James Edward Smith, the founder of the Linnean Society, that:

> I fear you will differ from me in opinion when I fancy Jussieu's natural orders to be superior to those of Linnaeus. I do not however mean to allege that he had even an equal degree of merit in having compiled them – he has taken all Linnaeus had done as his own; and having thus possessed himself of an elegant and sub-stantial fabric, has done much towards increasing its beauty, but far less towards any improvement in its stability.[67]

As Banks's words suggest, debates as to its merits did not substantially challenge the Linnean achievement and were more an invitation to refine and improve it rather than to demolish it.

Accurate charts and botanical and zoological collecting were all part of a common venture: to know as much of the world as possible. The better the maps and the more comprehensive the charting of the animal, vegetable and

mineral kingdoms the more subject such areas became to the European metropolitan powers. In the late eighteenth century, voyages of exploration were
more and more justified by Enlightenment values of curiosity and the quest
for knowledge. Such motives were, of course, combined with the familiar quest
for strategic or economic advantage.[68] Cook's great *Endeavour* voyage was prompted by the desire to participate in the observation of the transit of Venus
and had the additional scientific advantage of assisting Banks's work in natural
history. But it was also intended to promote the more accurate mapping of
New Zealand and the east coast of Australia, and thus to lay the foundation
for the eventual incorporation of these territories into the British Empire.
Explorers and naturalists like Banks and his clients expanded the realm of
science and of knowledge generally. They provided maps of geography and
natural history that opened up new sectors of the globe, and they also provided
the intellectual resources that made effective imperialism possible. Exploration made possible the building of centres of calculation that made the world
appear more rationally explicable but also recreated it in the image of an elite
imbued with such Enlightenment ideals. A world thus constituted made the
task of empire building both more manageable and more familiar.

Banks's involvement in the expedition of George Vancouver from 1791 to
1795 reflects this dual quality. The voyage itself was intended to consolidate a
British presence on the western coast of America and Vancouver's mapping
was a means to that end (see Chapter 2). To ensure the quality of the mapping and thus to secure its authority for scientific and imperial ends, Banks
was directly involved in drawing up the surveying instructions along with
Rennell and William Bligh.[69] When he gave instructions to Archibald Menzies,
the voyage's naturalist, Banks dwelt on the extent to which the voyage would
'promote the interest of Science, & contribute to the increase of human
knowledge'. Banks further instructed Menzies to assess 'whether, should it
any time hereafter be deemed expedient to send out settlers from England,
the Grains, Pulse and Fruits cultivated in Europe [that] are likely to thrive,
and if not what kind of produce would in your opinion be the most suitable'.[70] Maps and empires were made to appear natural allies.

If imperial botanical geography was a further instance of Banks's enthusiasm for bringing order to the world, there were, nevertheless, limits to his
willingness to endorse the changing map of natural knowledge. Reared in the
traditions of the gentleman collector with its long pre-history of the virtuoso,
Banks was unsympathetic to the growing claims for disciplinary specialisation. For him, science was a unified continent. Attempts to divide it into
different realms ran counter to a gentlemanly ethos where all forms of knowledge were open for edification or practical use without the obstacles of
excessive specialist expertise or organisations. Such views accounted for his
strong opposition to the attempt to found scientific bodies that might challenge

the Royal Society. The foundation of the Geological Society in 1807 and of the Astronomical Society in 1820 led the aged Banks to remark bitterly: 'I see plainly that all these new-fangled associations will finally dismantle the Royal Society, and not leave the old lady a rag to cover her.'[71] Banks's *cri de coeur* was in some ways that of a man of the old regime hostile to the spirit of reform and revitalisation that was beginning to reshape the political and intellectual institutions of a Britain being remoulded by the forces unleashed by the French and industrial revolutions.

Yet it was also a plea for the unity of knowledge, a plea that came naturally to a natural historian who regarded all objects, whether animal, vegetable or mineral, as being linked by their common location. Such a sense of the unity of nature was further promoted by the way in which Banks, as a member of the landed elite, had a sense of the importance of local knowledge as a way of understanding the natural and civil history of the countryside on which power and prestige were ultimately based.[72] Although, for Banks, as for other eighteenth-century naturalists,[73] such a sense of the interconnected nature of the geography of knowledge was local in its origin, it was given an imperial and even global dimension through his promotion of scientific exploration. In some ways, this was an insight that he shared with Alexander von Humboldt, another explorer whose sense of the unity of knowledge had been heightened by his dedication to the promotion of natural history in its widest sense. As Cannon writes, 'this idea of the interconnectedness of things was to be the theme that ran like a high voltage current through [Humboldt's] *Kosmos*'.[74]

For Banks, the man of the Enlightenment, the scientific specialisation and professionalisation which was becoming apparent in the early nineteenth century meant that the map of knowledge was being subdivided into separate compartments.[75] This was a development he saw as undermining that drive to overall order which sustained his own enquiries. It meant, too, a move away from the dominant goal of late eighteenth-century geography which was, as Godlewska puts it, to establish 'the reflection of the unity and coherence of the world'.[76] This was an ambition to which Humboldt remained committed. For Banks, too, a lifetime devoted to the promotion of improvement and of system was based on a firm belief in the unity of knowledge: its increasing fragmentation meant a new form of intellectual cartography which the ageing President of the Royal Society was ill-equipped to undertake.

NOTES

1 S. Harris, 'Introduction: thinking locally, acting globally', *Configurations*, 6 (1998), 131–9, quote on p. 136; L. Daston, 'The ethos of Enlightenment', in W. Clark, J. Golinski and S. Schaffer (eds), *The Sciences in Enlightened Europe* (Chicago: Chicago University Press, 1999), 495–504, quote on p. 502.

2 C. W. J. Withers and D. N. Livingstone, 'Introduction: on geography and Enlightenment', in D. N. Livingstone and C. W. J. Withers (eds), *Geography and Enlightenment*
(Chicago: Chicago University Press, 1999), 1–32; C. W. J. Withers, 'Towards a history
of geography in the public sphere', *History of Science*, 37 (1999), 45–78; W. Clark, J.
Golinski and S. Schaffer, 'Introduction', in Clark, Golinski and Schaffer (eds), *Sciences
in Enlightened Europe*, 3–31.

3 R. Yeo, *Encyclopaedic Visions: Scientific Dictionaries and Enlightenment Culture*
(Cambridge: Cambridge University Press, 2001).

4 N. Fisher, 'The classification of the sciences', in R. C. Olby, G. N. Cantor, J. R. R.
Christie and M. J. S. Hodge (eds), *Companion to the History of Modern Science*
(London: Routledge, 1996), 853–85, quote on p. 862.

5 *Ibid.*, 861–2.

6 D. Turnbull, 'Cook and Tupaia, a tale of cartographic *méconnaissance?*', in M. Lincoln
(ed.), *Science and Exploration in the Pacific: European Voyages to the Southern Oceans
in the Eighteenth Century* (Woodbridge: Boydell & Brewer, 1999), 117–31.

7 A. M. C. Godlewska, 'The Napoleonic survey of Egypt: a masterpiece of cartographic
compilation and early nineteenth-century fieldwork', *Cartographica*, 25 (1988), 1–
171.

8 For an overview of these issues, see J. B. Harley, 'Maps, knowledge and power', in
D. Cosgrove and S. J. Daniels (eds), *The Iconography of Landscape: Essays on the
Symbolic Representation, Design and Use of Past Environments* (Cambridge: Cambridge
University Press, 1988), 277–312.

9 D. N. Livingstone, *The Geographical Tradition: Episodes in the History of a Contested
Enterprise* (Oxford: Blackwell, 1993), 98.

10 B. Latour, *Science in Action: How to Follow Scientists and Engineers through Society*
(Milton Keynes: Open University Press, 1987), 215–37. On the application of Latour's
work to Joseph Banks, see D. P. Miller, 'Joseph Banks, empire, and "centers of calculation" in late Hanoverian London', and J. Gascoigne, 'The ordering of nature and the
ordering of empire: a commentary', in D. P. Miller and P. H. Reill, *Visions of Empire:
Voyages, Botany, and Representations of Nature* (Cambridge: Cambridge University
Press, 1996), 21–37 and 107–13 respectively.

11 M. H. Edney, 'Reconsidering Enlightenment geography and map making: reconnaissance, mapping, archive', in Livingstone and Withers (eds), *Geography and
Enlightenment*, 165–98.

12 J. Black, *Maps and Politics* (Chicago: Chicago University Press, 1997).

13 C. C. Gillispie, *Science and Polity in France at the End of the Old Regime* (Princeton:
Princeton University Press, 1980); R. Hahn, *The Anatomy of a Scientific Institution: The
Paris Academy of Science, 1666–1803* (Berkeley: University of California Press, 1971).
For a discussion of the continuation of one aspect of this tradition under Napoleon,
see A. M. C. Godlewska, 'Napoleon's geographers (1797–1815): imperialists and soldiers
of modernity', in A. M. C. Godlewska and N. J. Smith (eds), *Geography and Empire*
(Oxford: Blackwell, 1994), 31–55.

14 S. Widmalm, 'Accuracy, rhetoric, and technology: the Paris–Greenwich triangulation,
1784–88', in T. Frängsmyr, J. L. Heilbron and R. E. Rider (eds), *The Quantifying Spirit
in the Eighteenth Century* (Berkeley and Oxford: Science History Publications, 1990),
179–206; C. W. J. Withers, 'Situating practical reason: geography, geometry and mapping in the Scottish Enlightenment', in C. W. J. Withers and P. Wood (eds), *Science
and Medicine in the Scottish Enlightenment* (East Linton: Tuckwell Press, 2002), 54–78.

15 R. A. Gardiner, 'William Roy, surveyor and antiquary', *The Geographical Journal*, 143
(1977), 439–50.

16 C. Close, *The Early Years of the Ordnance Survey* (Newton Abbot: David & Charles, 1969), 5–29.

17 Gardiner, 'William Roy', 445.

18 On this project, see Widmalm, 'Accuracy, rhetoric, and technology', *passim*.

19 G. R. Crone, *Maps and their Makers: An Introduction to the History of Cartography* (Folkestone: Dawson, 1978), 86–8; N. J. W. Thrower, *Maps and Man* (Englewood Cliffs, NJ: Prentice Hall, 1972), 75–80.

20 H. B. Carter, *Sir Joseph Banks 1743–1820* (London: British Museum, 1988), 203–4.

21 Royal Society, CMO (Council Minutes), Vol. 7, 276, 29 June 1787.

22 W. Roy, 'An account of the measurement of a base line on Hounslow Heath', *Philosophical Transactions of the Royal Society of London*, 75 (1785), 385–478, quote on p. 385.

23 *Ibid.*, 389.

24 On Banks and the tensions between national and cosmopolitan uses of sciences, see J. Gascoigne, *Science in the Service of Empire: Joseph Banks, the British State and the Uses of Science in the Age of Revolution* (Cambridge: Cambridge University Press, 1998), 147–65.

25 A. M. C. Godlewska, *Geography Unbound: French Geographic Science from Cassini to Humboldt* (Chicago: Chicago University Press, 1999), 68–71.

26 Widmalm, 'Accuracy, rhetoric, and technology', 201.

27 Close, *The Early Years*, 37.

28 W. A. Seymour, *A History of the Ordnance Survey* (Folkestone, Kent: Dawson, 1980), 1.

29 M. H. Edney, *Mapping an Empire: The Geographical Construction of British India, 1765–1843* (Chicago: Chicago University Press, 1997), 9 and 333.

30 *Ibid.*, 337.

31 A. M. C. Godlewska, 'Map, text and image: the mentality of enlightened conquerors – a new look at the *Description de l'Egypte*', *Transactions of the Institute of British Geographers*, 20 (1995), 5–28, quote on p. 5.

32 Dawson Turner copies (DTC) of Banks's correspondence in the Botany Library, British Museum (Natural History), 23 volumes, Vol. 6, 101–2, Rennell to Banks, 22 December 1788.

33 Crone, *Maps*, 101.

34 DTC, Vol. 11, 275–6, Rennell to Banks, 22 August 1799.

35 Carter, *Sir Joseph Banks*, 425.

36 DTC, Vol. 18, 288, Rennell to Banks, November 1813.

37 Carter, *Sir Joseph Banks*, 261, 448, 507.

38 C. R. Weld, *A History of the Royal Society, with Memoirs of the Presidents*, 2 volumes (London: J. W. Parker, 1848), Vol. 2, 11–12.

39 On Banks as an improving landlord, see J. R. Farnsworth, 'A History of Revesby Abbey' (unpublished PhD thesis, Yale University, 1955); J. Gascoigne, *Joseph Banks and the English Enlightenment: Useful Knowledge and Polite Culture* (Cambridge: Cambridge University Press, 1994), 185–236; W. M. Hunt, 'The Role of Sir Joseph Banks, KB, FRS, in the Promotion and Development of Lincolnshire Canals and Navigations' (unpublished PhD thesis, Open University, 1986).

40 Lincolnshire Archive Office, RA 2/B/16, T. Stone, Survey of Revesby.

41 Carter, *Joseph Banks*, 392.

42 *Ibid.*, 344–5.

43 *Ibid.*, 398. See also Sutro Library, San Francisco (SL), Banks MSS, Geol. 1:2, Map, 9 September 1808, 'For explaining the Faults, shewn in J. Farey's small map of the great Limestone District in Derbyshire, made for Sir Joseph Banks.'

44 R. Porter, *The Making of Geology: Earth Science in Britain, 1660–1815* (Cambridge: Cambridge University Press, 1977), 179.

45 Yale University, Beinecke Library, Osborn Files, Banks to Palmerston, 28 March 1784.

46 SL, Banks MSS, Coal 1:20, 22 March 1797.

47 SL, Banks MSS, Coal 1:12, 1794.

48 Carter, *Joseph Banks*, 397.

49 J. Black, *Maps and History: Constructing Images of the Past* (New Haven: Yale University Press, 1997), 15.

50 J. Brewer, *The Sinews of Power: War, Money and the English State, 1688–1783* (London: Unwin Hyman, 1989), 221.

51 DTC, Vol. 16, 86, Rickman to Banks, 25 July 1805.

52 DTC, Vol. 16, 62, Banks to Rickman, 19 June 1805.

53 DTC, Vol. 16, 66, Rickman to Banks, 26 June 1805.

54 On Banks's connections with Sir George Mackenzie and agricultural improvement and clearance in the Highlands of Scotland, see C. D. Waterston, 'Late Enlightenment science and generalism: the case of Sir George Steuart Mackenzie of Coul, 1780–1848', in Withers and Wood (eds), *Science and Medicine in the Scottish Enlightenment*, 301–26.

55 DTC, Vol. 16, 66, Rickman to Banks, 26 June 1805.

56 R. Zupko, *Revolution in Measurement: Western European Weights and Measures since the Age of Science* (Philadelphia: The American Philosophical Society, 1990), 165–9.

57 R. D. O'Connor, *The Weights and Measures of England* (London: HMSO, 1987), 249–50, 253.

58 J. Hoppit, 'Reforming Britain's weights and measures, 1660–1824', *English Historical Review*, 108 (1993), 82–104.

59 Weld, *History of the Royal Society*, Vol. 2, 262.

60 British Library, Add. MSS 8099, f.140v, Banks to A. Lebland, 30 January 1802.

61 Yale University, Sterling Library, Historical Manuscripts Collection, Banks Correspondence, Banks to Blagden, 31 March [1817].

62 Gascoigne, *Science in the Service of Empire*, 121–3.

63 H. Cavendish and C. Hatchett, 'Experiments and observations on the various alloys, on the specific gravity, and on the comparative wear of gold', *Philosophical Transactions of the Royal Society of London*, 93 (1803), 43–194.

64 Edney, 'Reconsidering Enlightenment geography', 186.

65 H. B. Carter, *Sir Joseph Banks (1743–1820): A Guide to Biographical and Bibliographical Sources* (Winchester: St Paul's Bibliographies and the British Museum, 1987), 242.

66 On Kew Gardens as a site for promoting imperial 'improvement' from Banks's day to the twentieth century, see R. Drayton, *Nature's Government: Science, Imperial Britain, and the 'Improvement' of the World* (New Haven: Yale University Press, 2000).

67 P. Smith, *Memoir and Correspondence of the late Sir James Edward Smith*, 2 volumes (London: Longman, Rees, Orne Brown, Green and Longman, 1832), Vol. 1, 498, Banks to Smith, 25 December 1817.

68 On this, see J. Gascoigne, 'Motives for European exploration of the Pacific in the age of the Enlightenment', *Pacific Science*, 54 (2000), 227–37.

69 D. Clayton, 'On the colonial genealogy of George Vancouver's chart of the northwest coast of north America', *Ecumene*, 7 (2000), 371–401.

70 DTC, Vol. 7, 197, printed in N. Chambers (ed.), *The Letters of Sir Joseph Banks: A Selection, 1768–1820* (London: Imperial College Press, 2000), 128.

71 J. Barrow, *Sketches of the Royal Society and the Royal Society Club* (London, 1849), 10.

72 On this, see V. Jankovic, 'The place of nature and the nature of place: the chorographic challenge to the history of British provincial science', *History of Science*, 38 (2000), 79–113.

73 A. Cooper, 'From the Alps to Egypt (and back again): Dolomieu, scientific voyaging, and the construction of the field in eighteenth-century natural history', in C. Smith and J. Agar (eds), *Making Space for Science: Territorial Themes in the Shaping of Knowledge* (Basingstoke: Macmillan, 1998), 39–63.

74 S. F. Cannon, *Science in Culture: The Early Victorian Period* (New York: Dawson and Science History Publication, 1978), 105.

75 T. Broman, 'The Habermasian public sphere and "science *in* the Enlightenment"', *History of Science*, 36 (1998), 123–49.

76 Godlewska, *Geography Unbound*, 4, 239, 264.

9

Arcadian instincts: a geography of truth in Georgian England

❦

Vladimir Jankovic

PUBLISHED SOMETIME in the early eighteenth century, a thin octavo entitled *The Shepherd's Kalender* featured a story about a gentleman and a shepherd meeting in the countryside and hitting on the subject of the weather. The gentleman asked about the prospects for the day and the shepherd predicted rain in an hour. Since it was sunny, the gentleman laughed but soon found himself soaked by a proverbial English shower. Returning several days later, the gentleman looked for the fellow and asked him for the secret of his expertise. The shepherd at first refused to respond, but consented for a half crown and pointed to his horse, saying: 'When he runs his head into the hedge, and turns his arse to the weather-gage, than it will certainly rain, tho the weather promises at that time otherwise to those that are ignorant of the skill in prognosticating.' The gentleman thought the money well spent.[1]

The *Kalender* presented shepherds' knowledge as a commodity which, for some, was no less than an eighteenth-century symbol for legitimacy, modernity and, in no small degree, truth itself. This view has been substantiated by modern historical scholarship. Jack Plumb, John Brewer, Simon Schaffer, Margaret Jacob and Roy Porter amongst others have cast long shadows over the eighteenth century and set the tone for a historical practice which has, in recent years, achieved a thorough recasting of the theory and method of natural knowledge into a theory and method of Enlightenment business, public spectacle and commercialised leisure. For these scholars, and for the period studied, natural knowledge flourished in a quintessentially urban setting.[2] The 'urban renaissance', to use Peter Borsay's term, was in no small degree concerned with a rejuvenation of the visibility of experimental life and rational entertainment among coffee-house astronomers, improving landlords and aspirant clerical botanists.[3] But when provincials herborised and counted stars, it was because they were overly impressed by 'made in London' and for the surrogate associationism of enterprises such as the flower-shows of the club 'Sons of Flora' and Lichfield's 'Society of Gardeners,' or in Spalding's and other societies of omnivorous learning.[4] 'To provincial eyes,' wrote Roy Porter, 'enlightenment values offered a leg-up from rusticity, associated with barbarity and riot, towards metropolitan – indeed, cosmopolitan – urbanity.'[5]

This pairing of the city with legitimate knowledge had a normative effect: there was a tendency in the eighteenth-century literature to describe non-urban people as an inchoate crowd deprived of the powers of rational understanding. Rustic intellect was one of prejudice, superstition and, at best, imitation of urban mores. The stereotype of rural idiocy was the Siamese twin of urban intelligence. Robert Vaughn wrote in his *Age of Great Cities* (1842) that 'as we pass from the town to the country, from the crowd to the comparative solitude, we soon become sensible to another kind of diminution than that which meets the eye. It is soon perceptible that men are losers in intelligence, in proportion as they are losers in the habit of association.'[6] Solitude, hard work, ignorance, isolation and conservatism barred the rural population from joining the eighteenth-century republic of letters. How could a life behind the plough ever give rise to 'true' knowledge when the warrant for such knowledge was defined through detachment from work.[7]

But if Georgian science was said to have flourished in leisurely Palladian halls, city coffee houses and lecture theatres, this had consequences for the epistemology of pasture, cottage or mill. How earnest and how rational was the knowledge of country people removed as they were from the privileged sites of Enlightenment learning? Was the eighteenth-century shepherd, following Nicholson Baker's allegory, capable of producing a thought that 'may one day pack everything noble and good into its briefcase, elbow past the curators of purposelessness, travel overnight toward Truth, and shake it by the indifferent marble shoulders until it finally whispers its cool assent?'[8]

To show that some Georgians believed that thinking of this scope could occur in the countryside, this chapter investigates the geographical and social boundary between the 'rural' (or 'rustic') and 'urban' and the ways in which such a boundary developed into a philosophical dichotomy. My interest is to show that despite those asserting the supremacy of urban intelligence, there were numerous Georgian authors – mostly agricultural – who extolled the virtues of rustic thought and rustic practice. Writers such as John Mills, Walter Harte and Adam Dickson considered the rustic way of doing superior to the urban because they held that what their rural countrymen did was not about mere truth, but about important and useful truths. Such views had little to do with either eighteenth-century popularisations of science or with that sense of outdoor naturalising associated with the riding-cum-gardening routine of the provincial clergy. Rather, they were symptomatic of the still powerful identification of moral, political, social and intellectual elements of Georgian rural society.[9] In addition, these claims appeared to have addressed the phenomenon of – to use modern parlance – a 'situated' knowledge which does not split the subject and the object, context and content. And because so much in recent history of science has been about deconstructing the rationality of the Enlightenment, a study of rural science may put the bias toward urban reason into a broader perspective.[10] It is with these issues that this chapter is concerned.

EXPERIENCE AND EPIPHANY IN GEORGIAN NATURAL KNOWLEDGE

Let me begin with an example. In 1799, Alessandro Toaldo, Professor of Astronomy and Geography at the University of Padua, published a meteorological essay in the *Philosophical Magazine*. His essay was entitled 'On the signs exhibited by animals which indicate changes of the weather'. He argued that people who lived in the cities – 'who in their way of life deviate from the simplicity of nature, and are distracted by a thousand other objects – scarcely feel the impressions of the air; and if they speak of them to fill up a vacuum in their miserable and frivolous conversations, they do it without thinking of their causes and effects'.[11]

Toaldo's criticism addressed the status of meteorology as a science, an issue raised by a number of eighteenth-century naturalists. By the end of the century, metropolitan chemists, doctors, and readers of French and Swiss literature on the atmosphere made it clear that freak weather reports of provincial gentlemen and clerics had no place in a newly-fashioned meteorology. It was necessary and urgent to replace the failings of anecdotal weather reporting. Consequently, Erasmus Darwin, Jean-Baptiste Lamarck and Samuel Horsley looked for weather cycles, Luke Howard classified clouds, Charles Wells experimented with dew, John Capper conjectured on wind patterns. Despite such enthusiasm, no grand theory of weather was forthcoming. 'Projectors' were ridiculed: when, in 1806, for example, John Williams proposed to administer a gargantuan electrical shock to the entire British atmosphere to evaporate its humidity, it was observed that many of his contemporaries 'lay no great stress upon meteorological theories, and even deride speculations of philosophers'.[12] Toaldo believed that the problem was with who did the science. Theories of weather were weak precisely because they were laid down by philosophers, not peasants. For Toaldo, the question of reliable knowledge was whether something more visceral might replace the use of instruments, chemistry or the mathematics of clouds. If closely observed, he argued, the signs given off by animals would teach naturalists more than the barometer.

This argument was neither Toaldo's nor was it new. At the height of the barometer craze in the 1720s, for example, the geographer Charles Leigh recorded the skill of the common people in Lancashire in 'making as early and certain a Prognostick of the Changes of Weather, as the Modern Virtuosi can do by their Mercurial *Tubes*'. His contemporary John Pointer might have crippled the business of instrument making – if he had been read widely enough – when he insisted that animals and vegetables were nothing but 'a Contexture of Hygrometers, Barometers, and Thermometers'. Referring to Pliny and Lucan, Pointer explained that crows foretell rain when they beat the waters with their wings, a consequence of the 'pleasure' they take in the humid atmosphere. Just before rain, ants, directed by a 'secret instinct', would quit their labours and hide their eggs in a drier place. Pointer's and Leigh's statements were far from being unique. Yet while we have abundant histories of hygrometers, barometers, thermometers and their sellers and users, we lack accounts of prognostic birds, bees, and horses, and of the farmers, sailors and shepherds who understood animal behaviour.[13]

In part, the problem is heuristic. If we have learned from Shapin, Golinski and others that the accreditation of experimental science had to do with the pragmatics of virtual witnessing, literary inscriptions and gentlemanly trust, we do not as yet know how to explain the legitimacy – if such existed – of 'rustic science'. If Georgian peasants made strong claims about the natural world – as we are told they did by those who wrote on their behalf – then how did these claims square with those made by the Royal Society, the Greenwich Observatory or the British Museum? If experimental science appealed to reason and to courtesy, to what did Lancastrian common sense appeal? What, indeed, was the meaning of words 'common' and 'sense' which some Georgian writers used of rustic knowledge and arcadian insight over and against the urban philosophical fashions?

To answer these questions, I will begin by looking at what may best be described as a manifesto of rustic science, that much reprinted octavo volume by John Claridge, *The Shepherd of Banbury's Rules to Judge of the Changes of the Weather* (1744). It is a compendium of aphoristic weather rules based on the appearance of the sky and the behaviour of plants and animals which aimed to show that 'great progress [the shepherd] makes in observations, and a great certainty at which he arrives by mere dint of comparing Signs and Events'.[14] Katherine Anderson has recently pointed out that animal life and chronically sick people – 'women, the rough and uneducated, rural populations, and other races of man' – were traditionally considered more sensitive and reactive to the changes in the natural environment than urban Europeans. For Claridge, 'we, city folk, live much within doors, by which the atmospheric changes are less obvious to us'. In people whose business keeps them outdoors, however, these changes are more obvious as they are felt by their inner sense, what Claridge and other writers on the subject refer to as 'instinct'. For Claridge, this knowledge took the form of epiphany: it was the light acquired by studies in which 'Experience is a Kind of Revelation, that is to say, it is a sort of Knowledge that comes to us from without, and is infallible in itself.' Naturally, the shepherd does not require meteorological instruments – in Claridge's opinion they are useless because they cannot predict, but can only indicate the already occurring atmospheric change. The shepherd uses the instruments of 'real knowledge', namely, the sun, the moon, stars, trees, flowers, herbs and the behaviour of animals. The signs associated with them are not 'superstitious signs, but natural tokens, and as such they were worthy of notice by Aristotle, Virgil and Pliny'. But where Virgil saw agriculture as an art forged in a fight against hunger, Claridge's shepherd proved that all knowledge – that is, all meaningful knowledge – ought to come from a communion between, as it were, swain and rain. This was an experience that could not be concocted in laboratories, colleges or museums, an experience that assured infallible truth about the natural world.[15]

Claridge and his like-minded contemporaries used the image of synergetic relationship between the 'knower' and the natural world to voice their discontent with the, then, generally accepted models of knowledge production. These authors set themselves against the 'mundane means' involved in the making of science – non-epistemological vehicles of knowledge accreditation – when they rejected the class and political denominations underpinning eighteenth-century natural philosophy.[16] In the view of the apologists of rustic science, there was something socially, morally and even literally suffocating about the conventional sites of natural philosophy – museums, laboratories, lecture theatres, circulating libraries. In contrast, Claridge's science represents a democratic providentialism: the best use of one's talent is to follow one's duty, defined as an occupation in which providence has placed the individual. For Claridge, however, regardless of occupation,

> it is the manner in which we perform and not the character that makes the player, and in this sense what man is not a player? Here is an instance of one who has for many years studied his part, and now communicates his discoveries freely. In a Physician, in a Philosopher, in a Mathematician, this would be highly commendable, and why not in a Shepherd. We do not cast our own Part in the Drama of Life, no, this is performed by the great author of nature.[17]

Living under the skies and tending a flock was not only a fact of unalterable social arrangement, but a source of important natural knowledge. One finds variations of Claridge's view in other contemporary works.

Thomas Short, a Sheffield physician, advised his countrymen to study that to which they had daily access. Citizens, he argued, might attend to their barometers but these were often deceptive. In contrast, the countrymen's knowledge was legitimised by providence which would not leave 'rational Inhabitants of some Parts of [the] Globe [without understanding] of Marks, and Signs of Weather, especially when a total Incapacity to prepare for some extraordinary Changes might be of the worst Consequence'.[18] That people are doomed either to knowledge or to extinction constitutes the centrepiece of Virgil's theodicy of labour – known also as the Jupiter Theodicy. Virgil's *Georgics* – where the argument is classically stated – celebrates divinely-created natural disasters such as famines, inclement weather and disease as measures to prevent the moral decay of humankind. These troubles force humans to fight back and thus to advance civilisation. God 'sent worries to sharpen our wits' says Virgil, so that practice (*usus*), by taking thought, might little by little hammer out diverse arts.[19] For Virgil, adversity is a necessity, not an evil, yet, paradoxically, its very necessity is in its evil: storms force people to prosper by finding 'technologies' of survival. This is the perennial test. The Greeks and the Romans considered the art of reading weather signs as a *veterum praecepta* (a teaching of the ancients) 'hammered out' through exposure to air, earth, wind and fire. This line of thought enabled people like William Paley to argue that the cultivation of the earth remained poor precisely in places where the soil was of highest quality and the seasons temperate: 'Uncertainty, therefore, has its use even to those who sometimes complain of it the most.' Seasons of scarcity, Paley went on, are not without their advantages as they encourage new exertion and set contrivance and ingenuity at work.[20]

Such ingenuity is derived from belonging to the natural environment rather than being separated from it: to know, one has to be at a certain place. But the question is where? The argument is, therefore, about the place of knowledge. Neo-Virgilians were quick to point out that the place is in the country, not the city: 'We, city folk, live much within doors, by which the atmospheric changes are less obvious to us, and it is by this reason that the husbandmen, seamen, fishermen, but above all shepherds are better acquainted with the signs of the Alterations of the weather.'[21] More generally, in his 1753 *Spiritual Companion* for husbandmen, John Hildrop explained that the wise son of Sirach (in Ecclesiastes) was right to doubt whether he that 'holds the plough' can attain wisdom, but was wrong in equating such wisdom with knowledge of nature. Rural dwellers could not master that which was taught in courts and universities but they might 'learn the language and philosophy of nature'.[22]

The context of theodicy provides a vantage point from which to unravel the Georgian rustication of the intellect. To say that necessity commands invention is perhaps no less tautological than to speak of the survival of the fittest, but what makes this reasoning relevant is a unique ensemble which combined an idiosyncratic social theory of science with a political economy of British society. Claridge, Short and the mid-eighteenth-century neo-Virgilian poets astutely appreciated the link between the emplacement of society and the embodiment of knowledge. When these authors appealed to the grass-roots experience of farmers, they envisioned a kind of society in which such experience would make sense: a society that could use such knowledge in daily life, and not in the sphere of 'mere' truth.

Neo-Virgilian thought flourished during the third quarter of the eighteenth century, coinciding with the rampant expansion of the British market economy. Since Dryden's 1697 translation of the *Georgics*, the poem symbolised an aesthetic and ethical model for authors who, from John Phillips's *Cyder* (1708) via Christopher Smart's *Hop Garden* (1752) to Oliver Goldsmith's *Deserted Village* (1770), celebrated the cult of farming, gardening and the civic value of agriculture in the nation's economic affairs and foreign trade. Such literature placed a high premium on ancient agriculture and attempted to romanise British husbandry and, less successfully, the British climate. Their writings emphasised the advantages of practices such as a reliance on vegetative rather than astronomical signs of the seasons and the onset of seasonal tasks such as sowing.[23] Anthony Low has called this a 'Georgic Revolution,' a Virgil-inspired recognition of the crucial role of agriculture in the national economy. Patriotic parallels were drawn between the imperial causes of Roman decline and the danger of Britain going the same way if it let the fiscal vagaries of the city determine its public and political life. John Dyer in his *Fleece* (1757), for example, addressed the means of avoiding that entropy which had destroyed earlier societies and sought to relocate the moral centres of civilisation to accommodate the momentous socio-economic shift in land ownership to the new bourgeoisie.[24]

Such worries coincided with changes in the eighteenth-century British countryside. The increased production of grain between 1730 and 1750 lowered the price of bread in London and tended to increase depression in rural areas. Landscape gardening devoured villages. Parliamentary enclosure and emparkments generated displacement in the rural populace. New ideas about land improvement streaming from the metropolis conflicted with a traditional, sometimes inert community of self-reliant farmers and landlords who rarely identified the pecuniary incentives associated with untried practices. In some ways this was a replica of the situation which had ruined Virgil's Rome. And yet demographic facts and the expansion of foreign trade, not to mention the demand for luxury goods, called for optimisation of agricultural production. The problem, however, was to overcome the limited nature of the agricultural economy and to make improvements which would appeal both to landlords and tenants.[25] Frans de Bruyn is correct in suggesting that the conundrum facing the Georgian agricultural improver was how to transform the inherited skill of the farmer into knowledge that could command the attention of the gentleman. Charles Withers has shown that the same concerns were debated by Scottish agricultural writers, James Hutton, Francis Home, Lord Kames, Andrew Wight and others.[26] To resolve this problem was to combine *techne* and *logos*, or, as in Claridge, to pronounce *techne* a new *logos*. This might invite the transformation of existing practical experience into normative knowledge, apprenticeship into textbook.[27] In such a transformation, nothing approximated better to truth than what people already knew, and what they had known for a very long time. Agricultural 'truth' is the experience of those who till the land. But this is the truth neither of Jethro Tull's innovations nor of chemical husbandry: it is the body of thought associated with Adam Dickson, Walter Harte and John Mills.

OLD, SLOW AND TRIED: THE AGRICULTURE OF CUSTOM IN THE AGE OF REASON

Adam Dickson gained agricultural knowledge living on his father's farm in East Lothian. In 1750, he was ordained Minister of Dunse in Berwickshire. The first volume of Dickson's *Husbandry of the Ancients* was published in 1764 as a work intended to recommend Virgilian agriculture to landowners. He praised Virgil, Cato, Varro and Columella because they gave accounts of practices the value of which they themselves had experienced. Dickson's vision of agricultural improvement was, in this sense, rooted in the past. He blamed the moderns for claiming that their forefathers were fools. What one learns from Romans in the first place, argued Dickson, is the importance of local practice rather than universal theory. Local practice is adapted to the local soil and climate, and is acquired by a 'man of plain sense'. Dickson thought it was no accident that generations of common cultivators possessed an oral compendium of proverbs on the method and timing of cultivation – to regard these as primitive would be to negate their foundation, daily work, trial and error, the incontrovertible experience of survival. Samuel Trowell, Dickson's contemporary, put this view succinctly when he wrote that in agriculture, one must 'reason only from Experience, and the Use of such Means as have been accidentally discovered'.[28]

In Dickson's view, land improvement is most harmful when masterminded by those 'armchair' farmers who say that 'he is a slothful or ignorant farmer, who does not raise upon his fields at least one crop every year. But the real status of British agriculture with its practices and weed on the fields does not allow for the new methods'.[29] Dickson's view was that the husbandman himself should decide. Similarly, Walter Harte confessed in his *Essays on Husbandry* (1764) that he had:

> made husbandmen my first and almost only critics through the course of this work and have listened to their remarks not only with attention, but docility;

being sensible that many a great genius, of this sort, lives concealed in a thatched dwelling: and therefore we may compare such husbandmen to some of the oaks which grow on their farms, the bark is rough, thick, and knotty, but excellent sound timber lies concealed beneath it.[30]

For such reasons, there are in Harte's essays neither chemical observations nor mathematical reasonings, but only natural sagacity and matters of fact: 'Such a plain practical writer, as Gabriel Plattes, pays a little contingent to the republic of knowledge, with a bit of unstamped real bullion, whilst the vain-glorious men of science throw down an heap of glittering counters, which are gold to the eye, but lead to the touch stone.'[31] What should be emphasised here is Dickson's and Harte's identification of natural sagacity, local know-ledge and the common farmer as pillars of modern land improvement. This is perhaps obvious enough, but the polemical tone with which they argued these points suggests that they could have been on the defensive against what they perceived to be the encroachment of modern theory into a domain where theory had nothing to do. One may describe commitment to rustic knowledge as symbolic resistance to the philosophical appropriation of agri-culture, but that claim would not fully capture the meaning of the polemics. For if improvement led to increased production, why would philosophy not make for better business?

It may seem dishonest for an improver like Dickson to use the ancients and weeds to show that philosophical ideas cannot increase production. With John Mills, one finds such issues debated in a broader perspective and developed into reasoned economic policy. A Fellow of the Royal Societies of London and Dublin, the Royal Society of Agriculture at Paris, Rouen and of the Oeconomical Society at Berne, John Mills wrote on agricultural improve-ment in several works. His translation in 1762 of Duhamel du Monceau's *Practical Treatise of Husbandry* was followed in 1766 by a memoir on the management of bees: he also wrote one on cattle. In 1772, he published an essay on weather, but his main work was his *A New System of Practical Husbandry* (1767).[32]

Duhamel du Monceau's book caused controversy in France, pitting aggressive improvers and an advocacy of plough, drills and rotation against piecemeal reformers. Monceau was accused of importing 'a fanciful English system of husbandry' with clumsy drills and losses of ground caused by cultivation in beds. Desplace claimed in 1762 that peasant custom alone was enough to maintain healthy husbandry. La Salle de l'Etang praised cantonal customs.[33] The fiercest criticism, which referred to Monceau's rendition of Tull, was penned by Monnet: 'our agronomes will no doubt have noticed the uselessness of their general principles of agriculture'. The consequences of these (English) principles were all held to oppose established practice or accepted opinion. Monnet contended that the sole instinct of the cultivator could attain more agricultural knowledge, especially if the cultivator followed the customs of the place where he lived. 'I know how much it costs various farmers to have unadvisedly thrown themselves into the new speculations ... they have learned how to distrust our agronomes' systems.'[34]

Alert to the possibility of such accusations, Mills balanced praise for innovation and tradition by combining natural philosophy, political conservatism and a utilitarian criticism of British education. The bedrock of this heady blend was Mills's obsessive mistrust in the spirit of the system: the desire to combine all truths, he wrote, 'makes men adopt arbitrary data, which will be exploded by posterity'.[35] Since the early eighteenth century, this had been the position of followers of John Locke – D'Alembert and Condillac in France, and Mandeville and Hume in Britain. But in 1772, Mills adamantly sought to replace an abstract notion of experience with practical know-how and charted a pessimistic history of mind from Classical Greece to Baroque France in support of his thesis. In the recent past, he argued, philosophy had fallen into such disrepute that modern politicians regarded 'a philosopher as not only a useless member of community, but even a bad citizen'.[36] Philosophy had become a fashion: a few men of genius might acquire a reputation in a particular branch of knowledge and people immediately applied themselves to it without considering whether it merited such detailed attention. Successive ages had witnessed the reign of erudition, wit and geometry: the present was ruled by the cult of natural philosophy. But Mills's quasi-social-constructivist critique did not end in relativism. It was, rather, a pretext for the identification of the central issue, that of competence and authenticity rather than sophistry, something akin to Harte's 'real unstamped bullion'. It is instructive to read Mills pontificating on the failures of Enlightened science: academies 'ring of nothing but physical experiments': natural history has degenerated into trifles, mere cabinets of curiosities and shells – in short, 'the fair name of philosopher is debased, by lavishing it upon the frivolous maker of experiments, upon the bloodbesmeared anatomist, the busily prying botanist, the sooty chemist'.[37]

But Mills's diatribes did not reject natural philosophy in its entirety. His heroes were Bacon, Descartes, Newton and Locke as much as they were Buffon and Linnaeus. He did, however, reject the kind of specifically urban philosophy designed either to gratify scholastic vanity or to provide entertainment in a public venue. Mills was concerned with authenticity, and his argument amounts to a theodicy of labour writ large. Natural philosophy, he argued, 'requires time and labour', not genius. For him, the pace of knowledge acquisition played a crucial role in rustic science: as slowly accumulated agricultural wealth was held superior to the rapid wealth of the stockmarket, so, in the mental sphere, the slowly achieved wisdom of shepherds surpassed the ready-to-wear speculations of court philosophers. Furthermore, no individual naturalist can see everything – he must be guided by what others observed before him. One cannot 'attain real skill even in philosophy, but by experience, by a knowledge of the world and of men'. Such forms of experience have, however, little to do with methodological recipes on how to conduct an experiment, make measurements, or describe anatomical curiosities. In modern science, argued Mills, one sees 'nothing but methods, which have the fate of metaphysical systems: one destroys and swallows up the other, like the serpents of the magicians'. Like Claridge, Mills defined experience not as a propaedeutics – a preparatory drill which would lead to general truths – but as communion between knower and the social and natural environment, driven by an 'instinct of curiosity' implanted in humans by God.[38]

That knowledge comes from hard work is for Mills proven by the fact that great men had always been born in poverty – so much for the greatness of Robert Boyle or of Montesquieu – and in countries without extensive trade or a luxury economy. Human achievements did not coincide with times of prosperity – witness ancient Persia – but, rather, followed times of 'trouble, ferments, and civil war, in which personal merit fires the mind' – at times, in other words, in which languishing commerce had not seduced the mind by the prospect of gain. This seduction had of course taken place in cities as centres of trade. Cities, therefore, do not encourage, but rather stifle science. Those who wish to succeed in urban society must live by its rules: adopt an air of frivolity and seek spectacle, glory and pleasure. Great minds have always come from the countryside, or have been shaped amid adversity: little wonder that Linnean agriculture, recently introduced to Britain by Benjamin Stillingfleet, commanded such respect, not least since it was inspired by the barrenness of the Swedish soil.[39]

This, then, is the heart of Mills's argument. Following French agronomes like Duhamel and Mirabeau – or the doctrine of *economistes grands seigneurs*[40] – Mills invested the cultivation of the land with primacy in the moral economy of the nation. The land persists. It is the opposite of the city in which everything falls prey to fashion and speculation. Agriculture is about the 'teaching' of the land and so is the opposite of the business of newfangled experimentalism. But what is truly remarkable about his position is how readily it translated a moral economy into knowledge claims and how such claims carved up the topography of eighteenth-century truth. As the science conducted in lecture theatres and coffee houses reflected the fashions and fortunes of the newly-emerged cash nexus, so the science of pastures and open fields delivered the honest truth of virtuous labour. A wise government would thus do well to promote agriculture not only because it could act as a countervailing force to the vices of the free market but also because agricultural knowledge had been in the making and in use from times immemorial. If the experiment were to prove expensive and farmers unwilling to take the risk, the government must pay for it. Parenthetically, Mills suggested, neglect of agriculture would create a 'brain drain' in the rural population and trigger the migration of unemployed peasants to the cities.[41]

Mills's 1770 essay on weather, like Claridge's handbook, includes a discussion on the 'Shepherd of Banbury Rules'. The argument is familiar in its slant towards the ancients. Despite two centuries of the new science, no account of weather could match those made by the earliest authors, even though 'it may be presumed that the operations of nature are set in much clearer light to us, than they could be to the ancients'. Mills surmised that this might have been due to the neglect of observation. A more likely explanation, however, is modern contempt for 'the remarks of illiterate country people'.[42] Yet, like the ancients, ordinary people were well aware of the implications of their own actions – fishermen rarely unfurl their sails when a storm is brewing: why should a farmer not act with the same degree of practical confidence? Like Thomas Short, Mills's advice to farmers is to turn to personal observation, to what Harte called *empiria* and *autopsia*, to observe periods in the annual vegetative cycle, the foliation of trees that determine the sowing season. Optimal sowing time would lead to plentiful crop yield and thus lay the foundations for national welfare. Nor could general principles be trusted. Mills diplomatically praised Tull's methods for enriching the soil by frequent plowing, but also drew attention to demographic and agricultural restraints which inhibited the success of those methods. Rather, he argued, we should return to natural, traditional and locally-recognised techniques such as using manure in the form of marl, chalk and lime. Mills's preference was for a literal local knowledge: 'Good crops depend on this local knowledge, just as the welfare of the country depends on good crops.'[43]

Mills's mission was nothing short of a patriotic manufacturing of rustic science. But in contrast to the political nostalgia of pastoral sentimentalism, his project was about innovation, not aristocratic retreat. It had little to do with oxymorons such as the architectural *rus in urbe*, or with a desire to recreate sylvan purity in the streets of London in the manner of Marie Antoinette playing a milkmaid.[44] There was nothing antiquarian or nostalgic, or even anti-modernist about Mills's project. He called himself a 'projector', and deplored the disrepute into which the term had fallen amongst sceptics. Paradoxically, however, his project incorporated actors – commoners, ancients, and instinct – who sit uneasily with the iconography of either the Enlightenment or of modern culture itself. The French philosopher Bernard Le Bovier Fontenelle observed that culture required minds which could either raise themselves above the needs of life or become polished through social intercourse, but shepherds, 'always lacked one or the other: in the golden ages when they lived in abundance, the world was not polished, while in the following centuries, they were simply too miserable'.[45]

The problem, however, of making good use of local knowledge, centred on what Mills called the 'absolute inability of the husbandman'. Poor, weighed down with taxes, peasants had neither the power nor the inclination to spend money on soil. An over-loaded beast, the peasant had no incentive either to learn or to improve. Mills's solution had several parts. First, cut dues, fines and taxes (although not to the extent of destroying industry, since low taxes do not necessarily lead to prosperity). Secondly, hand land over to the people, not least since absent landowners have no long-term interest in innovation. At the same time, he insisted that the husbandman cannot enjoy any of these measures if he is not allowed to cultivate the land according to his own understanding. And the individual's own understanding is best used when one actually possesses property (or an extended lease). In England, in Mills's and Harte's opinions, this had been achieved by enclosures which should be permitted and encouraged by Parliament: the legislator should direct the husbandman to manage his own land.[46]

With this radical agenda, Mills transformed a theory of rustic knowledge into a political economy of the small independent farmer, who, according to Georgic agriculturalists, had suffered in the wake of Roman imperial adventurism. The agenda worked on the premise that farmers could use their experience only to the extent that they possessed the economic motivation to do so. This motivation came from enclosure. The economic autonomy of the independent farmer expressed the kind of social and intellectual autonomy symbolised by Georgic images of the shepherd, the sailor and the husbandman.

CONCLUSION

How do we make sense of these correlations between geography, epistemology and economy? We may begin with Kurt Heinzelman's remark that the Georgic as a literary/didactic form 'vanished at the end of eighteenth century as "a named genre" because of its excessive burden of referentiality. It was so entwined with didactic purposes of Georgian economic improvement and foreign policy that it become unthinkable as an aesthetic norm.'[47] But more intriguing than this transformation is the problem of whether historians can always understand the economic and cultural forces behind pronouncements about rural custom and rustic knowledge. There is limited evidence to help here, such as that of John Lawrence, a rector in Northamptonshire, who observed that in the course of his study of gardening he met with resistance from local gardeners who disliked the fact that he 'meddled' in their business. If in such circumstances the gentleman-scholar lacked determination, he had to follow old methods, or risk offending the locals. 'What (say they), does this man come and pretend to teach us, to make our masters think we do not understand our business? It is fitter for him to be at his Study's making sermons.' As a rule, farmers laughed at gentlemen's abilities in agricultural affairs even when the outward respect appeared to have been preserved.[48]

For Harte, the reason for such disrespect was due not only to the clash of tradition and innovation. Rather, both the husbandman and the bailiff knew that it was not 'for their interest that a gentleman be intelligent in matters of husbandry'.[49] No doubt the clash lay in the economic sphere where the bailiff's mastery over the estate was often exercised via customary short-cuts and illegal manoeuvring. Such attitudes accord with farmers' reluctance to experiment, given their attachment to the practice of their predecessors. As Mills's teacher Duhamel du Monceau observed, they would be foolish to risk limited competence against the improbable success of new experiments. Nothing less than professional integrity, if we may be allowed to use an ana-chronism, was at stake here. When farmers asserted that tradition was the judge in matters of land cultivation, this was merely a less controversial assertion of their social and political autonomy.

The irony is that this rustic pathos and shepherdly love were quintessen-tially urban products which coincided with the prominence of agronomes, physiocracy, industrialisation and the growth of suburbia as well as with nostalgic criticism of enclosures. These changes occurred in a context which they sought to deny. The masochistically anti-urban output of people like John Dyer, Christopher Smart, Walter Harte, Adam Dickson or Robert Dodsley mobilised an enormous (if literary) sympathy for the Arcadian ethos of 'native geniuses'.[50] Not quite in the country, and not quite on good terms with urban kitsch, the mid-eighteenth-century literati used an ancient genre to define a mentality of Georgian suburbia which 'introduced bourgeois taste to the rural environs of cities to such an extent that it gave rise to an entirely new setting', a setting imbued with a rosy imagery of the rural realm. The cult of the picturesque and a programmatic reversion to a rustic aesthetic extended into the philosophic domain where the theme of 'native truth' became a norm.[51]

The deconstruction of Mills's, Harte's or Dickson's motivations in writing modern Virgiliana might be an enticing project in its own right. Their deconstruction of Hanoverian natural philosophy into fashion and business reflected, however, their own simultaneous construction of rustic science. What they insisted on was that farmers' and peasants' knowledge embodied the farmers' and peasants' economic interests, and that this was as it should be. Georgian writers held that good agricultural theory ought to use local knowledge. This theory should also acknowledge, but not eradicate, peasants' unwillingness to cooperate with their superiors. Harte thought that philo-sophers should learn about this unwillingness before committing themselves to improvement. In other words, true knowledge must integrate interest; and interest warranted true knowledge. Conversely, disinterestedness in natural knowledge was like absentee landownership: they both failed to take into account practical know-how in matters where such practice was most important. What the city traveller at the beginning of this chapter got by paying half a crown was not a rain rule derived from a horse's arse, but a finely-distilled need to seek shelter in the face of Jupiter's testing storms.

In the final analysis, however, the theodicy of rustic science is pre-eminently political: it is, as in Paley's leisurely praise of famine, apologetic of those who had the nerve to contemplate the benefits of hunger. Despite themselves, these endorsements of shepherds and farmers and their native intelligence seem at this point to betray any sympathy for their daily toil. To invoke a rustic truth was to reify a geography in which a region of hard post-lapsarian work surrounded urban islands of reflection, bank interest and, not least, Georgic poetry itself. It was a telling sign when Richard Bradley, amidst all the rapture about arcadian retreat, warned that his recommendation for agricultural labour 'ought not to be literally taken', because 'no man takes more upon himself than his degree, his condition, his age, his strength, and decency, will permit him'.[52]

NOTES

The research for this project was made possible in part by grants from the William Andrews Clark Memorial Library, UCLA, and the Wellcome Trust. I thank those who commented on early drafts, Charles Withers, Miles Ogborn and Bill Luckin in particular, the participants of the Georgian Geographies conference and the 2001 Oxford Michaelmas Seminar Series.

1 [J. S.], *The Shepherd's Kalender: or, the Citizens and Country Man's Daily Companion*, second edition (London: Printed by C. A. Milbourn for Tho. Norris, 1715?), 20.

2 J. H. Plumb, *The Commercialisation of Leisure in Eighteenth-Century England* (Reading: University of Reading Press, 1973); J. Brewer and R. Porter (eds), *Consumption and the World of Goods* (London: Routledge, 1994); S. Schaffer, 'Natural philosophy and public spectacle in the eighteenth century', *History of Science*, 21 (1983), 1–43; M. Jacob, *Scientific Culture and the Making of the Industrial West* (Oxford: Oxford University Press, 1997); J. Golinski, *Science as Public Culture: Chemistry and Enlightenment in Britain* (Cambridge: Cambridge University Press, 1992); L. Stewart, *The Rise of Public Science: Rhetoric, Technology, and Natural Philosophy in Newtonian Britain, 1660–1750* (Cambridge: Cambridge University Press, 1992); T. Broman, 'The Habermasian public sphere and "science in the Enlightenment"', *History of Science*, 36 (1998), 123–49; L. K. Nyhart and T. Broman (eds), 'Science and Civil Society', theme issue of *Osiris*, 17 (2002).

3 P. Borsay, *The English Urban Renaissance: Culture and Society in the Provincial Town, 1660–1770* (Oxford: Oxford University Press, 1989).

4 On provincial science, see G. Averley, 'English Scientific Societies of the Eighteenth and Early Nineteenth Centuries' (unpublished PhD thesis, Teesside Polytechnic, 1989); T. Fawcet, 'Measuring the provincial Enlightenment: the case of Norwich,' *Eighteenth-Century Life*, 18 (1982), 15–27; R. M. Wiles, 'Provincial culture in early Georgian England',

in P. Fritz and D. Williams (eds), *The Triumph of Culture: Eighteenth-Century Perspectives* (Toronto: A. M. Hakkert, 1972), 49–68; A. Goldgar, *Impolite Learning: Conduct and Community in the Republic of Letters, 1680–1750* (New Haven: Yale University Press, 1995).

5 R. Porter, 'Science, provincial culture and public opinion in Enlightenment England', *The British Journal for Eighteenth-Century Studies*, 3 (1980), 20–46, quote on p. 27; see also V. Jankovic, 'The place of nature and the nature of place: the chorographic challenge to the history of British provincial science', *History of Science*, 38 (2000), 79–113.

6 R. Vaughan, *The Age of Great Cities* (London: The Woburn Press, 1969), 146.

7 S. Shapin, ' "The mind is its own place": science and solitude in seventeenth-century England', *Science in Context*, 4 (1991), 191–218.

8 N. Baker, *The Size of Thoughts* (London: Vintage, 1997), 10.

9 A. Everitt, *Landscape and Community in England* (London and Ronceverte: The Hamledon Press, 1985); C. Estabrook, *Urbane and Rustic England: Cultural Ties and Social Spheres in the Provinces, 1660–1780* (Manchester: Manchester University Press, 1998). On the politics of regional antiquarian scholarship, see N. T. Phillipson, 'Culture and society in the eighteenth-century province: the case of Edinburgh and the Scottish Enlightenment', in L. Stone (ed.), *The University in Society* (Princeton: Princeton University Press, 1974), 407–48.

10 D. J. Haraway, 'Situated knowledges: the science question in feminism and the privilege of partial perspective', in M. Biagioli (ed.), *The Science Studies Reader* (New York: Routledge, 1999), 172–88.

11 A. Toaldo, 'On the signs exhibited by animals which indicate changes of the weather', *Philosophical Magazine*, 4 (1799), 367–75, quote on p. 367.

12 *The Anti-Jacobin Review and Magazine*, 9 December 1806, 339, in a review of J. Williams, *The Climate of Great Britain; or Remarks on the Change it has Undergone, Particularly within the Last Fifty Years* (London: C. and R. Baldwin, 1806). On the 'crisis' in eighteenth-century meteorology, see V. Jankovic, *Reading the Skies: A Cultural History of English Weather, 1650–1830* (Chicago: Chicago University Press, 2000), 126–9.

13 C. Leigh, *The Natural History of Lancashire, Cheshire, and the Peak in Derbyshire, with an Account of the British, Phoenician, Armenian, Greek and Roman Antiquities in those Parts* (Oxford: the Author, 1700), 6; J. Pointer, *A Rational Account of Weather, Showing the Signs of its Several Changes* (London: Aaron Ward, 1738), 40. Animal instrumentation such as the use of seaweed, leeches, tree-sap, is mentioned in W. C. Hazlitt, *Faiths and Folklore of the British Isles* (London: Murray, 1846), 625; W. Hone, *The Table Book* (London: Hunt and Clarke, 1827); [Lover of the Sciences], *A Succinct Treatise of Popular Astronomy . . . to which is subjoined Prognostics of the Weather* (Edinburgh: W. Creech, 1780), 47–8; E. Tonge, 'Some observations concerning the variety of the running of sap in trees', *Philosophical Transactions of the Royal Society of London*, 5–6 (1670–71), 2070–1.

14 J. Claridge, *The Shepherd of Banbury's Rules to Judge of the Changes of the Weather* (London: W. Bickerton, 1744), iv.

15 K. Anderson, 'Instincts and instruments', in C. D. Green, M. Shore and T. Teo (eds), *The Transformation of Psychology: Influences of Nineteenth-Century Philosophy, Technology, and Natural Science* (Washington: American Psychological Association, 2001), 65; Claridge, *Shepherd*, 34, 41. Instinct is the preferred trope of Georgic writers such as John Dyer, for whom the calculating 'artful men' should be held liable for rural evils, while the humble swain in his care for the flock and in his knowledge of 'the fickle seasons of the sky' follows infallible 'sacred instinct': see J. Dyer, *Poems* (London: John Hughes, 1761), 65.

16 On 'mundane means', see S. Shapin, 'Rarely pure and never simple: talking about truth', *Configurations*, 7 (1999), 1–14.

17 Claridge, *Shepherd*, viii.

18 T. Short, *New Observations, Natural, Moral, Civil, Political and Medical on City, Town, and Country Bills of Mortality* (London: T. Longman, 1750), 457.

19 Virgil, *Georgics* 3 volumes, ed. R. A. B. Mynors (Oxford: Clarendon Press, 1990), Vol. 1, 129–35. On theodicy and alternative readings, see C. G. Perkell, 'Virgil theodicy reconsidered,' in J. D. Bernard (ed.), *Vergil at 2000: Commemorative Essays on the Poet and His Influence* (New York: AMS Press, 1986), 67–83.

20 W. Paley, D. D., 'On the seasons', in A. Hunter (ed.), *Georgical Essays*, 8 volumes (London: T. Wilson and R. Spence, 1804), Vol. 5, 347.

21 Claridge, *Shepherd*, 34.

22 J. Hildrop, *The Husbandman's Spiritual Companion* (London: John and James Rivington, 1753), 2–3.

23 Neo-Virgilian writing was also represented in poems such as William Somerville, *The Chase* (1735); John Armstrong, *The Art of Preserving Health* (1744); James Dodsley, *Agriculture* (1754); John Dyer, *The Fleece* (1757); James Grainger, *The Sugar Cane* (1763); William Mason, *The English Garden* (1772–82); and William Cowper, *Task* (1785). On this subject, see L. P. Wilkinson, *The Georgics of Virgil* (Cambridge: Cambridge University Press, 1969), 299, and W. P. Jones, *The Rhetoric of Science: A Study of Scientific Ideas and Imagery in Eighteenth-Century English Poetry* (London: Routledge & Kegan Paul, 1966), 200–12.

24 A. Low, *The Georgic Revolution* (Princeton: Princeton University Press, 1993); see also G. E. Fussell, *The Classical Tradition in West European Farming* (Rutherford: Fairleigh Dickinson University Press, 1972), 138–74, and J. Goodsridge, *Rural Life in Eighteenth-Century Poetry* (Cambridge: Cambridge University Press, 1995).

25 M. Overton, *Agricultural Revolution in England: the Transformation of the Agrarian Economy, 1500–1850* (Cambridge: Cambridge University Press, 1996).

26 C. W. J. Withers, 'On georgics and geology: James Hutton's "Elements of Agriculture" and agricultural science in eighteenth-century Scotland', *Agricultural History Review*, 42 (1994), 38–48.

27 F. de Bruyn, 'From Virgilian georgic to agricultural science: an instance in the transvaluation of literature in eighteenth-century Britain', in A. J. Rivero (ed.), *Augustan Subjects: Essays in Honor of Martin C. Battestin* (Newark: University Of Delaware Press, 1997), 47–67.

28 A. Dickson, *The Husbandry of the Ancients*, 2 volumes (Edinburgh: for J. Dickson and W. Creech, 1788); S. Trowell, *A New Treatise of Husbandry, Gardening, and other Matters relating to Rural Affairs* (London: for Olive Payne, 1738), preface.

29 Dickson, *Husbandry of the Ancients*, Vol. 1, 467.

30 [William Harte], *Essays on Husbandry*, 2 volumes (London: W. Frederick, 1764), Vol. 1, 189–90.

31 *Ibid.*, Vol. 1, 194.

32 John Mills in *Dictionary of National Biography*. J. Mills, *A New and Complete System of Practical Husbandry* (London: R. Baldwin, 1762). Subsequent editions appeared in 1763, 1765 and 1767. J. Mills, *An Essay on the Management of Bees* (London: J. Johnson and B. Davenport, 1766); J. Mills, *Treatise on Cattle* (London: printed for J. Johnson, 1776); J. Mills, *An Essay on the Weather with Remarks on Shepherd of Banbury Rules and Directions for Preserving Lives and Buildings from the Effects of Lightning* (London: S. Hooper, 1770); M. Duhamel du Monceau, *A Practical Treatise of Husbandry*, second edition (London: C. Hitch and L. Hawes, 1762).

33 See A. Bourde, *The Influence of England on the French Agronomes, 1750–1789* (Cambridge: Cambridge University Press, 1953), 64; E. Fox-Genovese, *The Origins of Physiocracy: Economic Revolution and Social Order in Eighteenth-Century France* (Ithaca: Cornell University Press, 1976), 93.

34 'Dissertation de M. Monnet sur les Terres', *Journal de Physique*, 4 (1774), 183, quoted in Bourde, *Influence*, 66.

35 [J. Mills], *Essays Moral, Philosophical and Political* (London: S. Hooper, 1772), 3.

36 *Ibid.*, 5.

37 *Ibid.*, 30–3.

38 *Ibid.*, 31–2, 37–8. On an 'instinct of curiosity', see p. 204.

39 *Ibid.*, 212, 240, *passim*. 'The great men of a nation seldom spring from the bosom of the capital [note the double meaning of 'capital']: they are produced in the country, where more simple ways of life permits the infant genius to strengthen itself in silence, afterwards to shine in a more conspicuous place': *Ibid.*, 240.

40 J. Q. C. Mackrell, *The Attack on 'Feudalism' in Eighteenth-Century France* (London: Routledge & Kegan Paul, 1973), 136.

41 Mills, 'Of agriculture', in *Essays*, 273–340.

42 Mills, *An Essay on the Weather*, 1–2.

43 *Ibid.*, iv, x–xi; Mills, *Essays*, 297.

44 R. Porter, 'The urban and the rustic in Enlightenment London', in M. Teich, R. Porter and B. Gustafson (eds), *Nature and Society in Historical Context* (Cambridge: Cambridge University Press, 1997), 176–94.

45 B. Le Bovier Fontenelle, *Digression sur les Anciens & les Modernes* (Paris: Chez Michel Guerout, 1688), quoted in L. Rothkrug, *Opposition to Louis XIV: The Political and Social Origins of the French Enlightenment* (Princeton: Princeton University Press, 1965), 112.

46 Mills, *Essays*, 318–28.

47 K. Heinzelman, 'Roman georgic in the Georgian age: a theory of Romantic genre', *Texas Studies in Literature and Language*, 33 (1991), 182–214, quote on p. 200.

48 J. Lawrence, *The Clergy-Man's Recreation: Shewing the Pleasure and Profit of the Art of Gardening* (London: for Bernard Lintott, 1714), iv.

49 Harte, *Essays on Husbandry*, 196–7.

50 For Harte, farmers were the first and only critics to whom he listened not only with attention, 'but docility, being sensible that many a great genius live concealed in a thatched dwelling . . . for there is more plain, strong, unadorned sense, more native truth, genuine beauty, and solid matter of fact, in the writings of the shop-keeper Gabriel Plattes and day laborer Peter Somer than in the well turned periods of a French academician': Harte, *Essays on Husbandry*, 190.

51 Estabrook, *Urbane and Rustic England*, 257.

52 R. Bradley, *A Survey of the Ancient Gardening Collected from Cato, Varro, Columella, Virgil, and others of the most eminent Writers among the Greeks and Romans* (London: B. Motte, 1725), preface.

10

Geography books and
the character of Georgian politics

Ƈ

Robert J. Mayhew

T HE CONTEMPORARY preoccupation with the politics of geography and
of broader forms of geographical knowledge is by no means a new
departure in the geographical tradition. The view that geography was vital to
politics was a commonplace that ramified down the centuries in European
intellectual life. The meaning of this commonplace to the geographical
culture of Georgian Britain will be examined in this chapter in ways which
engage with both the history of the Georgian era and with the historiographical
frameworks through which the political and geographical cultures of that era
have been understood by recent commentators.

To approach the Georgian conjunction of geography and politics, this
chapter adopts the approaches established by historians of the book and
recently deployed profitably by historians of science.[1] In other words, it takes
geography to be a textual arena peopled by authors, publishers and readers
rather than a static idealist realm of enquiry with defined and well-delimited
boundaries.[2] The chapter will initially canvass the main frameworks through
which Georgian politics and geography have been conceptualised in recent
writings to suggest lines by which we might expect the two areas to be conjoined. The bulk of the chapter then pursues these intimations to further our
understanding of how Georgian geography books can meaningfully be read
as political. While there are hundreds of books for which such an analysis
might be conducted,[3] this chapter concentrates on the writings of two geographical authors from the mid-Georgian period, namely Thomas Salmon
and William Guthrie. Other geographical writings from the era are used to
deepen the analysis and to create a context in which this detailed investigation of Salmon and Guthrie can be more meaningfully situated.

Salmon and Guthrie have been selected because of the range and popularity of their geographical works. Thomas Salmon wrote in all the major genres of eighteenth-century geography. His first text, *Modern History* (1725–38), was a monumental multi-volume compilation of geographical and historical information. Salmon's other major geographical projects, his *Modern Gazetteer* (1746) and his *New Geographical and Historical Grammar* (first published in 1749) were more standard, falling neatly into the two most common genres of geographical writing in the eighteenth century. These two genres will be explored in more detail below. Salmon's geographical grammar, by some way his most popular project, went through thirteen editions by 1785.[4] William Guthrie's *New Geographical, Historical and Commercial Grammar* (1771) was intended by its author to be the lineal successor to Salmon's *Grammar*, being modelled on it in terms of title, content and audience. Guthrie's work surpassed its model, becoming by a wide margin not only the most popular geographical grammar, but also the most popular geography book produced in Georgian Britain, going through some 46 editions between 1770 and 1840.[5] As such, Guthrie's work influenced British geographical culture throughout the second half of the Georgian era.

STRABO *REDIVIVUS* – GEOGRAPHY'S POLITICAL UTILITY

Geography's utility to politicians has been asserted from ancient times, so much so that the assertion ossified into a commonplace repeated uncritically by authors from the Renaissance to the late nineteenth century. Taking Strabo's *Geography*, written around the time of the birth of Christ, as founding the European tradition of producing texts called 'geographies' (older fragments remain, but no earlier complete geography exists),[6] the connection of geography and politics is already apparent. In Book 1.1, Strabo asserts that his work will be useful to statesmen. Strabo wrote at a time of Roman imperial aggression and expansion when the citizen, to perform his role in the polity, needed to have a sound grasp of the disposition of the empire and of neighbouring powers. Recent studies have focused on the chronological and causal link between the emergence of Roman geographical writings and the development of the Roman empire. Rome's hunger for geographical knowledge was tied up with its geopolitical expansion.[7]

In the Renaissance, interest in Roman geography was revived, and Strabo's prefatory comments on the utility of geography to those in political life took on the status of a commonplace. We can see this in an early English geography book, William Cunningham's *Cosmographical Glasse* (1559), which claimed the subject was vital to 'the defence of our Country':

Cosmographie herein do so much profite, that without it both valeaunt Corage, Policy and Puisaunce oftentimes can take no place. For by her we are taught whiche way to conduct most safely our ooste; where to pitch our tentes, where to winter; yea, and where most aptlye to encounter them in the fielde.[8]

One other Renaissance commonplace about geography's role in the structure of knowledge also implicitly aligned it with political life, and that was the claim that geography was an 'eye' of history. The phrase gained currency through Abraham Ortelius's late sixteenth-century *Theatrum Orbis Terrarum*, and probably owed something to Ptolemy's discussion of geography's relationship with chorography in his *Geography*, a text which Renaissance scholars keenly seized upon when it became available in Latin.[9] As history was a crucible for political debate throughout the period with past examples being drawn upon in present political debates, to give geography a propaedeutic role for historical enquiry was to give it a politicised identity.[10]

Clearly, how Strabo's commonplace about geography's political utility was understood varied according to the conception of politics being invoked. In Strabo's *Geography*, politics was clearly an imperial realm. By contrast, Cunningham's conception of politics was altogether more 'practical' and spatially more parochial, being limited to battlefield tactics, where to camp and how to provision. Finally, Ortelius linked geography to an intellectual's conception of politics. Ortelius's realm of politics was one of debate and discussion, drawing on history and theology in the prosecution of doctrinal arguments. As such, the mere claim that geography was useful to the statesman might ossify into a truism, but, I want to suggest, the rhetorical contexts in which that truism was invoked varied greatly according to the aims of authors and their conception of the political realm.

Strabo's commonplace continued to make regular appearances in geographical writings in Georgian Europe. Thomas Salmon in his *New Geographical and Historical Grammar* stated that 'here the Senator and Politician may view the Constitution, Forces, and Revenues of the respective Kingdoms and States'.[11] Similarly, Anton Büsching's *New System of Geography* (1762) was anything but novel in its prefatory discussion 'Of the Utility of Geography': 'None can pretend to be a Statesman without a competent skill in Geography: For, how should he come to the knowledge of the weakness and strength of the dominions of his sovereign, and of the princes with whom he is connected by alliances, without a treatise on political Geography?'[12]

Both of these authors suggested that geography could advise the statesman about the interrelations between states, something which might sound like a new departure appropriate after the Treaty of Westphalia (1648), which crystallised a Europe of nation states.[13] In fact, the standard vision of geography and its relation to politics survived, and the age of Enlightenment was really one of late humanism as far as geography was concerned, continuing the scholarly techniques and mores forged in the fifteenth and sixteenth centuries.[14] This can be seen by looking at two further prefaces, which show fundamental lines of continuity between Strabo's view, that of Cunningham and Ortelius in the Renaissance, and that of Georgian Britain.

William Guthrie's *New Geographical, Historical and Commercial Grammar* connected what he called 'political geography' – knowledge of the interrelation of modern states – and history: 'We are sensible that a reader could not examine the present state of nations with much entertainment or instruction, unless he was also made acquainted with their situation during the preceding ages, and of the various revolutions and events, by the operation of which they have assumed their present form and appearance.'[15] Guthrie, then, tied geography to history. Even if he did not use Ortelius's commonplace that geography was the eye of history, he continued to operate within a conception of politics wherein precedent had sovereign authority.

As Guthrie retained Ortelius's connection between geography and politics, so in the work of James Rennell we can see elements of Cunningham's linkage of these two spheres continued in the Georgian era. Rennell was map maker to the East India Company, and in this capacity constructed his enormously influential map of India, together with a *Memoir* which detailed how that map had been constructed (see also Gascoigne's discussion in Chapter 8 of Rennell's connections with Banks, pp. 159–61).[16] The 'Preface' to the *Memoir* opened as follows:

> Whilst the theatre of the BRITISH WARS in HINDOOSTAN was limited to a particular province of it, little curiosity was excited towards the general Geography of the country: but now that we are engaged either in wars, alliances, or negotiations, with all the principal powers of the Empire, and have displayed the BRITISH STANDARDS from one extreme of it to the other; A MAP OF HINDOOSTAN, such as will explain the local circumstances of our political connections, and the marches of our Armies, cannot but be highly interesting.[17]

For Rennell, the nation's interest in geography would be sparked by imperial expansion. He was writing in just the sort of rapid phase of imperial expansion which had provided the context for Strabo's geography. We should note also that Rennell's conception of the political sphere was every bit as militaristic as Cunningham's, albeit inflected by the 'military revolution' which had transformed warfare, the only difference being that the geography embodied in Rennell's *Memoir* was designed retrospectively to illuminate military actions in the Indian theatre rather than to direct them.[18] Yet Rennell argued elsewhere that a key factor behind Britain's defeat in the American War of Independence was its woeful geographical ignorance, so he clearly did view geography as militarily useful.[19]

In short, whether politics was taken to be a realm of intellectual argument, of imperial aggrandisement, or of military strategy, Georgian geographers asserted the role geography had to play in politics, and they did so in ways consonant with exemplars stretching back centuries. What follows is further concerned with what precisely the commonplace idea that geography was vital to politics meant in Georgian Britain. To investigate this, we need first to see what geography and politics meant in Georgian Britain, and then precisely how they were conjoined.

THE REALMS OF GEOGRAPHY AND OF POLITICS

Geography

Modern studies have adopted a number of overlapping conceptions of geography in the Georgian era, the diversity of these conceptions being well represented in this volume.[20] What, however, were the ways in which the Georgian period itself distinguished geography as a form of knowledge, and what were the textual forms in which they encapsulated such knowledge?

Looking at dictionary definitions, it is apparent that 'geography' in the Georgian era was defined as a scale of enquiry. Geography was the discussion of the whole globe, as opposed to 'cosmography', which studied the operation of the universe, or 'chorography' and 'topography', which discussed regions and nations.[21] By extension, a geography book was a structured discussion of all the nations of the world, primarily in terms of their history, laws, religion and the like, but also in terms of their mathematical delimitation.

As mentioned earlier, it is an acceptable generalisation that there were two main varieties of geography book in this period, varieties which used different organisational methods. First, the geographical gazetteer arranged material under place names, these names then being arranged alphabetically. It is worth noting that Johnson's *Dictionary* (1755) defined 'gazetteer' as a newspaper, and, as such, the geographical gazetteer was an offshoot of the general gazetteer whose ambition was to provide information about the present political state of the various nations of the globe. Many geographical gazetteers were little more than embellished and plagiarised political gazetteers such that the generic construction of alphabetical geographies made them inseparable from political digests. Secondly, there were geographical grammars, which arranged information by continent and nation, using a series of standard headings for each national description. As an example, we can again mention Thomas Salmon, whose *Modern History* (1725–38) was a political gazetteer of the present state of all nations. He later wrote both his gazetteer and grammar essentially as methodised abridgements of the *Modern History* organised along geographical lines. Beyond Strabo's commonplace that geography was vital to the statesman, it is apparent that the generic conventions of the two dominant forms of Georgian geographical compendium of necessity brought them within the ambit of political writings, from which their content was frequently drawn.

Politics

The political character of Georgian Britain has been the source of considerable attention and contention. In what follows, three comprehensive pictures of Georgian politics are canvassed, and then deployed to inform our understanding of the politics of Georgian geography.

The first synoptic characterisation of Georgian politics is that generated by Lewis Namier, most notably in his *The Structure of Politics at the Accession of George III* (1957). Namier's influence has been immense, both through his own work and through his influence on a generation of graduates. His approach focused on a particular set of spaces as defining politics and upon the operation of those spaces. For Namier, the realm of politics was coextensive with Parliament. He ignored other political spaces, notably the court and popular protest, focusing on Parliament and the hustings.

Namier is more notable, however, for the way he characterised human behaviour in those spaces. He opened his *Structure of Politics* by depicting the Commons as 'a modified, socialized arena for battle, drive, and dominion' wherein people sought personal gain, not the common good.[22] Namier portrayed a very closed political system, in which most appointments to government posts occurred by private patronage, and where most who participated in the political process did so as a birthright, their families controlling a parliamentary seat. Namier's original position is often simplified and caricatured: he did in fact recognise the importance of personal qualities in MPs, Parliament acting for some as a career open to the talents.[23] He made it clear that any parliamentary seat could be lost, however great the local influence, if an election were poorly managed.[24] Further, while Namier's picture of politics revolved around self-interest not scruples (which he said had driven the political life of the previous century), he accepted that in some cases party feeling was both genuine and grounded in religious differences.[25]

The second approach to Georgian political life which has been widely influential might be seen as an attempt to reverse Namier's functionalist picture. A number of political and intellectual historians have been intent on demonstrating the intellectual underpinnings of politics in Georgian Britain. J. G. A. Pocock's work is devoted to showing how eighteenth-century political actors adapted the Renaissance language of civic humanism in the altered circumstances of a commercialising economy. The language of virtue and corruption and the advocacy of a political and martial citizenry resonated from Machiavelli to early eighteenth-century England, and thence to American political thought in the War of Independence.[26] In the wake of Pocock, the importance of other discourses fashioning Georgian political consciousness has been demonstrated, perhaps most importantly in the work of Jonathan Clark which has shown the centrality of religious argumentation to British and American political life.[27] Both Clark and Pocock also show that conceptions of English law were vital to political thought.[28] This focus on intellectual languages as structuring Georgian political life also extends to plebeian or popular politics in the period. E. P. Thompson's reconstruction of the 'moral economy' argumentation of the English peasantry clearly shows that they drew on ideas of customary law and the moral life which were part of the nexus of religion and law which Clark and Pocock have studied for 'high' politics.[29]

If Namier's political spaces were the election and the Commons, and Pocock and Clark's arguments revolve around the library and the pulpit, a third coherent depiction of Georgian political life has opened up yet further political spaces to our scrutiny. John Brewer's *Sinews of Power* (1989) gives a synthetic picture (towards which others such as Dickson and Langford have gestured) of Georgian politics as the functioning of a 'fiscal-military state'.[30] For Brewer, what distinguished political life after the Glorious Revolution was the transformation of Britain into a major world power. For him, Britain saw the emergence of a meritocratic cadre of administrators poles apart from Namier's image of corruption and nepotism. While the system functioned by influence and patronage, it also consistently produced diligent and scrupulous bureaucrats. These bureaucrats administered a political system which involved Britain ever more closely in European affairs and in the projection of these affairs onto a global imperial canvas (Gascoigne's attention to Banks is illustrative here: see Chapter 8). As Britain became more embroiled, she needed larger armed forces, and ever greater taxes to pay for them. Taxation of the 'middling sorts' became essential, where previously land taxes aimed at the gentry had been sufficient. The financial revolution in English government changed the dominant social constituencies of political life away from the aristocracy and gentry. The political spaces of the fiscal-military state might be said, then, to be the confined ones of the bureaucrat's desk and the expansive ones of the theatres of imperial outreach, the two being connected by a world of taxes, trading and territorial conflict.

These three depictions of Georgian political life need not be seen as conflictual, but, rather, as overlapping pictures emphasising different elements of the whole. My concern is not to adjudicate between them, but to deploy each to deepen our understanding of the politics of geographical writing in Georgian Britain, and to consider how the enduring Strabonic commonplace of geography's political utility was enacted.

THREE READINGS OF THE POLITICS OF GEORGIAN GEOGRAPHY

Namierite geography

The texts of most Georgian geography books seem to have very little in them pertaining to the Namierite picture. Taking the geographical *oeuvre* of Thomas Salmon as a reference point, which elements of his work relate to the Namierite world? The *Modern Gazetteer* does at some points gesture to a world of patronage and of Parliament. In common with many gazetteers, there are two types of information consistently given within Salmon's alphabetical treatment which relate to Namier's interpretation. First, under numerous British place-names, Salmon also tells us that they confer a title to a member of the aristocracy, as at Abingdon, where he comments that 'from hence the noble family of Bertie take the title of Earl'. This might seem a reasonable inclusion under a place name, but it is important to take the whole entry into consideration: 'ABINGTON, W. lon. 1.20 lat. 51.35 a borough town of Berkshire, sit. on the river Thames, 55 m. W. of London, and 5 m. S. of Oxford; sends one member to parliament, and from hence the noble family of Bertie take the title of Earl.'[31]

The entry is very short, and mostly gives the information that a modern gazetteer would, namely, a mathematical description of a place's location. The entry's only elaborations beyond this are twofold: first, a note on the parliamentary status of Abingdon as a borough town, and, secondly, the fact of its giving a title to a peer of the realm. Both of these elaborations might be seen as related to a Namierite world, in that one is about the Commons, and the other about the Lords, but one which also discloses an aristocratic culture of patronage and influence.

Salmon's *Modern Gazetteer* is in no way judgemental about this parliamentary system of ambition that it notes in passing. His entry on Old Sarum, for example, a notorious pocket borough that sent two members to Parliament despite having no permanent residents, only notes the fact that it sends parliamentary representatives. Namier showed that this political system was a coherent one which had distinct rules of engagement, a finding recapitulated by O'Gorman who has emphasised both that many did not see unequal representation as unfair, and that it was only in the later Georgian era that calls for an overhaul of the franchise became significant.[32] In geography books, James Bell's *System of Geography* (1832) articulated such a position at the time of the Reform Act which recast electoral politics away from the system Namier anatomised: 'Edinburgh, the metropolis of the kingdom, has only one representative in the national senate, while an English hamlet of six old houses sends two representatives to the same assembly! The whole kingdom [of Scotland] sends 45 members to parliament; a single county in England, namely Cornwall, sends 44!!'[33]

If we look to Salmon's other major geographical work, the *Geographical and Historical Grammar*, we find a critique of the English political system which is more in tune with Bell, and which suggests it was only constraints of space or genre which made his gazetteer so indifferent to these issues. In discussing the English constitution, Salmon's picture is of an impossible balancing act between crown, aristocracy and people, which is always being pushed towards extremes of tyranny and corruption by self-interested parties who want to monopolise power. Salmon starts by criticising the notion that power does (or can) come directly from the people:

> The commons are said to represent the People, 'tho they do not in Reality represent a fourth Part of them . . . If there was any stress therefore to be laid on that Maxim, *That all just and legal Power is derived from the People* (from the Multitude), then there has been very few just or legal Governments in this or any other nation.[34]

Salmon's point is that full representative democracy is an impossibility, but in making it he exposes the nature of British 'representative' democracy and opens up a world akin to Namier's portrayal of Georgian parliamentary life. It would seem that the geographical genre in which Salmon wrote made a significant impact on the picture of political life he was able to sketch.

Yet we must not see Salmon's *Grammar* as elaborating his true and plausibly Namierite view of Georgian politics in a way that his gazetteer could not, for the simple reason that his *Grammar*'s position was strongly tied to a political language, the 'country' rhetoric which Tories adopted on their exclusion from government under the first two Georges.[35] For Salmon, it was the proscription of the Tories which made Georgian politics an oligarchic exclusion, not the political system per se as Namier argued. Not only did Salmon view democracy as impossible, there is no sign that he saw it as desirable. His only complaint was that half of the political nation was being excluded from its birthright by the tyrannical misuse of the patronage system.

If we look beyond the texts of geography books, further ways emerge in which Georgian geography is illuminated by reference to Namier. First, as became apparent in the case of Salmon, it is worth considering the authorial biographies of geographers. If Salmon's geographical *œuvre* is viewed not in isolation, but in the context of his other writings, it becomes apparent that they are of a piece. Salmon consistently wrote as a Tory who had been alienated from the levers of power by the accession of the Hanoverian dynasty. In other words, if Salmon strikes the pose of a critic of political corruption, it is for the very Namierite reason that in a political system where power was all, the dispossessed such as Salmon had no recourse but to lambast the whole system.

More generally, it is important to look to the authorial contexts in which geographical authors wrote, as these often explain the political positions encoded in their texts. Authors frequently used their publications to curry favour with the politically powerful. Geography books were no exception. Flattering references to aristocratic families and royalty were rife in geographical works, especially in dedications and prefaces. It is the massive and expensive geographical publishing projects that unveil this world most obviously. Such works required substantial financial backing and often reflected it in the form of dedications, of cartouches to sponsors on maps and illustrations, and in subscription lists. The anonymous update of Herman Moll's *Complete System of Geography* (1747), for example, was an elaborate two-folio project dedicated to George II. Similarly, Charles Middleton's equally ambitious *Complete System of Geography* (1778) had a long list of subscribers at the end of the second volume. The listing was alphabetical, but, under each letter, names were arranged in an order determined by social status, with titled nobility listed first, followed by commoners – men and, finally, women. Like dedications, subscription lists could both aggrandise a publishing project by demonstrating the significance of the subscribers and mirror a hierarchical and enduringly deferential social system. In both respects, geography books reflect the political world that Namier depicted. If the geographical genre in which authors wrote was important to the way in which they portrayed Georgian political life, the nature – and, above all, the expense – of publishing projects could also affect the political world which books disclosed. Larger and more expensive projects tend to give a window onto a socio-political system of patronage, hierarchy and deference, if only because such projects needed to tap into that system to become financially viable.

How, then, if we take a Namierite view of the character of Georgian political life, did Georgian geography books update the Strabonic commonplace that geography was useful to the politician? In a political system of patronage and influence, the geography book could, on the one hand, be a mode of address to those with access to the levers of power. The statesman, on the other hand, often sought to play the role of Maecenas, and patronising projects such as geographical descriptions of the British empire or the home nation was one route to such cultural capital. Of course, the activities of both courting and lavishing patronage, and thereby linking politics and geographical scholarship, were by no means limited to the Georgian era. Yet Namier never suggested that the political motivations he discerned in Georgian politics were restricted to that era: quite the contrary. Geography's need to court its Maecenases is an enduring way in which it has been and remains in the ambit of political life.

Geography and political languages

Georgian geography books could encode complex political languages. The sophistication with which this could be done varied according to the genre in question and the projected scale of the book. As a general rule, the format of the 'grammar' allowed for the deployment of political languages rather more than did the gazetteer, as it routinely included under each nation a discussion of its constitution and laws, its monarchy and parliament, and its religious and political history. The grammar, moreover, was normally written in continuous prose, as opposed to the often heavily abridged presentation of gazetteers.

We can look to Guthrie's *Grammar* as an example of the ways in which political languages could be incorporated into a geographical grammar. Guthrie self-consciously used the format of the grammar to inculcate a political position. I say 'self-consciously' in that the 'Preface', in common with a number of other geographical texts such as the *Complete System* (1747), argued that a comparative analysis of the nations of the world, as facilitated by a geographical grammar, aided political insight. As Guthrie put it, 'by comparing together our accounts of the European nations, an important system of practical knowledge is inculcated, and a thousand arguments will appear in favour of a mild religion, a free government, and an extended, unrestrained commerce'.[36] The message of Guthrie's work is that a church–state nexus notably akin to Georgian Britain (at least in its self-image) is the apogee of political wisdom, this being presented as the objective finding of geographical enquiry. How, then, was this system of political knowledge inculcated in Guthrie's *Grammar*?

For Guthrie, in accordance with the stadial theory of the Scottish Enlightenment, Europe was by far the most civilised continent, such that 'little for our entertainment or instruction' was offered by the other continents.[37] Yet within Europe, not all nations demonstrate the same degree of political wisdom and Guthrie feared the exercise of too extensive power by any one group within a polity. Both Russia and Denmark were said to possess monarchies with despotic powers. In both cases, the virtues of individual monarchs are said to have ensured virtuous political life despite a vicious constitution.[38] Equally, however, the monarchy can, as in Sweden after the death of Charles XII, be brought 'too low' and replaced by the overweening ambition of a parliament:

> the king of Sweden can scarcely be called by that name, being limited in every exercise of government . . . Thus, upon the whole, the government of Sweden may be called republican . . . It would be endless to recount the numerous subordinate courts, boards, commissions, and tribunals, which the jealousy of the Swedes have introduced into the administration of civil, military, commercial, and other departments; it is sufficient to say, that though nothing can be more plausible, yet nothing is less practicable than the whole plan of their distributive powers.[39]

Finally, as becomes clear in Guthrie's commentary on the Polish political system, excess power can be vested in the aristocracy, a situation he calls 'Gothic' independency: 'It is founded, however, upon Gothic principles, and that unlimited jurisdiction which the great lords, in former ages, used to enjoy all over Europe. The want of subordination in the executive parts of the constitution, and the rendering noblemen independent and unaccountable for their conduct, is a blemish.'[40] According to Guthrie, translating from space to time, this Polish Gothic system once existed throughout Europe: 'When we examine the best accounts of the present constitution of Poland, and compare them with the ancient history of Great Britain, and other European kingdoms, we may perceive a wonderful similarity between what these were formerly, and what Poland is at present.'[41] Guthrie argues that the Polish political system can be transformed into a modern one 'by the introduction of arts, manufactures, and commerce'.[42]

In looking at the modern political system, Guthrie's implicit benchmark is Britain. Yet even here his picture is not one of unalloyed modernity: 'this Gothic system still prevails in Poland; a remnant of it continued in the Highlands of Scotland so late as the year 1748. And even in England, a country renowned for civil and religious liberty, some relicks of these Gothic institutions are perceivable at this day.'[43] His criticism is that the Anglican church preserved 'Romish' tendencies, and that the Revolution of 1688 'was not altogether so perfect as might have been wished'.[44] But, in the main, his picture is highly positive. England has clearly learned the lesson which the *Grammar* inculcates via its geographical survey, 'maintaining an equal poise, that no one part of the three estates overpower or distress either of the other'.[45]

In his argumentation, Guthrie deploys a number of the languages of political thought which dominated Georgian Britain. In brief, Guthrie appealed to rhetoric about the English and British system as a *via media* between the extremes, both religious and constitutional, of tyranny and anarchy.[46] This was the traditional fare of English and then British patriotism, especially after the settlement of 1688–89. His concerns about the British state were also squarely within one political language, the British adaptation of the Machiavellian language of civic humanism to a commercialising world. This language feared the corruption of political virtue that would ensue when citizens no longer defended their own state, employing instead a paid standing army. In Guthrie's version: 'in a land of liberty, it is extremely dangerous to make a distinct order of the profession of arms. In such, no man should take up arms, but with a view to defend his country and its laws: he puts not off the citizen when he enters the camp.'[47] The modern political system which Guthrie thought a geographical survey would advocate to the statesman should, in other words, be a commercial one, but not a venal one of debt financing. In these terms, Guthrie's whole geographical structure, with its emphasis on stadial theory and its defence of Presbyterianism, fits into the political language of the Scottish Enlightenment.[48]

Arguably, showing that geography books such as Guthrie's deployed specific political languages is hardly revelatory. It might be seen as akin to Molière's Monsieur Jourdain, who was delighted to discover that he spoke prose. The whole thrust of those who have analysed languages of political thought has been that political expression cannot but be both constrained and enabled by the extant repertoire of paradigmatic languages. To say, then, that geographers made interventions into the discussion of politics is to say that they deployed political languages. It is certainly not to say anything distinctive about the Georgian period, given that all geographers in all eras have drawn on political languages. But the rubric of languages of political thought does make us aware that we should look for specific types of political commentary in the Georgian era, as particular forms of political language dominated. Above all, the contortions of civic humanism, and the theologico-political arguments which emanated from the events of 1688 are to be expected and they are indeed what we discover in geography books. Similarly, the clerical and conservative English Enlightenment's contact with the Presbyterian and reforming Scottish Enlightenment generated much political argument, and this, too, is reflected in geography books.

This leads us back to the question of what the Strabonic commonplace about geography's utility in the political sphere meant in the Georgian era. The analysis of the languages of political thought suggests that geography books, thanks to their discussions of religion, the constitution and the like were useful to the political commentators who wished to make their position clear. As a textual tradition, the geography book contributed to the propagation and adaptation of the political languages through which thought and action were structured. If, as J. L. Austin said, 'words are deeds', the geography book was useful to those who wished to intervene in political life.[49]

Fiscal-military geography

In discussing the emergence of a fiscal-military state in Georgian Britain, Brewer has pointed out that the growing fascination with trade statistics, empire and bureaucratic efficiency led to a parallel demand for works of useful knowledge. Useful knowledge was, he says, 'applicable to everyday life and reducible, through the science of number, to a series of figures or tables. This knowledge was not confined to information either produced by or descriptive of government activity. It included not only state statistics but information about the population, the economy and society at large.'[50] Simply put, Brewer's description of works of useful knowledge, if arranged spatially, encapsulates the sorts of information which Georgian geography books contained.

For some support for this contention, we can look again at the gazetteer and the grammar. Looking to Salmon's *Modern Gazetteer*, his 'Introduction' discussed the findings of political arithmetic about England's wealth. Salmon, he admitted, in fact drew on a 'computation made by Dr Davenant fifty years ago'.[51] Of course, half a century of precocious growth in the Georgian economy made the calculations Salmon transcribed all but worthless. Yet as Brewer points out, it was not the accuracy of books of useful knowledge that was the issue: 'at bottom the emphasis on "useful knowledge" constituted a change in perception, the growth of a new vision of state and society'[52] (see also the discussions in Chapters 2 and 8). Salmon's *Modern Gazetteer* also contained large sections of more up-to-date information about the functioning of the British empire, facts which accord with Brewer's picture. Frequently, Salmon's entries concerning colonial outposts of the British empire were a catalogue of trading relations between homeland and empire, or of trading potential yet to be realised. Discussing New Hampshire, for example, Salmon opined: 'this country seems very proper for producing naval stores; a great part of it is appropriated by act of parliament, for furnishing masts, yards &c. for the royal navy'.[53] Even outside the imperial context, the key trading posts for British trade received far longer entries than other locations, as for example Aleppo in Turkey because 'every European nation almost has its factors here: the English factors are about 40 in number'.[54]

The same comments could be made of the geographical grammar. Guthrie's *Grammar*, for example, is with good reason called the *New Geographical, Historical and Commercial Grammar*, for commerce bulks large. The Preface justified Guthrie's extensive coverage of the Americas, since 'whether considered as an immense continent . . . or as a country intimately connected with Europe by ties of commerce and government, [it] deserves very particular attention'.[55] Guthrie's discussion of the Americas duly covered over four times as many pages as either Asia or Africa. If Guthrie's work inculcated a political message in praise of Georgian Britain and her constitution, it also assumed a commercial and imperial political world as the context in which British political life was situated. Similarly, if (as we have seen) Guthrie displayed civic humanist fears about a standing army, this in no way meant he was critical of the military machine which the British state was developing in other respects. The section on 'Military and Maritime Strength' in which Guthrie voiced his fears about the army also eulogised the navy as 'more agreeable to the principles of our free constitution. The royal navy of England hath ever been its greatest defence and ornament; it is its ancient and natural strength; the floating bulwark of the island; an army, from which, however strong and powerful, no danger can ever be apprehended to liberty.'[56] Appended to this section were tables listing the entire British fleet and the daily rates of pay for both naval and land-based officers. These tables show that the works of useful knowledge which a fiscal-military mentality engendered significantly inflected the format of the geographical grammar. It is noticeable that as more tabulated and statistical information became available, especially in the last fifty years of the Georgian era, so it progressively came to dominate geography books, forming one of the most notable transitions in Georgian geography between a work such as Salmon's *Grammar* in the mid-eighteenth century and James Bell's *System* nearly a century later.[57]

So, the genres of the Georgian geography book and their contents accord rather well with the mentality which, Brewer argues, developed as the British political system came to pivot around money, military might and manufactures. Yet within the texts under discussion, very different mental worlds coexist with the preoccupation with commerce and empire. This should be apparent from the claims of previous sections which have shown elements of a Namierite worldview and also the articulation of complex political languages within the selfsame texts. The most restrictively 'useful' geography books, such as Salmon's *Modern Gazetteer*, contained types of information which could by no means be justified by a fiscal-military mentality alone. The following entries are good examples:

> Calcedon . . . Once the capital of the country [of Lesser Asia] . . . Here the 4th general council was held, anno 451, and it made a great figure at that time, but is now dwindled to a little village.

> Babylon, once the capital of the Babylonish empire has now no remains of it left, but is supposed to have lain in 44 degrees of E lon. and 32 degrees of N lat. on the river Euphrates, but not on the present channel; and hereabouts is supposed to have been the seat of Paradise.[58]

In both entries, there was confessedly no utilitarian rationale to justify their inclusion. Babylon cannot even be located precisely, the basic function of a gazetteer, and is linked to that other great geographical imponderable to a still Christian culture, the location of Paradise.[59] Calcedon, though of mathematically determinable location, was of no present significance in commercial, imperial or military terms: its inclusion related to its role as the site of one of the great Patristic councils. Clearly, even the Georgian geography book as a modern text of useful knowledge had not relinquished all its connections to the culture of humanist learning with its emphasis on Christian and classical history. This finding applies *a fortiori* to geographical grammars, which always contained substantial sections of far from useful learning.

In the Georgian context, how does the view of geography books as tied to the emergence of a fiscal-military state update the Strabonic commonplace of geography's utility to the statesman? Above all, in a political world of figures and statistics, the geography book was one of a series of means by which knowledge could be disseminated to a reading public ever more eager to garner such information. If political culture was becoming more commercial and imperial, the geography book was an ideal tool. Most of the data in geography books was hopelessly inaccurate, not only in comparison with modern attempts at historical quantification, but also with the best information available at the time. As such, the utility of these geographical works to the political culture of the time was as much as a way of responding to a demand for information as for their truth content. The statesman would not straightforwardly rely on the calculations contained in geography books, and to that extent they were not useful to political life. Yet such works, by responding to a perceived need for efficient and fair government, served a political function by their very publication.

CONCLUSION: THE MANY POLITICAL WORLDS OF GEORGIAN GEOGRAPHY

The three paradigmatic characterisations of Georgian politics that this chapter has discussed are obviously not mutually exclusive. Recognising this, it is unsurprising to find that the geography book, the *ne plus ultra* of structured miscellanies, encompassed elements of all three variants. It is true, nevertheless, that we can discern certain trends over time in the politics of Georgian geography books which this chapter's structure has tended not to highlight. The proliferation, for example, of statistics and tables in geography books of the later eighteenth and early nineteenth centuries is noticeable if one looks at works such as Bell's *System* in comparison with, say, Guthrie's *Grammar* of only sixty years before. This might seem to accord with the characterisation of a fiscal-military state, but if so the rise of statistics to textual prominence was much delayed, as the fiscal revolution which Brewer sees as initiating this new form of politics began almost a century earlier in the late seventeenth century. Similarly, the role of empire in geographical texts increased markedly in later Georgian texts, a language of empire becoming important as the categories of civic humanist discourse seem to have become marginalised. Yet this shift was handled within a fairly static conception of Britain as a 'fair' empire, in contradistinction to the rapacity of the Dutch and the 'Black Legend' of the Spanish.[60] It was also the case that more extensive discussions of the British empire operated largely in the sphere of trading relations and the ambit of the fiscal military state. Finally, and right at the end of the Georgian period, there came a sustained attack on the British political and electoral system which Namier depicted, this being reflected in geography books only on the eve of the Reform Act.

The evidence from eighteenth-century geography books about the nature of Georgian political life can also be organised in ways other than the chronological, and can thereby suggest different patterns from those constructed around a binary of secular change or stasis. In particular, taking the approach of historians of the book, we can see that different geographical books and genres produce different pictures of the political life of the time. Starting with the nature of the book, the more grand publishing projects which involved lavish illustrations and maps needed to court patronage and aristocratic subscriptions. These works reflect a Namierite world of influence, hierarchy and clientage networks far more readily than the more modest geographical grammars and gazetteers in octavo or smaller, with either no illustrations or with plagiarised ones. These latter works fit Brewer's category of works of 'useful knowledge' more closely and better reflect the fiscal-military state worldview. Further, turning to the genre of the book, regardless of its physical grandeur and expense, geographical grammars created a picture of Georgian political life far more akin to that provided by historians of political thought than most geographical gazetteers. The geographical grammar allowed for long prose discussions of constitutions, religion, law and international relations, wherein paradigmatic languages of political expression such as that of civic humanism, of the ancient constitution, and of empire and universal monarchy, could not but be deployed. By contrast, all but the most expansive gazetteers were condensed digests of information, with little continuous prose, and, therefore, had little scope for creating coherent political arguments.

Beyond geography books themselves, one might look to authorial issues and readership in determining the character of politics in Georgian geography. Different authors clearly operated in very diverse political worlds: James Rennell's world was one of patronage by the East India Company, which he then staunchly defended in his geographical works, as he rose to a position of scientific respectability in late eighteenth-century London in the Royal Society and the African Association. By contrast, John Walker, author of *Elements of Geography* (1789), was a Quaker schoolmaster in Dublin. Walker's *Elements* lambasted British colonialism and its connection to the slave trade, and he refused (in true Quaker fashion) to refer to anyone by a title such as 'Sir' or 'Lord'. Walker no doubt sought patronage as much as Rennell, but within a geographical and intellectual space which made his political world one whose orbit touched Rennell's only to condemn it.

If authorial positions could connect geography to very different political worlds, so readers could position them differently again. Any reader could take, for example, Guthrie's political message and subvert it. North American colonists in the War of Independence might agree about the sanctity of freedom but place Britain roughly as Guthrie had Sweden and Denmark, namely as a political system that lacked the wisdom to restrain the monarch constitutionally.[61] Further, and more importantly perhaps, geography books, by their formats, with an array of headings arranged either alphabetically or geographically, were clearly designed to act as works of reference, to be browsed rather than read. As such, the dominant mode of reading Georgian geography books perhaps mitigates against any simple authorial argument being taken into account.

Georgian geography books, then, show a myriad of political worlds in coexistence, rather than adjudicating about the nature of political life in the period. We can cut into their meanings in different ways to provide vastly different pictures of the political life of the period. But one thing is clear: geography books did operate within the ambit of political life owing to the economics of publishing, the generic conventions of the geography book, and the authorial ambitions of those who wrote them. As such, Strabo's commonplace that geography was useful to the statesman remained a truism at least in part because it was true.

NOTES

1 For a representative sample of recent work, see M. Frasca-Spada and N. Jardine (eds), *Books and the Sciences in History* (Cambridge: Cambridge University Press, 2000).

2 See R. J. Mayhew, 'The character of English geography, *c.* 1660–1800: a textual approach', *Journal of Historical Geography*, 24 (1998), 385–412.

3 For a listing, see O. F. G. Sitwell, *Four Centuries of Special Geography* (Vancouver: University of British Columbia Press, 1993).

4 For more on Salmon, see R. J. Mayhew, 'Introduction', in Thomas Salmon, *The New Geographical and Historical Grammar* (Bristol: Thoemmes Press, forthcoming); R. J. Mayhew, *Enlightenment Geography: The Political Languages of British Geography, c. 1650–1850* (London: Macmillan, 2000), 132–40.

5 For more bibliographic information, see Sitwell, *Four Centuries*, 271–86. An analysis of the work is provided in R. J. Mayhew, 'William Guthrie's *Geographical Grammar*, the Scottish Enlightenment and the politics of British geography', *Scottish Geographical Journal*, 115 (1999), 19–34.

6 For this, see C. van Paassen, *The Classical Tradition of Geography* (Groningen: J. B. Wolters, 1957).

7 C. Nicolet, *Space, Geography and the Politics of the Early Roman Empire* (Ann Arbor: Michigan University Press, 1991); K. Clarke, *Between Geography and History: Hellenistic Constructions of the Roman World* (Oxford: Clarendon Press, 1999).

8 W. Cunningham, *The Cosmographical Glasse* (London: John Day, 1559), sig.Aiiiir.

9 A. Grafton, *Commerce with the Classics* (Ann Arbor: University of Michigan Press, 1999), 53–94.

10 A. Grafton and L. Jardine, ' "Studied for action": how Gabriel Harvey read his Livy', *Past and Present*, 129 (1990), 30–78.

11 T. Salmon, *A New Geographical and Historical Grammar* (London: William Johnston, 1749), sig.A3v.

12 A. Büsching, *A New System of Geography*, 2 volumes (London: A Millar, 1762), Vol. 1, 5.

13 M. Heffernan, *The Meaning of Europe* (London: Edward Arnold, 1998).

14 This point about the continuities between humanism and Enlightenment thought has been made more generally for the culture of European scholarship by, among others, John Pocock and Joseph Levine: see J. G. A. Pocock, *Barbarism and Religion*, 2 volumes (Cambridge: Cambridge University Press, 1999); J. Levine, *Humanism and History: Origins of Modern English Historiography* (Ithaca: Cornell University Press, 1987) and *The Battle of the Books: History and Literature in the Augustan Age* (Ithaca: Cornell University Press, 1991).

15 W. Guthrie, *A New Geographical, Historical and Commercial Grammar* (London: J. Knox, 1771), v.

16 On Rennell's cartographic activities, see M. H. Edney, *Mapping an Empire: The Geographical Construction of British India, 1765–1843* (Chicago: University of Chicago Press, 1997) and C. Markham, *Major James Rennell and the Rise of English Geography* (London: Cassell, 1895).

17 J. Rennell, *Memoir of a Map of Hindoostan* (London: M. Brown, 1783), i.

18 G. Parker, *The Military Revolution* (Cambridge: Cambridge University Press, 1988).

19 For Rennell's repeated assertions of British ignorance of the geography of America, see, for example, J. Rennell, *The Geographical System of Herodotus Examined* (London: W. Bulmer and Co., 1800), 41, 430.

20 See also D. N. Livingstone and C. W. J. Withers (eds), *Geography and Enlightenment* (Chicago: University of Chicago Press, 1997) for some of the diverse rubrics through which the interconnections of geography and eighteenth-century culture have been conceptualised.

21 See Mayhew, 'Character of English geography'; for an earlier period, see L. Cormack, *Charting an Empire: Geography at the English Universities, 1580–1620* (Chicago: University of Chicago Press, 1997).

22 L. Namier, *The Structure of Politics at the Accession of George III*, second edition (London: Macmillan, 1957), 1.

23 *Ibid.*, 7–11.

24 *Ibid.*, 134–43.

25 *Ibid.*, 90 and 113.

26 J. G. A. Pocock, *The Machiavellian Moment: Florentine Political Thought and the Atlantic Republican Tradition* (Princeton: Princeton University Press, 1975).

27 See J. C. D. Clark, *English Society, 1688–1832* (Cambridge: Cambridge University Press, 1985), and J. C. D. Clark, *The Language of Liberty, 1660–1832: Political Discourse and Social Dynamics in the Anglo-American World* (Cambridge: Cambridge University Press, 1994).

28 J. G. A. Pocock, *The Ancient Constitution and the Feudal Law* (Cambridge: Cambridge University Press, 1987).

29 E. P. Thompson, *Customs in Common* (London: Merlin Press, 1991).

30 J. Brewer, *The Sinews of Power: War, Money and the English State, 1688–1783* (London: Unwin Hyman, 1989); see also P. G. M. Dickson, *The Financial Revolution in England: A Study in the Development of Public Credit* (London: Macmillan, 1967); P. Langford, *Public Life and the Propertied Englishman, 1689–1798* (Oxford: Clarendon Press, 1991).

31 T. Salmon, *The Modern Gazetteer* (London: S. & E. Ballard, 1756), *sub.* Abington.

32 F. O'Gorman, *Voters, Patrons and Parties: The Unreformed Electorate of Hanoverian England, 1734–1832* (Oxford: Clarendon Press, 1989).

33 J. Bell, *A System of Geography* 5 volumes (Glasgow: Blackie, Fullarton and Co, 1832), Vol. 3, 180.

34 Salmon, *Grammar*, 314–15.

35 On languages of political expression, see Pocock, *Machiavellian Moment*; L. Colley, *In Defiance of Oligarchy: The Tory Party, 1714–1760* (Cambridge: Cambridge University

Press, 1982); and C. Gerrard, *The Patriot Opposition to Walpole: Politics, Poetry, and National Myth, 1725–1742* (Oxford: Clarendon Press, 1994).

36 Guthrie, *Grammar*, vii.

37 *Ibid.*, vii.

38 *Ibid.*, 81 and 113–14.

39 *Ibid.*, 95–6.

40 *Ibid.*, 450.

41 *Ibid.*, 450.

42 *Ibid.*, 450.

43 *Ibid.*, 58.

44 *Ibid.*, 238.

45 *Ibid.*, 246.

46 For this rhetoric, see J. G. A. Pocock, 'Within the margins: the definition of orthodoxy', in R. D. Lund (ed.), *The Margins of Orthodoxy: Heterodox Writing and Cultural Response, 1660–1750* (Cambridge: Cambridge University Press, 1995), 33–53.

47 Guthrie, *Grammar*, 263.

48 This argument is made at length in Mayhew, 'William Guthrie's *Geographical Grammar*', *passim*.

49 See J. L. Austin, *How To Do Things With Words* (Oxford: Oxford University Press, 1962).

50 Brewer, *Sinews of Power*, 228.

51 Salmon, *Modern Gazetteer*, sig.a3r.

52 Brewer, *Sinews of Power*, 229.

53 Salmon, *Modern Gazetteer*, sub. Hampshire-New.

54 *Ibid.*, sub. Aleppo.

55 Guthrie, *Grammar*, vii.

56 *Ibid.*, 266.

57 Mayhew, *Enlightenment Geography*, 207–28.

58 Salmon, *Modern Gazetteer*, sub. Calcedon and Babylon.

59 C. W. J. Withers, 'Geography, Enlightenment and the paradise question', in Livingstone and Withers (eds), *Geography and Enlightenment*, 67–92.

60 A. Pagden, *Lords of All the World: Ideologies of Empire in Spain, Britain and France, c. 1500–c. 1800* (New Haven: Yale University Press, 1995); D. Armitage, *The Ideological Origins of the British Empire* (Cambridge: Cambridge University Press, 2000).

61 J. P. Greene, *Peripheries and Center: Constitutional Development in the Extended Polities of the British Empire and the United States, 1607–1788* (Athens GA: University of Georgia Press, 1986).

Index

⁊

Notes: page numbers in *italic* refer to illustrations; literary works can be found under authors' names; references to items in the notes are given by page number and note number.